D1520313

NIGERIA'S DIVERSE PEOPLES

Other Titles in
ABC-CLIO's
ETHNIC DIVERSITY WITHIN NATIONS
Series

Canada's Diverse Peoples, J. M. Bumsted

The Former Yugoslavia's Diverse Peoples, Matjaž Klemenčič and Mitja Žagar

FORTHCOMING

Australia's Diverse Peoples, Andrew Wells and Julia Theresa Martínez

The Former Soviet Union's Diverse Peoples, James Minahan

NIGERIA'S
DIVERSE PEOPLES

A REFERENCE SOURCEBOOK

April A. Gordon

A B C ⬥ C L I O

Santa Barbara, California   Denver, Colorado   Oxford, England

Library of Congress Cataloging-in-Publication Data
Gordon, April A.
  Nigeria's diverse peoples : a reference sourcebook / April A. Gordon.
    p. cm. — (ABC-CLIO's ethnic diversity within nations series)
Includes bibliographical references and index.
  ISBN 1-57607-682-2 (alk. paper) ISBN 1-57607-683-0 (eBook)
  1. Ethnicity — Nigeria. 2. Ethnic groups — Nigeria. 3.
Nigeria — Colonization. 4. Nigeria — Ethnic relations. 5.
Nigeria — History — Civil War, 1967–1970. I. Title. II. Series: Ethnic
diversity within nations.

  GN653.G67 2003
  305.8'009669 — dc22

                                2003016243

07 06 05 04 03   10 9 8 7 6 5 4 3 2 1

ABC-CLIO, Inc.
130 Cremona Drive, P.O. Box 1911
Santa Barbara, California 93116-1911

This book is also available on the World Wide Web as an eBook.
Visit www.abc-clio.com for details.

This book is dedicated to the late Robert Mundt, a devoted Africanist scholar and a special friend and colleague. Bob, you are missed.

Contents

11 The Future of Nigeria   255

Series Editor's Foreword

WE THINK OF THE UNITED STATES AS A NATION OF PEOPLES, with some describing it as a mosaic, a stew, an orchestra, and even yet as a melting pot. In the American vision of diversity the whole is perceived as greater than the sum of its parts—groups of peoples unify into a national identity. Not all Americans have shared that vision, or, to the extent that they initially did, they considered diversity as groups of people with shades of difference—such as shades of whiteness or variants of Protestantism. Many of the early newcomers would come to represent the core of an American society wherein distinctions were expected to fade by and large because a unity was anticipated that would be greater than any one homogeneous racial or ethnic national community. That unity would be forged through a common commitment to the American system of republicanism and a shared set of political principles and values—collectively, America's civic culture. For decades the diversity that was recognized (essentially in terms of religion and nationality) did not appear to be so formidable as to constitute a barrier to nationhood—as long as one did not look beyond the whiteness to the African and Native American (and later Latino and Asian) peoples. By rendering such groups invisible, if not beyond the pale, majority groups did not perceive them as representing a challenge to, or a denial of, the national unity. They were simply left out of the picture until, eventually, they would compel the majority to confront the nation's true composition and its internal contradictions. And, even before that more complex confrontation took place, streams of (mostly) European newcomers steadily stretched the boundaries of the nation's diversity, requiring a reexamination of the bonds of nationhood, the elements of nationality, and the core society and values. By World War II and in the ensuing two decades it became more and more difficult to ignore the impact of a dual development—the expanding Latino and Asian immigration and arrival of far more diverse groups of European newcomers. To secure their national vision, Americans had (albeit reluctantly and not without conflict) to make rather profound and fundamental adjustments to many of those components that had served as the nation's bonds, particularly the perception of America as a multicultural society and the belief that pluralism was a legitimate and inherent part of American society and culture.

To what extent has this scenario of a nation of peoples been present elsewhere in the world? Where have others struggled to overcome racial, religious, tribal, and nationality differences in order to construct—or to preserve—a nation? Perhaps one might even ask where, by the late twentieth century, had others *not* experienced such struggles? In how many of the principal nations has there long been present a homogeneity of people around which a nation could be molded and shaped with little danger of internal discord threatening the overall fabric of national unity? On the other hand, in how many countries has there been present a multiplicity of peoples, as in the United States, who have had to forge a nation out of a disparate array of peoples? Was that multiplicity the product of in-migrations joining a core society as it has been in the United States, or was there a historic mosaic of tribes, bands, and other more-or-less organized entities that eventually adhered together as their discovered commonalities outweighed their differences? Or, do we see invasions from without and unity imposed from above, or the emergence of one group gradually extending its dominance over the others—installing unity from below? Did any of these variations result in nation-states comparable to the United States—the so-called first new nation—and, if so, what have been the points of similarity and difference, the degrees of stability or unrest? Have their diversities endured, or have they been transmuted, absorbed, or suppressed? How much strain have those states experienced in trying to balance the competing demands among majority and minority populations? In other words, where nation-states have emerged by enveloping or embracing (or subjugating) diverse peoples, what have been the resulting histories in terms of intergroup relations and intergroup strains as well as the extent of effective foundations of national unity?

The challenges of coexistence (voluntarily or otherwise) remain the same whether two or twenty people are involved. The issue is what traditions, institutions, concepts, principles, and experiences enable particular combinations of peoples to successfully bond and what factors cause others to fall prey to periodic unrest and civil wars? Finally, many upheavals have taken place over the past 150 years, during which in-migrations have penetrated nations that were previously homogenous or were sending nations (experiencing more out-migration than in-migration) and were less prepared to address the rather novel diversities. Have these nations had institutions, values, and traditions that enabled them to take on successfully such new challenges?

Examples abound beyond the borders of the United States that require us to examine the claims of American exceptionalism (that America's multiculturalism has been a unique phenomenon) or, at the very least, to understand it far better. Canada and Australia have had indigenous peoples but have also long been receiving nations for immigrants—however, usually far more selectively than has the United States. Brazil and Argentina were, for decades in the late nineteenth and early twentieth centuries, important immigrant-receiving nations, too, with long-term consequences for their societies. Long before there were Indian and Yugoslavian nation-states there were myriad peoples in those regions who struggled and competed and then, with considerable external pressures, strained to carve out a stable multiethnic unity based on tribal, religious, linguistic, or racial (often including groups labeled "racial" that are not actually racially different from their neighbors) differences. Nigeria, like other African countries, has had a history of multiple tribal populations that have competed and have endured colonialism and then suffered a lengthy, sometimes bloody, contest to cement those peoples into a stable nation-state. In the cases of South Africa and Russia there were a variety of native populations, too, but outsiders entered and eventually established their dominance and imposed a unity of sorts. Iran is representative of the Middle Eastern/Western Asian nations that have been for centuries the crossroads for many peoples who have migrated to the region, fought there, settled there, and been converted there, subsequently having to endure tumultuous histories that have included exceedingly complex struggles to devise workable national unities. In contrast, England and France have been tangling with about two generations of newly arrived diverse populations from the Asian subcontinent, the West Indies, and Africa that are particularly marked by racial and religious differences (apart from the historic populations that were previously wedded into those nation-states), while Germans and Poles have had minorities in their communities for centuries until wars and genocidal traumas took their toll, rendering those ethnic stories more history than on-going contemporary accounts—but significant nonetheless.

The point is that most nation-states in the modern world are not like Japan, with its 1 percent or so of non-Japanese citizens. Multiethnicity and multiculturalism have become more the rule than the exception, whether of ancient or more recent origins, with unity from below or from above. Moreover, as suggested, the successes and failures of these experiments in multiethnic nation-states compel us to consider what traditions, values, institutions, customs, political precedents, and historical encounters have contributed to those successes (including that of the United States) and failures. What can Americans learn from the realization that their own history—by no means without its own conflicts and dark times—has parallels elsewhere and, as well, numerous points of difference from the experiences of most other nations? Do we come away understanding the United States better? Hopefully.

An important objective of the Ethnic Diversity Within Nations series is to help readers in the United States and elsewhere better appreciate how societies in many parts of the world have struggled with the challenges of diversity and, by providing such an understanding, enable all of us to interact more effectively with each other. Thus, by helping students and other readers learn about these varied nations, our goal with this series is to see them become better-informed citizens that are better able to comprehend world events and act responsibly as voters, officeholders, teachers, public officials, and businesspersons, or simply when interacting and coexisting with diverse individuals, whatever the sources of that diversity.

Elliott Robert Barkan

Introduction

WHILE ON A VISIT TO THE UNITED STATES IN 2001, Nigeria's president, Olusegun Obasanjo, was asked to name his major achievement since being elected to office in 1999. He responded, "Nigeria is still united" (Dare 2001). For readers unfamiliar with Nigeria's tumultuous history since its independence in 1960, Obasanjo's remark may appear to be odd and to indicate little in the way of tangible accomplishments. However, after reading this book, which explores the history and dynamics of the relationships among the diverse people of Africa's most populous country, readers will better realize the significance of Obasanjo's statement.

Understanding Nigeria is more than just a subject of casual intellectual interest. For one thing, Nigeria is of importance to the United States. It is the ancestral home of many African-Americans and the fifth largest supplier of oil to the U.S. market. It is also a major economic and political power on the African continent and an ally of the U.S. government in promoting U.S. interests in Africa. If Nigeria should fail as a nation, it would have profound destabilizing economic and political consequences on the African continent, which is already reeling from decades of political and economic crises.

The issue of national unity to which President Obasanjo referred is related to three lines of fragmentation in Nigerian society, which will be discussed throughout this book. One is ethnic diversity. Nigeria is home to at least 250 distinct ethnic groups. The three largest groups are the Hausa-Fulani, the Yoruba, and the Igbo (sometimes spelled Ibo). The country is also divided into rival groups based on region, the most basic division being the north versus the south. Religion is a third area of concern. Roughly half of the population is Muslim, with a large Christian minority numbering about 40 percent. About 10 percent of Nigerians continue to embrace indigenous religions.

All of these lines of fragmentation, ethnicity, region, and religion, are crosscutting. Specifically, the Hausa-Fulani live mainly in the north and are mostly Muslims. The Yoruba are found mainly in the southwest. Most are Christian, with a sizeable number of Muslims among them, especially in the more northern parts of Yorubaland. The Igbo are mainly in the southeast, although many are found in urban areas throughout the country. They are also a largely Christian population. Complicating the ethnic mix is the large number of smaller ethnic groups scattered throughout the north and the south. Holding this sometimes contentious assortment of people together has been a challenge not only to Obasanjo but to all of his predecessors as well, which will be shown in the following chapters.

Before this exploration of diversity in Nigeria begins, it is important to clarify several interrelated misconceptions about Africa and the nature of ethnic diversity there. Perhaps readers will have noticed that this book refers to Nigeria's various peoples as "ethnic groups" and not as "tribes," as is common among most people, including some Africans. Most Africanist scholars avoid the term *tribes* because of the connotations it has. The idea of tribe implies that Africans are organized into ancient and "primordial" groups usually based on descent from a common ancestor. Tribes share a common history and culture (including language) and have deep and abiding loyalties to each other that are the primary basis of identity. These tribal loyalties are seen as "traditional" and backward, for they override and prevent the formation of more "modern" sources of identity and affiliation, such as those of nationality and class. Thus, Africans are seen to be qualitatively different and inferior to people who live in developed countries like those of Europe or the United States, whose culturally diverse groups are called ethnic groups or nationalities, anything but tribes! Scholars also avoid the term *tribe* because of the common tendency to use tribalism as the main explanation for political conflict and violence in African countries. Instead of analyzing the complexity of contemporary factors involved in conflict, too often conflict is reduced to "a resurgence of long-standing tribal hatreds."

The deeply ingrained notion of tribes and tribalism in people's thinking is rooted in nineteenth-century European racialist and evolutionary colonial conceptions of non-Western people. Most colonized people were seen as primitive, uncivilized, and at an early stage of social evolutionary development compared to Europeans. Europeans saw themselves as superior, especially in comparison with Africans. Africans were described as living in primitive tribal communities, whereas Europeans supposedly lived in modern nations. According to such thinking, a tribe was like a large family or kinship group held together by real or perceived blood ties. By contrast, nations were made up of people loyal to a state structure regardless of their different ancestral origins. Tribalism was then, and still is, seen as a leftover of the past that is supposed to disappear with modernization. Seen this way, tribalism's powerful persistence in Africa becomes a justification for viewing

Africans as backward and their problems as being rooted in their inability to change and adapt to the modern world or to manage modern nations.

The term *ethnic group* escapes the problems associated with the concept of tribe. It recognizes the existence of identities and loyalties rooted in common language, culture, or territory that people of *all* societies have, even those who live in modern nation-states. Being an Igbo in Nigeria is thus an ethnic identity, just as being an Italian-American is in the United States. Such identities do not preclude a sense of being Nigerian or American as well. When Africans are seen as members of ethnic groups like the rest of the world, they will be less likely to be thought of as the "other" and as backward anomalies. Perhaps then, as is true of other areas of the world, the fragile condition of African nations will be analyzed in terms other than "tribal conflict."

The concept of tribal conflict explains nothing about the political, economic, or social bases for conflict among most African groups (or the lack of conflict). To make this point more clearly, compare some world conflicts that were not in Africa. When civil war broke out in the former Yugoslavia between the Serbs, Croats, and Bosnians, it was not described as a tribal war. The same is true for the disintegration of the former USSR. Its breakup was not explained as the result of tribalism. Secessionist sentiments among the French-Canadians and their antagonisms with English-speaking Canadians are also not seen in tribal terms. People view these conflicts as in part ethnically based, but the major explanation rests on understanding the political, economic, and social causes for conflict along ethnic lines.

By contrast, when civil war broke out in 1994 in the East African country of Rwanda, it typically was blamed on ancient tribal hostilities between the Hutu majority and the Tutsi minority. Often unanalyzed were the origins of contemporary violence in colonial policies and in current economic and political rivalries and inequities. Also ignored in understanding allegedly ancient tribal hatreds were such facts as the cultural similarity and years of intermixing between the two groups, and the fact that there were long periods of peaceful coexistence in earlier times. If there is violence now, what has changed? And why did it progress from isolated cases of violence by certain extremists to wholesale genocide? (On this issue, one can point to the inaction of the outside world in the early stages of the violence.) It is these questions people need to be asking, rather than finding easy answers in "tribalism."

If Africans lived in small, isolated communities where identities have been stable for many generations, it might be appropriate to refer to them as living in tribes. This is not the case for most groups, however, and certainly not for the three Nigerian ethnic groups. As we will see, the Hausa-Fulani, the Yoruba, and the Igbo include millions of people. Each group's population is larger than the populations of many European countries, is made up of diverse peoples due to centuries of intermixing, and has long had contact with outsiders. Current identities and cultures are not unaltered extensions of the past, rooted in "tradition" and untouched by "modernity." Therefore, it is inaccurate to portray them as having ancient and primordial identities when their identities have changed and continue to change over time.

Some scholars go so far as to claim that in many respects, a large number of the so-called tribes of Africa have been "invented" by Europeans and by Africans themselves during the colonial period (that is, during the nineteenth to twentieth centuries). Not only are tribes invented, but they have also undergone modification in response to the changing political and economic context in which groups found themselves. For example, in Nigeria, the Yoruba did not exist as an ethnic group or tribe in their own self-perceptions until Europeans came and applied this name to them based on the language they spoke. Even the term *Nigerian* is a European concept invented to apply to all Africans living within the boundaries of their newly created colony, which they called Nigeria. All of the people living within the colony of Nigeria were assigned to a tribal group and given a tribal name for administrative purposes. Tribal labels were applied regardless of the size or the actual fluid boundaries and differences in political organization, social complexity, or history of the groups in question. As with any self-fulfilling prophecy, subjugated Africans soon came to perceive themselves and to relate to each other and to other groups along these imposed tribal lines.

Once tribal identities were systematically applied, they had major consequences with regard to altering identities and relationships. For instance, tribal identities were soon followed by the application of distinct boundaries between one tribe and other tribes. Divisions and conflicts not previously present then developed, as groups vied to enjoy the benefits or minimize the costs of colonization, as these were often dependent on tribal affiliation. As readers will discover, in Nigeria most of the alleged ancient tribes and tribal conflicts referred to today are actually legacies of colonialism that were continued and modified in the present postcolonial society. In fact, in many other parts of the world as well as in Africa, ethnicity is becoming a growing issue and for similar reasons. Rather than sweeping away the concept of ethnicity, the forces of modernization in a postcolonial, globalizing world—including the spread of capitalism, democracy, nationalism, and Western culture—are behind the growth of ethnic divisiveness. Such conflicts are not inevitable but reflect the uneven and often inequitable impact of modern and global forces on societies and on groups within society. As readers will see, this is certainly the case in Nigeria.

Rejecting the descriptive and explanatory value of the concept of tribe does not mean that divisions and conflicts in Africa are not connected to ethnicity and to a heightened sense of ethnic identification in many places. Ethnic identity has become for many Africans a primary basis for identity and for mobilizing people, sometimes in opposition to other ethnic groups. Often, ethnicity does outweigh national identity and loyalty or class consciousness. Nonetheless, one must keep in mind that ethnicity is neither the only identity people have nor always the primary one. In Nigeria, for example, many people have regional and religious identities that do not necessarily coincide with ethnicity. In some situations, religion may be more important than ethnicity or region, or vice versa. There are cases in which class interests can forge ties of solidarity that override ethnicity, as when workers organize and engage in strikes or demonstrations as members of labor unions. Other identities exist as well, such as those of gender, age, political party, or kinship that can create alliances across ethnic groups, regions, or religions.

What this demonstrates is that, like people everywhere, Nigerians possess a variety of identities and loyalties, including a national identity. One should avoid the mistake of assuming, however, that nationalism is inherently superior and more culturally advanced than ethnicity. Both forms of identity can be used to promote xenophobic discrimination, conflict, violence, and even genocide. If national identity is weak and ethnicity comes to be of primary relevance or to be related to conflict in a country, those who study the nation need to look for the underlying causes. Even if ethnicity has precolonial roots, researchers need to look for the contemporary forces at work that make ethnic identity vital to individuals and communities and that set certain ethnic groups in competition or conflict with each other.

This study of Nigeria will focus on the precolonial, colonial, and postcolonial development of ethnic relationships, but the emergence of regional and religious differences will be examined as well. The book will examine the underlying social, economic, and political forces that have shaped and modified these relationships over time, which will allow readers to see why such identities have been of little or no importance at one time but of major importance in influencing events at other times. The book will also closely examine the present problems of national unity in Nigeria. The root problem is not ethnic (or regional or religious) diversity; it is more a symptom of underlying problems associated with the failure of the Nigerian state to serve the interests of the nation. This has led people to rely on those subnational communities and groups they believe can provide the resources and protection necessary for survival and, in the case of the privileged few, power and prosperity. Since gaining its independence, the country has flip-flopped between corrupt and ineffectual civilian rule and repressive and corrupt military rule. Political instability, economic decline, and divide-and-rule policies are among the problems that have increased group divisions within the country to the dangerous point at which the nation may not survive.

One effect of Nigeria's fractious and unstable recent history is that millions of Nigerians have left the country to work and live for extended periods. In some instances, they are in neighboring African countries, but many have gone to Europe or the United States. As migrants, most retain close ties with their homeland, families, and communities of origin. They form vibrant associations in host countries, some of which can be accessed on the Internet. Their impact on politics and development in Nigeria will be a topic of discussion in the latter part of the book.

A major issue to be discussed is whether or not Nigeria can survive as one nation. There is a recent historical basis for concern. Nigeria experienced a civil war in the late 1960s due to the Igbos' desire to secede and create their own nation, Biafra. Some observers conclude that Nigeria is too diverse to succeed as a unitary state. Yet the world has countries like the United States that include people of diverse ethnic, racial, regional, and religious identities but who manage to thrive as members of one nation. The problem is not diversity as such, but how diversity is managed. The task for Nigeria is to develop institutions and rules governing intergroup relations that can earn legitimacy and confidence from its people. Unfortunately, as will be seen in this book, such institutions do not currently exist. Much of the fault lies in the failure of the Nigerian state and political system to create conditions in which ethnicity is not the only or best way for people to promote their individual or group interests. Instead, in Nigeria, groups are placed in competition with each other for scarce economic and political resources that are controlled by the state and based largely on people's ethnic affiliations. This competition and the identities it promotes are intensified by the fact that ethnic groups tend to be concentrated in different regions of the country or within ethnic enclaves in cities outside their home regions.

Both the concentration of ethnic groups and the competition for such things as jobs, social and development services, political offices, and financial rewards are conducive to conflict along ethnic lines. Competition and conflict in turn heighten insecurity and further reinforce ethnic boundaries that separate groups from each other. Rather than being "ancient," these boundaries often were not present in the past. They are, like ethnicity itself, circumstantial—that is, they are the result of current conditions and social tensions. Ethnic conflict is ultimately about the struggle for political rights and an equitable share of material and social resources. When people feel that as a group they are excluded or unfairly treated by the state, which controls these resources and their distribution, ethnic solidarity promises to be the most effective way to organize to acquire a bigger slice of the resource pie.

One might ask why in Africa ethnicity and not some other identity is most often used to pursue collective or individual interests. One might contrast Africa with the United States, where the claim is that individuals and groups organize into ideologically or class-based political parties and interest groups to seek access to state power and resources and where such organizing is infrequently done along ethnic lines. (There is no political party in the United States for the Italians versus the Irish, for example.) Interest groups also tend to reflect issues, such as the environment or gun control, or economic interests, such as those of professional or business groups. These groups are not limited to specific ethnic groups, nor do most members of ethnic groups see ethnic mobilization as a primary means to achieve their goals.

Although these claims are true to a point, if one thinks critically one can see many exceptions. For one, there are tendencies for some ethnic/racial groups to identify with one of two major U.S. parties. African-Americans usually vote Democratic by a wide margin, as do many Latinos (other than Cubans). Also, some ethnic groups (especially minorities) do have associations and interest groups to promote group interests. Jews, Arabs, and African-Americans come to mind.

The difference between African countries and the United States, which explains the difference in the potency of ethnicity, is that in the United States there is more opportunity for economic and political advancement by individuals (although discrimination does exist). In countries like Nigeria, the private sector is weak, and individual advancement often depends on access to political office or officeholders. Government, rather than the private sector, provides most of the means to acquire wealth and influence. Political and economic resources are relatively scarce, and competition for them is intense. Too often, access to these resources depends on using ethnic group ties and networks. Although groups also organize along class or occupational group lines, such groups are usually smaller and weaker than ethnic groups. Ethnic groups also have the advantage of being more tangible and localized, thus more "real" to the average Nigerian. Ethnic identities are constructed on the basis of real or imagined social bonds of shared culture, history, religion, or descent. These are analogous to family and kinship, with which people can readily identify. Moreover, members of some ethnic communities may have greater access to political and economic advancement than others if state power is concentrated in the hands of one or a few ethnic groups who favor members of their own group over others. In these circumstances, rather than individuals or families achieving social mobility in a relatively open competitive system, an individual's class or occupational advancement is often more dependent on ethnic group membership.

The main problem in Africa is that since independence most states have failed to deliver on their promises to provide development and good governance for their people. Instead, authoritarian, often military, governments resort to a combination of patron-client relationships and repression to remain in power. Patron-client relationships are those in which people in positions of economic and political power (the patrons) distribute the benefits of their positions (such as jobs, loans, or public services) to communities, groups, or individuals in exchange for their loyalty (such as with their votes at election time). In countries like Nigeria, it is of critical importance to have a member of one's own ethnic group in a position of power if one hopes to receive resources from the government. Otherwise, access to jobs, schools, business licenses, government contracts, health clinics, or roads may be difficult or impossible to get. By the same token, politicians are expected by their clients to make decisions favoring them, otherwise those clients may transfer their support to another patron who provides more benefits.

Although patron-client politics are designed to create ties of mutual obligation among politicians and their constituents, using ethnicity, region, or religion as the criteria for distributing government resources results in sacrificing impartial and rational criteria for such decisions. Waste and inefficiency too often are the results, and, if done on a large enough scale, this system can severely hamper development of the country. Ultimately, patron-client relationships may also be unsustainable because widespread corruption and mismanagement can lead to a decline in government resources as the economy falters. This often intensifies ethnic group competition and conflict over a shrinking pie.

If the government attempts to make the competition more equitable by creating an ethnically sensitive system for providing government resources to all, it then tends to formalize and harden ethnic boundaries in the political system. This is done in Nigeria through the creation of numerous states reflecting the concentration of ethnic groups in various parts of the country. Ethnicity becomes formally recognized as the means to political participation and political resources. Rather than lessening ethnic conflict and identification, the opposite may occur. New ethnic groups proliferate in an effort to gain political recognition and legitimate minority group claims for their own separate states and budgets. In this way they can claim a piece of the resource pie from the central government that would be unavailable otherwise.

As already mentioned, the patronage-based state fails to serve the needs of its people. Indeed, the idea of "nation" loses legitimacy and meaning. People are compelled to seek more aid, protection, and meaning from subnational groups and affiliations. Ethnic, regional, and religious identities increase in significance, as is occurring in Nigeria. As state resources shrink, states cut back on the services and resources they can provide. People turn to local groups, such as churches, religious groups, militias and vigilante groups, and hometown and ethnic associations to meet their needs for economic development, social services, poverty alleviation, and even crime control.

Repression and violence are also linked to the failure of government and may manifest themselves along ethnic, regional, or religious lines. Poverty and inequality have increased in many African countries, in part as a result of global forces but also as a result of the corruption and mismanagement mentioned above. In some countries, the government has unfairly favored some ethnic groups with benefits at the expense of others. A sense of victimization grows among groups who feel left out. These can be religious groups or regions as well as ethnic groups. Feeling victimized, groups develop a heightened perception of loss of autonomy or rights, of unjust or discriminatory treatment, or of a lack of power or parity in the economy or government. The scarcer the resources for which people compete, the greater the likelihood of ethnic or religious mobilization and conflict. In response to conflict among groups or threats against the government itself, the state responds with growing repression. This further reduces its support from the populace. If ethnic or religious conflict and violence intensify, ethnic or religious identification and solidarity become even more vital. As the state neither meets people's needs nor protects people (in fact, the state may be encouraging intergroup conflict), people have no choice but to take refuge in kinship, region, ethnicity, or religion. These become the only safe havens. At the same time, separation from and distrust of others not in one's group are reinforced, and violent conflict among such groups becomes more likely. In Nigeria, for example, these forces are evident in the growing number of clashes between Muslims and Christians as well as in ethnic group conflict.

All of the above issues apply to Nigeria and have led to the present fragile state of this young nation. Does this mean that Nigeria is doomed to fail as a unified country? Is separation into different countries along ethnic, regional, or religious lines the only answer to the instability the country has endured since its independence in 1960? Or can equitable and legitimate institutions be created to defuse the tensions and lack of unity among the volatile mix of peoples who comprise the Nigerian nation? These are among the questions that are addressed in this book and that must be resolved by Nigerians themselves.

Before beginning the discussion, it is important to point out some features of the chapters ahead. At the end of each chapter is a timeline of the major events mentioned in the chapter. Following the timeline is a section of significant people, places, events, and information with which the reader may not be familiar. This section is not a glossary; it adds additional germane information to what is discussed in each chapter. Last, the reader will find a bibliography, which lists the major references used in the chapter.

Bibliography

Atkinson, Ronald R. 1999. "The (Re)Construction of Ethnicity in Africa: Extending the Chronology, Conceptualisation, and Discourse." Pp. 15–44 in *Ethnicity and Nationalism in Africa*. Edited by Paris Yeros. New York: St. Martin's.

Braathen, Einar, Morten Boas, and Gjermund Saether. 2000. "Ethnicity Kills? Social Struggles for Power, Resources, and Identities in the Neo-Patrimonial State." Pp. 3–22 in *Ethnicity Kills? The Politics of War, Peace, and Ethnicity in Africa*. Edited by Einar Braathen, Morten Boas, and Gjermund Saether. New York: St. Martin's.

Cornell, Stephen, and Douglas Hartmann. 1998. *Ethnicity and Race: Making Identities in a Changing World*. Thousand Oaks, CA: Pine Forge.

Dare, Sunday. 2001. "Two Years On." *The Nation* (Nigeria) 6 (June 11).

Eriksen, Thomas Hylland. 1999. "A Non-Ethnic State for Africa? A Life-World Approach to the Imagining of Communities." Pp. 45–64 in *Ethnicity and Nationalism in Africa*. Edited by Paris Yeros. New York: St. Martin's.

Farrar, Tarikhu. 1992. "When African Kings Became 'Chiefs': Some Transformations in European Perceptions of West African Civilization, c. 1450–1800." *Journal of Black Studies* 23 (December): 258–278.

Hobsbawm, Eric, and Terence Ranger, eds. 1983. *The Invention of Tradition*. Cambridge, UK: Cambridge University Press.

Olzak, Susan. 1983. "Contemporary Ethnic Mobilization." *Annual Review of Sociology* 9: 355–374.

Ranger, Terence. 1999. "Concluding Comments." Pp. 133–144 in *Ethnicity and Nationalism in Africa*. Edited by Paris Yeros. New York: St. Martin's.

Williams, Robin M., Jr. 1994. "The Sociology of Ethnic Conflicts: Comparative International Perspectives." *Annual Review of Sociology* 20: 49–79.

List of Maps

CHAPTER ONE

The Peopling of Nigeria

THIS BOOK'S INTRODUCTION discussed why the terms *ethnic group* and *ethnicity* are used here instead of the more common terms *tribe* and *tribalism* for referring to Nigeria's major cultural groups. The Introduction examined how such identities as that of ethnic group are created and redefined by people over time. Such identities are not primordial (ancient and primary) or unchangeable. More accurately, ethnic identities are circumstantial and reflect the complex interplay of social, economic, and political forces. The three largest ethnic groups in Nigeria are the Hausa-Fulani, the Yoruba, and the Igbo (sometimes called Ibo), and they will be the focus of study in this chapter and throughout the book. The discussion that follows will examine the origins of these three groups and their relationships to the earliest people of Nigeria. Migratory movements, language families, and the intermixing of people in the past are all elements that reveal how today's ethnic groups came to be where they are in Nigeria and that provided the early foundations for developing some cultural similarities.

Readers should be aware, however, that there is much that scholars do not know about these topics because of the scarcity of reliable archeological and historical data. Most African societies relied in the past on oral traditions as a way to transmit their history and origins. Although often having some basis in fact, most of this information is imbued with supernaturalism and other embellishments. In addition, different subgroups may have different versions of the same story. Obviously, one cannot rely on these accounts without corroborative data, which is currently unavailable.

Ethnic Diversity in Nigeria

Today, the West African country of Nigeria is a large and diverse place. It has an area of 356,669 square miles, twice the size of California, with more than 120 million people. Nigeria has the largest population of any African country and is the world's tenth largest country; it will be the seventh largest by 2025. Nigeria's immediate neighbors are Benin, Burkina Faso, Niger, Chad, and Cameroon.

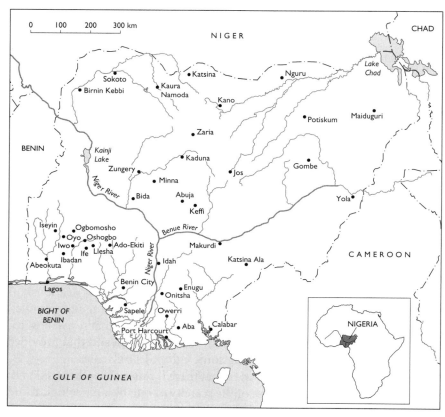

Map 1.1
Federal Republic of Nigeria

Nigeria has approximately 250 different ethnic groups and languages, but the four largest groups are the Hausa (21 percent), the Yoruba (21 percent), the Igbo (18 percent), and the Fulani (9 percent). Because of extensive inter-mixing, the Hausa and Fulani have become hard to distinguish. Usually they are discussed as one group, the Hausa-Fulani. Therefore, this study will focus on Nigeria's three main ethnic groups—the Hausa-Fulani, the Yoruba, and the Igbo. The rest of the population is a diversity of minority groups, including the Igala, the Nupe, the Kanuri, the Ibibio, the Tiv, the Ijaw, and many others. Each group tends to be concentrated in a specific region of the country.

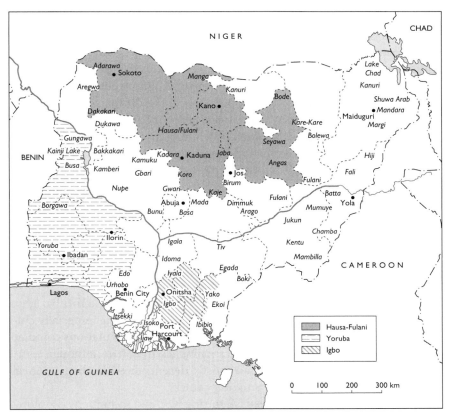

Map 1.2
Major Cities and Ethnic Groups

As religion has become such an important element in Nigerian intergroup relations, it will also be discussed where relevant. Currently, about 50 percent (mostly in the north) are Muslims, 40 percent are Christians (mostly in the south), and 10 percent follow indigenous religions.

Nigeria and Nigerians did not exist until the twentieth century. These concepts are recent inventions or constructions of identities. The name *Nigeria* was reputedly suggested by Flora Shaw in 1897. She was the wife of Lord Frederick Lugard, who at the time was the British colonial ruler of what was to become the Northern Nigerian Protectorate. When the Northern and Southern Protectorates were combined in 1914, what is now Nigeria came into existence. In other words, Nigeria is the result of British colonial conquest rather than an African creation that reflected the affiliations and sentiments of the people living there. Before becoming a British colony,

Nigeria was a loose geographical area made up of many diverse groups with widely varying cultures and political systems. Their societies varied from highly independent, small villages to large, complex states. Boundaries shifted as a result of population movements and warfare. In many cases, peoples in Nigeria are related to groups in surrounding countries. This reflects the mixing and movement of people over the centuries and the arbitrariness and recency of today's nation-state boundaries.

The peopling of Nigeria has been much influenced by geography. There are several geographic zones that affected such things as access, population density, subsistence strategies (for example, fishing, farming, or pastoralism), and social organization. Mangrove swamps and rainforests dominate the coast. This area also has many creeks and islands, and it also includes the Niger River delta. Along the coast, fishing and farming have long been practiced. Because there is little dry land, settlements and farms were usually small-scale. The Ijo and Kalabari are among the peoples who live along the coast. They traded salt and fish with interior groups, traveling by boat along the creeks and rivers.

Moving inland, one finds the forest belt. Here are located the Yoruba, Igbo, Edo, and Ibibio, among others. They specialized in farming, especially cultivating root crops and tubers. In the forest belt, larger populations could be supported by the land. Many large and small states arose here, although some groups, such as the Igbo, remained mostly decentralized in their political structure and had no chiefs or hereditary rulers.

There are more hills and plateaus in the interior, and mountains rise along the eastern border. The Niger-Benue River valley is another distinctive zone in the country's interior and an area that supported many different societies of varying sizes and complexities.

Lastly, one arrives at the northern savannah region, which is part of the Sahel and Western Sudan. Here the climate is more hot and dry, and grass fields replace forests. Livestock herding and farming, including the cultivation of cereal crops, have been practiced here since ancient times. Much of the soil in the north is infertile, making it more difficult to make a living. Nonetheless, many early states and city-states developed here, often supported by long-distance trade. The Hausa-Fulani are the major group in the North, although several minorities, notably the Kanuri, also live here.

Scholars know which groups inhabit these areas of Nigeria now and which groups have inhabited them as far back as the past few centuries, but much less is known about where these groups came from, how long they have lived where they are, and how they are connected to prehistoric occupants of Nigeria or elsewhere. There is still only limited archeological, linguistic, or reliable historical evidence to shed light on the ancient past. Despite these deficiencies in current knowledge, there is some tantalizing information available, and more will surely become available as more research is done.

Nigerian Prehistory

Perhaps 5 million years ago, the earliest hominids began evolving in Africa. The first true humans evolved in Africa from these hominid ancestors about 100,000 years ago. The evidence to date is that the earliest, most varied, and longest-lived hunter-gatherer societies were in Africa as well. These early societies adapted to a wide range of environments, from deserts to rainforests to coastal swamps. Tropical diseases killed many individuals, and these diseases also limited agriculture and the use of domesticated animals, such as horses or cattle. Also limited was the size and growth of human populations.

Most of the fossils and artifacts showing the evolution of early ancestors and human culture come from eastern and southern Africa. By contrast, there are no clear-cut, datable fossils or artifacts of early hominids in Nigeria or West Africa in general. There are two possible reasons for this. One is that such material has not yet been discovered. The other is that bones and perishable tools (such as bone, wood, or basketry) have not been preserved due to the nature of West African soils and moisture.

Although rare, some artifacts have been discovered in Nigeria. Among the finds are stone choppers, which were found at Beli in northern Nigeria. Hand axes and cleavers were also unearthed on the Jos Plateau and in the country of Ghana. Because they were in a disturbed location, scholars are unable to date these materials with certainty. The existence of primitive stone pebble tools suggests the presence of what is called Olduwan technology, which dates from 2 to 5 million years ago in other parts of Africa. Other stone artifacts point to the presence of homo erectus, the ancestor of modern homo sapiens, between 1,500,000 and 100,000 years ago. Many other ancient artifacts, such as bifacial spear points, knives, and scrapers, have been found in Nigeria. These are linked to a technology more advanced than the Olduwan, the Acheulian, which existed between 1,500,000 and 200,000 years ago. In southwest Nigeria, a hunter-gatherer people left stone artifacts of their microlith (small stone tools) technology in a rock shelter at Iwo Eleru, which dates to between 11,000 and 12,000 years ago. A burial site was also located. The skeletal remains in the site had negroid features similar to those of present-day West Africans. At other sites, pottery and ground stone tools dating to 5,500 years ago have been found. One such site is at Afikpo, in southeast Nigeria; another is in Cameroon. Other microlith sites without pottery have been discovered in such places as Mejiro, near Old Oyo, and at Rop, on the Jos Plateau. In some densely forested areas of Nigeria, Sierra Leone, and Guinea, crude axe-like stone tools were used for digging until the past few thousand years.

Climate change also affected human habitation in and around Nigeria. Before about 12,000 years ago, the Sahara was largely uninhabited, but after that date (and during the previous Ice Age) the area was wetter. Lake Chad was bigger then, and there were more lakes and streams in northern Nigeria. The people living in the area of Nigeria then were different than those living there today. Although few skeletal remains have been found, those that have been discovered show some resemblance to, as well as differences from, today's people. These remains suggest that there has been a long and ancient pattern of moving and mixing of peoples throughout Nigeria.

West Africans changed from primarily hunting and gathering to agriculture and pastoralism at least 5,000 years ago. This change in subsistence patterns was largely an indigenous development rather than the result of cultural diffusion from elsewhere. Almost all of the early food crops derived from local wild plants. These included such grains as sorghum (sometimes called guinea-corn) in the savannahs south of the Sahara. Oil palms and tubers, including the yam, were long used as staple food in southern Nigeria. Cattle, goats, and sheep were introduced from North Africa into the Sahara (during its wetter period) up to about 5,000 years ago. As the Sahara became drier, beginning about 5,000 years ago, Saharan cattle moved south. By 3,000 years ago, cattle were raised as far south as the forest edge in West Africa. Diseases of the forest zone prevented the further southward expansion of cattle. Other crops common to West Africa today, among them maize, manioc, and tomatoes, came from the New World in the past 500 years. Bananas were introduced even earlier as part of the Indian Ocean trade in East Africa.

Some intriguing evidence has been found of other Saharan influences on West African habitation and subsistence, besides the introduction of domestic animals. For example, some pottery decorations in West Africa are similar to Saharan ones. Also, the similarity of dates (about 5000 B.C.E.) for the appearance of pottery and ground stone tools in many parts of West Africa suggests common Saharan origins. By this time the Sahara was becoming dry again, likely precipitating new migrations of people into West Africa. Both the pottery and ground stone tools found at sites in Nigeria and other areas of West Africa were known in the Sahara at an earlier date. As another illustration of Saharan influence, in the Bornu plains in extreme northeastern Nigeria (bordering Lake Chad), permanent settlements date to 4000 B.C.E. Houses had wood walls and clay floors. Numerous artifacts were found indicating the use of bone tools, pottery, and domestic cattle and goats. The people engaged in hunting and fishing as well as agriculture and pastoralism. Similar communities were found in the Sahara at least 2,000 years earlier, which suggests that they were the origin of the Nigerian settlements. It is possible that such cereals as bulrush millet, fonio, and sorghum were brought to West Africa by Saharan migrants, but it is likely they are at least in part indigenous plants. Whatever the case is for origins, today these grains are found along a broad belt from the Nile valley to Senegal. Their cultivation and that of yams and rice (which seem to be indigenous crops) have been well established for thousands of years (perhaps as early as 5000 B.C.E.).

Another cultural influence from the north, perhaps as far away as the Nile valley, is the rectangular buildings found in the forest areas of Ghana and Nigeria. In both areas, the most common buildings are large, four-unit structures with verandahs and open, square courtyards. These buildings are more suitable for a dry climate than for areas like the forest belt that get heavy rain, because when it rains, water collects in the sunken courtyard and must be removed. Some argue that such an impractical architectural feature may be the result of cultural diffusion from elsewhere. Some oral tradition states that the courtyard was brought by the ancestors of the Akan (in Ghana) and the Yoruba and Edo (in Nigeria). These ancestors are said to have had Nile-area origins. Supporting these claims of a Nile connection, Egyptian houses were rectangular with open courtyards; this was also true of the palaces at Meroe in Kush, south of Egypt.

Linguistic evidence is another useful tool to trace the origins, movements, and intermixing of people from the distant past. There are four African language families to which all African languages belong. These include Niger-Congo, Khoisan, Afro-Asiatic, and Nilo-Saharan languages. In general, Niger-Congo languages are spoken by most people of sub-Saharan ancestry. Among the Niger-Congo languages in Nigeria are the Western Atlantic branch languages, including Fulfulde (or Fulbe), which is spoken by the Fulani, and the Central branch language of the Tiv. Kwa languages are spoken by the Yoruba, Afikpo, and Igbo. In some parts of eastern Nigeria, languages of the Adamawa-Ubangian branch are spoken. The term *Bantu languages* is often used to refer to the Niger-Congo languages that originated in the West African forest belt, including Nigeria. They are spoken throughout much of Africa as a result of the southward migration of people from the Cameroon-eastern Nigeria area about 3,000 to 4,000 years ago. The Hausa language is part of the Chadic branch of the Afro-Asiatic language family. Linguistics ties the Hausa with many other Saharan peoples and languages rather than with the people and languages of the forest belt to the south.

Iron Age Nigeria

Along the slopes of the Jos Plateau in Nigeria's Middle Belt region are several sites that reveal an early, sophisticated culture in which iron was being smelted as early as 500 B.C.E. The Nok culture, as it was named, produced such items as knives, arrowheads, spear points, and jewelry of iron. Equally impressive were life-size terra cotta figurines, mostly of humans. The human figures have Negroid features, similar to those of the current population. The Nok culture flourished until the second century C.E. The new iron technology spread rapidly by trade and population movements. Eventually, Bantu-speaking, forest-belt people extended the technology throughout most of the continent during their migrations.

Scholars continue to debate the origins of iron working in West Africa. One hypothesis is that traders or migrants introduced iron making from Meroe. It then moved across the Sahel, the semiarid region bordering the Sahara that has long been a major trade route. Another view is that iron came from earlier Sahelian settlements, which may have gotten the technology from Meroe. One such early settlement is Taruga. Iron smelting furnaces there date to at least 400 B.C.E. Other sites almost as old have been found in the Kainji dam area on the Niger River and near Yelwa. Others contend that iron working was independently discovered in more than one location. The new technology may have been based on earlier local copper smelting. The fact that iron working dates from between 600 to 300 B.C.E. in other sub-Saharan communities in east central Africa (for example, in Tanzania) and the Middle Nile suggests that the early iron industry radiated from one or more sources in the Sahara toward the equator.

Whatever the origins of iron technology in Nigeria, the items produced for agriculture, warfare, and domestic use reflect indigenous cultural influences. The early Iron Age cultures in Nigeria were associated primarily with peasant agricultural communities, which predominated in much of West Africa for at least the past 2,000 years. The Nok people, for example, cultivated such crops as sorghum and raised cattle. Iron Age West Africans also engaged extensively in interregional trade long before the trans-Saharan trade routes developed. This trade included grains and foods, animals and skins, and crafts such as pottery and iron tools. This trade was a major stim-

Reproduction of a Nok Nigerian sculpture, dated from between 500 B.C.E. and 500 C.E. (AFP/Corbis)

ulus to the growth of towns and cities, new technological and cultural developments, intermixing of people, and eventual state formation.

It is important to stress once again that, during this period, the people in Nigeria were not the same people we see today. Although there are some broad similarities linguistically and culturally, for the most part current groups have been in their present locales only during the past millennium. People have moved and intermixed extensively over time, sometimes displacing earlier peoples, and other times intermixing to produce new hybrid populations and cultures. In some cases, one can see a connection between today's cultures and earlier cultures; in others, one can see the introduction of elements from outside the region. The next section will explore the origins of the major ethnic groups found in Nigeria today as history has continued into more recent times.

The Origins of Nigeria's Present Ethnic Groups

A few points need to be reiterated before beginning a discussion of current ethnic groups in Nigeria. One is that most of these groups are of fairly recent origin; they are not ancient "tribes" whose identities have remained unchanged over a long period of time. Another point is that they are not uniform groups descended from a common ancestor in ancient times; they are instead a mixture of groups. Most group origins are shrouded in myth, with only some independent scientific data available to establish the facts. Whatever the facts, however, ultimately it is what people *believe* about their own identities and those of other groups that affects their social reality and, consequently, their relationship with others.

By the ninth century C.E., many highly developed cultures, some highly stratified by wealth and power, existed in many parts of Nigeria. The site of one such society is at Igbo Ukwu, near the present-day city of Onitsha in Igboland. Here, a burial site was discovered that contained extensive grave goods of a person of considerable power and status, perhaps a priest-king. The person's status is indicated by the fact that he was buried in a seated position on a stool, a symbol of rulership even today in many parts of West Africa. Other official regalia were also found. Further testifying to the status of the deceased was the discovery of the bodies of five attendants in an upper chamber. Other items associated with the burial were ivory tusks and superb cast bronze objects using the lost wax method. These grave goods included vases, bowls, models of seashells, and personal ornaments. The Igbo Ukwu site may be an antecedent of the later renowned forest belt states of Oyo and Benin, states associated with the Yoruba and Edo people, respectively. Many of the glass beads and some of the artwork techniques used at Igbo Ukwu are unlike any local work. Recent archeological investigations suggest that these latter items are similar to those found in Egypt at this time and thus may indicate the existence of long-distance trade between Igbo

Ukwu (and thus the forest belt) and Egypt prior to this date.

The forest belt, inhabited by such groups as the Yoruba, the Edo, the Igbo, and the Ibibio, produced numerous small and large states. These states developed despite their relative isolation, their climatic and agricultural limitations, and disease. The sophistication of many of these states is indicated by the early mastery of iron smelting (by 300 to 500 C.E.) and their use of the lost wax method to produce metal work of considerable craftsmanship. By 1000 C.E., trade in slaves, ivory, salt, glass beads, coral, cloth, weapons, brass, and other items was well established.

The Yoruba

One early settlement in southwestern Nigeria was at Ife, where a significant population of Iron Age agriculturalists had settled by 900 to 1000 C.E. Ife was the spiritual capital of the Yoruba kingdoms, but it never attained much military or political power due to a poor location within the forest belt. Ife, however, may have inspired the development of the greatest of the Yoruba kingdoms, Oyo, located in the better-situated savannah region and one of the oldest kingdoms in Africa. Little is known about the people who first settled Ife or of their relationship to the Yoruba. In fact, little factual information exists about the Yoruba before 1700. Before that time, oral tradition was the only record of their origins and history, and not all of the accounts agree with each other. Indeed, all of the main Yoruba towns have their own origin myths. According to some Yoruba origin myths, God let down a chain at Ife from which Oduduwa, the ancestor of the Yoruba (and, in some accounts, of all people), descended. He carried earth (which he threw into the waters), a cock (which scratched the waters to become land), and a palm kernel (which grew into a palm tree with sixteen branches). The branches of the palm tree represent the sixteen original Yoruba kingdoms. Subsequent migrations of Oduduwa's offspring and their followers from Ife led to the establishment of the other Yoruba kingdoms. In the Oyo version of the origin myth, Oduduwa came from the east, settled at Ife, and had seven sons. In Ife, legends recount that an earlier people lived in the area before Oduduwa but were conquered or driven out. The main area of agreement among the Yoruba about their origins, which has considerable significance even today, is that all Yoruba view Oduduwa as their common ancestor and Ife as their source and spiritual center.

Most Yoruba legends make no mention of a movement of people from outside the Nigeria area but instead suggest a process of state formation by people within the area. Linguistic evidence provides some basis to conclude that the Yoruba inhabited their present area for hundreds or perhaps more than 1,000 years, with some in-migration from other groups. There is also some speculation, however, that before that most of the Yoruba originated in the savannahs to the north, then migrated to the forest region some time in the distant past.

Whatever their origins, the Yoruba and their neighbors, the Edo (or Bini), became a link between the savannah to the north and the Niger delta, where the Efik and Ibibio (among others) lived, and to the Igbo in the southeast. Yorubaland, though mostly forest, also included areas of woodland savannah. Trade brought all of these groups in contact with each other. Both the Yoruba and Edo established kingdoms that were African creations uninfluenced by Islam. This was also true of the Hausa states to the north until the fifteenth century after which time Fulani and Muslim influence became significant.

There is little historically accurate information on the origins of the Yoruba kingdoms. The Oduduwa legend points to a king at Ife, who may have sent forth six or seven of his sons to found independent kingdoms between 1100 to 1400 C.E., or perhaps as early as the late eighth or early ninth centuries. More likely, however, Ife was an early kingdom, which reached its zenith in the eleventh or twelfth century. Ife then may have been a legitimating force in the founding of additional kingdoms. This legitimacy was based on the bestowing of beaded crowns on major rulers (*obas*), who trace their ancestry to Ife and to Oduduwa, a practice that still exists today. The myth of a common origin from Oduduwa and Ife provides rulers with legitimacy and is a source of common identity and ancestry for the Yoruba, along with the Yoruba language and various other cultural traditions.

Despite the common elements that can be a unifying force and a source of ethnic identity for the Yoruba, the Yoruba are, in reality, not a single "tribe." They are a group of diverse people who came to share a common language, dress, ideas of chieftaincy (or kingship), and sense of history. Eventually, the Yoruba did develop seven major kingdoms, but these differed culturally in significant ways and often competed with each other for power. The kingdoms were Oyo, Kabba, Ekiti, Egba, Ife, Ondo, and Ijebu. Some were linguistically different enough that they had trouble understanding each other (for example, the Oyo in the north and the Ijebu in the south). Even the name *Yoruba* was not an identity the Yoruba developed for themselves. The name was first given to them by the Hausa in the north. The term referred to the Yoruba-speaking people who were living among them. The Yoruba label was extended in the nineteenth century by Christian missionaries, who applied it to all of the various groups who shared the Yoruba language. These groups gradually came to apply the label to themselves. This process is a clear example of the invention of ethnic groups and identities.

Northern Nigeria and the Hausa-Fulani

Trade was the basis of organized communities in the savannah areas of northern Nigeria. Prehistoric communities had dispersed by the third millennium B.C.E. due to the drying up of the Sahara. Trans-Saharan trade linked the savannah with the upper Nile region from ancient times and with the Mediterranean from the time of Carthage (ca. third century B.C.E.). Trans-Saharan trade was also the source of the centralized states, notably the Hausa states and Kanem, that were in existence before the ninth century C.E. By the eleventh century, many of the Hausa states (actually city-states) had become well established, walled towns controlling a mostly agricultural and pastoral hinterland. Other states, such as Ghana and Gao, helped to spread Islam as well as trade to the area.

According to myth, Hausa civilization originated in the city of Daura (north of the city of Kano). The Hausa's ancestors descended from Bayajidda, an immigrant from North Africa or the Middle East. When Bayajidda came to Daura, he slew a snake that had kept the people from getting water from a local well. The queen of Daura married Bayajidda as a reward. Their son Bawo assumed power after his father's death. Bawo had six sons, who established dynasties in Kano, Aria, Gobir, Katsina, Rano, and Biram. Most Hausa see Daura as their founding city-state and the home of their civilization and ruling lineages.

Kano, one of the greatest of the Hausa city-states, has an ancient history of its own. It began as the site of an important local deity, who lived on a high rock outcrop called Dalla Rock. Between the tenth and eleventh centuries C.E., Berbers from North Africa overthrew the local cults and the priests that ruled the area. The Berbers laid the foundation for Kano, whose inhabitants were of diverse origins, to become a major center of trade.

Like the Yoruba, the Hausa never formed a unified people or single state. They established independent city-states with their own distinct histories. The Hausa's main commonality was their language, which has been influenced by contact with other peoples. Hausa is a Chadic language of the Afro-Asiatic family, which distinguishes it from most of the languages of the south of Nigeria. About 25 percent of the language has Arabic origins and, since the 1900s, many English words have also entered the language.

Many Hausa institutions and skills came from the Kanuri people in Borno, a neighboring kingdom. Borno was closely linked to Kanem, the power in the Lake Chad basin by the thirteenth century. Kanem's ruling Saifi dynasty descended from black pastoralists, called Zaghawa, who settled in the area in the seventh century. The name *Kanuri* was originally that of a particular clan, but the term was gradually applied to all the inhabitants of Kanem. The rulers of Kanem came to accept Islam, which was brought by traders in the eleventh century. The Kanuri came to be identified as an ethnic group in the late fourteenth and early fifteenth centuries in the aftermath of a civil war. The war forced the rulers of Kanem and their followers to move to Borno (southeast of Lake Chad) in the fourteenth century. There they imposed their authority over the local So villages and began to be identified as a distinct people called the Kanuri. In the sixteenth century, the Kanuri exiles became powerful enough to reestablish their rule over Kanem. Kanem-Borno became a unified state that prospered into the nineteenth century, when it was threatened by the expanding Hausa-Fulani theocratic states to the west. There was much contact between the Hausa and the Kanuri, and eventually the Kanuri adopted the Hausa language and much of their culture. This has contributed to the considerable regional homogeneity found in the north today.

The Fulani began to enter Hausaland as nomadic pastoralists in the thirteenth century. By the fifteenth century, they were also in Borno. Their original home was the Senegambia region of West Africa. The Fulani are known by various names. Among the Wolof in Senegal, they are known as the Peul. The Bambara of Mali call them Fula. Their language, often referred to as Fulfulde or Fulani, is in the Western Atlantic branch of the Niger-Congo family. The spread of the Fulani people from Senegambia began in about the eleventh century, but they had converted to Islam before then. The Islamic brotherhoods they formed played a major role in strengthening Fulani ethnic and linguistic solidarity. By the late sixteenth century, the Fulani reached Lake Chad. There they mixed with the local Shuwa people. Originally from upper Egypt, the Shuwa were a pastoral group who were a mixture of Arabic and local Nilo-Saharan peoples. By the eighteenth century, the Fulani were moving into Borno to escape drought. In the nineteenth century they moved into Hausaland and became its rulers in the jihad wars led by Uthman dan Fodio (this will be discussed more in the next chapter).

Once the Fulani began living in Hausa cities, they freely intermixed with the Hausa and other groups over the generations. Many of the Fulani adopted the Hausa language and customs, making it difficult to tell them apart. This has resulted in the term *Hausa-Fulani* being applied to them. Although both are mixtures of different people, in Nigeria they now are often identified as one ethnic group.

The Igbo

The Igbo are the third largest ethnic group in Nigeria. Their home area is in the southeastern part of Nigeria. Their origins are obscure. The Igbo language is part of the Kwa language branch of the Niger-Congo family, which suggests that the Igbo originated in regions east and south of their present home in Nigeria. About 5,000 years ago, as groups migrated to different areas and became more culturally distinct, the Igbo, Yoruba, Edo, and Ijo became separate groups after having had common ancestors. Also, like the Yoruba, until recently the Igbo were linguistic communities rather than a single or unified ethnic group. There were, in fact, more than 200 different groups who came to speak the Igbo language.

Like most Nigerian groups, the Igbo have a mainly oral tradition to explain their origins and migrations. Most of these traditions suggest that the Igbo originated from a core area in Awka and Orlu. From there they dispersed south toward the coast and east to the Nsukka-Udi highlands. Tradition also refers to a later massive migration into the southeast, into the eastern Isuama area, and into Aba. Other migrations dispersed various populations eastward and even northward, where they became isolated as the Northeastern Igbo. Present-day Ada, Item, and Ibibio ethnic groups also were migrating at the same time. Most of the traditions explain these movements as "a flight from the raids of white-eyed dwarfs who came up the river armed with muskets" (Jones 1963, 30–31). The area of Arochuku was developed by the Igbo and Ibibio who remained in the area rather than migrating. Some Igbo groups have a tradition of coming from a variety of areas rather than one central location.

Although the data are sketchy, what evidence there is suggests that the Igbo (and other related ethnic groups in the area) have a history of periodic movements of people into new areas, where they merged with other groups. Both the Igbo and the Ibibio, for instance, moved into the Kalabari area and merged with each other along the boundaries. Fighting occasionally broke out, but in the end a new ethnic group was created, the Ngwa. The Ngwa themselves report that they are indeed the result of a blending of the Igbo and the Ibibio. Most of the coastal and Niger River delta minority ethnic groups are culturally and linguistically related to the Igbo. On the other hand, on the west side of the Niger River and its delta are people such as the Bini and Urhobo, who see themselves as being related to the ancient kingdom of Benin.

The Middle Belt

Although most of this discussion has been focused on Nigeria's three main groups, it is important to mention the so-called Middle Belt, where a sizable minority of Nigeria's population lives. The Middle Belt runs from the Cameroon Highlands on the east to the Niger River valley on the west. Today, between fifty and one hundred different ethnic groups live in this rather sparsely populated area. Among the major groups are the Nupe, the Igala, and the Tiv. Many small states developed here. The Middle Belt was also home to such ancient civilizations as the Nok culture. In the eastern part of the Middle Belt are Chadic language-speaking groups. Chadic languages are linked to eastern and central African languages, which are part of the Afro-Asiatic family. The languages found in the west are related to those of Mende-speakers found farther west in Africa. There is evidence that these western groups are descendants of an earlier group of cultures that occupied most of northern Nigeria before the large, centralized Islamic emirates were established in the early nineteenth century.

Conclusion

Clearly, there is much to learn about the origins and intermixing of Nigeria's contemporary ethnic groups. What evidence researchers have indicates that the composition of today's ethnic group reflects a long history of migration of peoples from sometimes distant locales, those people themselves being a mixture of different stocks going back to very ancient times. Traditional accounts provide very fragmentary information and often take a group's history back only a relatively short period of time. In most respects, one can view these histories as efforts to create or legitimate a group's identity by providing a common ancestor, place of origin, and explanation for certain cultural or political practices. The past also reveals that identities were fluid and changing over time as groups moved around and intermingled. In the case of Nigeria's three major ethnic groups, none was a unified group either politically or culturally in the past. Typically, people did not see themselves in terms of the ethnic group labels they currently have. Perhaps the main basis for current identities one can establish from the discussion so far is that the Yoruba, Hausa-Fulani, and the Igbo are the descendants of people who came to occupy particular geographical locations, which then influenced their acquisition of some cultural and linguistic commonalities.

The next chapter will look more closely at the historical development of the cultures of Nigeria's peoples. The focus, as in this chapter, will be on the Yoruba, the Hausa-Fulani, and the Igbo. Obviously, being in a similar geographical area or having a similar language is not sufficient to make people identify with each other as the same people, especially as people who share common interests. The foundation for being an ethnic group depends on perceptions of commonality and peoplehood that arise from favorable political and economic circumstances. The question is whether these circumstances existed in the distant past.

Timeline

5–2 million B.C.E.	Olduwan culture in Nigeria
1,500,000–200,000 B.C.E.	Acheulian culture in Nigeria
1,500,000–100,000 B.C.E.	Homo erectus stone tools indicate presence of ancestors of modern humans
10,000–9000 B.C.E.	Iwo Eleru rock shelter site dates from this time (Paleolithic or Stone Age)
Before 10,000 B.C.E.	Sahara becomes wetter; settlements in northern Nigeria
5000 B.C.E.	Sahara becoming dry again; people migrate south, east, and west
5000 B.C.E. (or earlier)	The domestication of plants and animals begins in Nigeria
4000 B.C.E.	Permanent settlements develop in the Lake Chad area
500 B.C.E.	The Nok Culture (Iron Age) begins in northern Nigeria
800 C.E.	Development of stratified, sophisticated society at Igbo Ukwu
900–1500 C.E.	Kingdoms and city-states established (Oyo, Benin, Kanem, Kanem-Borno, Hausa states)

Significant People, Places, and Events

ACHEULIAN TOOL TECHNOLOGY This lithic (stone) technology is named after St. Acheul in France, where it was first recognized. Tools consist of chopping, cutting, piercing, and pointing tools used for processing plants and animals for food. These tools were developed about 1.5 million years ago by homo erectus and lasted until about 200,000 years ago in Africa, when they were replaced by more complex technologies.

AFRICAN LANGUAGE FAMILIES The four indigenous language families in Africa are Niger-Congo, Khoisan, Afro-Asiatic (or Hamito-Semitic), and Nilo-Saharan. Although some disagreement exists about aspects of the language classifications in each group, most scholars accept the overall system of classifications, which was established in the 1950s.

AFRO-ASIATIC LANGUAGE FAMILY This language family, which includes Hausa, originated about 15,000 years ago in or near Ethiopia. Its best-known branch is Semitic, which includes Hebrew, Arabic, and Aramaic (the now-extinct language spoken by Jesus). The other branches of Afro-Asiatic are entirely African in origin and distribution.

BANTU LANGUAGES Some scholars classify Bantu languages as part of the Benue-Congo branch of Niger-Congo languages. The ancestral Bantu language was spoken in eastern Nigeria, but by 300 C.E. it had spread into equatorial Africa and into eastern and southern Africa.

B.C.E./C.E. B.C.E. means "before the common era," and C.E. means "of the common era." These acronyms are used instead of B.C. or A.D. in order to provide a more universal, nonreligious-based dating system.

CHADIC LANGUAGES The Chadic branch of the Afro-Asiatic language sub-family includes about 100 languages spoken in Niger, northern Nigeria, Cameroon, and Chad. Hausa is the most important and widely spoken Chadic language. As such, Hausa is also considered one of the world's most important languages.

KUSH (CUSH) Kush is accepted by most scholars as the earliest black African kingdom (although some scholars argue that Egypt, which predates Kush, was at least in part a black kingdom). Located south of Egypt along the Nile River, Kush became so powerful that it conquered and ruled Egypt for about eighty years during the eighth century B.C.E.

LOST WAX METHOD This ancient method of casting bronze or brass involves making a wax model of an object inside of a clay mold. Molten metal is poured into the clay mold. The metal melts the wax and replaces it in the mold. When the metal cools and hardens, the clay is chipped away, leaving the metal object. The ancient Greeks also used this method, but so far there is no known connection between Africa and Greece. It remains a mystery how the Yoruba sculptors developed the technique.

MEROE Meroe was the capital of Kush and the center of its iron industry. Some scholars speculate that early Iron Age culture in Nigeria originated in Meroe.

NIGER-CONGO LANGUAGES Niger-Congo languages are found in about half of Africa, and the family includes several hundred different languages. It has six branches: Western Atlantic, Mande, Voltaic, Kwa, Benue-Congo, and Adamawa-Eastern.

SAHEL The semiarid region along the southern edge of the Sahara desert is known as the Sahel. This area was often used as a route for population migrations and trade and, consequently, the growth of many ancient African cities and states occurred across the Sahel.

WESTERN SUDAN This term is used in reference to the Sahel area located in West Africa beginning roughly at Lake Chad and ending at the Atlantic Ocean. Many of Africa's early states and empires were located here.

Bibliography

Collins, Robert O. 1990. *Western African History.* Princeton, NJ: Markus Wiener.

Falola, Toyin. 1999. *The History of Nigeria.* Westport, CT: Greenwood.

———. 2001. *Culture and Customs of Nigeria.* Westport, CT: Greenwood.

Hull, Richard W. 1976. *African Cities and Towns before the European Conquest.* New York: W. W. Norton.

Jones, G. I. 1963. *The Trading States of the Oil Rivers: A Study of Political Development in Eastern Nigeria.* London: Oxford University Press.

Lloyd, P. C. 1965. "The Yoruba of Nigeria." Pp. 549–582 in *Peoples of Africa: Cultures of Africa South of the Sahara.* Edited by James L. Gibbs, Jr. Prospect Heights, IL: Waveland.

Ottenberg, Phoebe. 1965. "The Afikpo Ibo of Eastern Nigeria." Pp. 3–37 in *Peoples of Africa.* Edited by James L. Gibbs, Jr. New York: Holt, Rinehart, and Winston.

Phillipson, David W. 1985. *African Archeology.* Cambridge, UK: Cambridge University Press.

Smith, Robert S. 1988. *Kingdoms of the Yoruba.* Madison: University of Wisconsin Press.

Stenning, Derrick J. 1965. "The Pastoral Fulani of Northern Nigeria." Pp. 363–401 in *Peoples of Africa: Cultures of Africa South of the Sahara.* Prospect Heights, IL: Waveland.

CHAPTER TWO

Cultures of Nigeria: An Overview of Ethnicity, Region, and Religion

T HE CULMINATION OF THOUSANDS OF YEARS of Nigerian settlement, movement, and mixing of peoples is the present configuration of more than 250 distinct ethnic groups and languages. This was, however, a long process in which groups moved in and out of different areas, mixed with each other, and absorbed or developed new languages and cultural practices. Group identity was fluid and changing and much different than what we find today.

This chapter will look more closely at important aspects of the cultures and religions of Nigeria's three main ethnic groups—the Yoruba, the Hausa-Fulani, and the Igbo—during these earlier years before contact with Europeans (beginning in the 1500s). The emphasis will be on cultural and historical developments that helped to lay the foundation for identities and intergroup relations before contact with Europeans and also later, when Europeans become an influence in Nigeria.

Chapter 1 discussed how the Yoruba- and Igbo-speaking people became concentrated in the southwest and southeast, respectively, and how the Hausa-Fulani came to be in the north. Each of these areas has distinctive geographic attributes that helped to shape the cultures located there. Among other developments, centralized states were created, especially among the Yoruba and the Hausa-Fulani. Long-distance trade was common in the savannah region, most notably the trans-Saharan trade between the ancient kingdoms and empires in the Sahel and in north Africa and the Middle East. In much of the southern region, more decentralized, village-based societies prevailed.

In general, trade played an important role in the development of Nigerian societies and cultures and in intergroup relations. Although often widely separated by geography and culture, Nigeria's people were not isolated from each other or the outside world. Trade was a source of local, regional, and international linkages. Local trading networks existed between towns and nearby villages. Regional networks linked many towns together, often over great distances. The savannah peoples often acted as intermediaries between producers from the forest or coast and people from international markets. Long-distance traders controlled these networks and organized large caravans and trading colonies to transport such goods as slaves, ivory, glass beads, salt, coral, cloth, weapons, leather goods, and brass rods.

For the most part, peaceful relations among Nigerian regions and states were facilitated by trade in earlier times. Coastal communities had salt and fish to sell to people inland. Forest people had kola nuts, which they traded for such goods as salt from the coast and horses (more northern areas did not have the disease problems that made the use of horses impossible elsewhere) and cattle products from the north (such as meat and leather). States were organized in part to manage this trade, and they had to cooperate with each other to use and maintain trade routes that cut across their territories. Cultural linkages also were promoted by trade. Such practices as age-grade systems, intermarriage, religion, and secret societies were spread from group to group, especially at the intervillage and intertown level, and helped to forge ties among people.

Although trade could help to spread religion from group to group, thus eliminating potential religious conflict, differences among indigenous religions were generally not a source of conflict. Before Islam and Christianity came to Nigeria, religions did not profess universality or compete for converts. Typically, families and locales had their own spirits, venerated ancestors, deities, and rituals. These were important to structure and regulate local group relationships but were not seen as applying to others outside the community. In some cases, however, cults did attract followers from groups outside the local area, as with the Igbo cult that focused on an important oracle. In more centralized states, such as those of the Yoruba, local beliefs were linked to reinforcing and providing legitimacy for the city-state form of social organization.

Facilitating trade and the political functions of the government were the main impetus for the growth of towns. Towns served as both market centers and as capitals for the government. Although most of Nigeria's early peoples were rural dwellers, there is a long history of cities existing throughout the country. This is especially true for the Yoruba, the Hausa-Fulani, and the Kanuri. By the sixteenth century, many communities of town dwellers existed. Many were part of centralized states, such as the kingdom of Oyo in the west, Ilesha and Ife, just within the forest region, and the northern Hausa city-states. In the east, amidst the grasslands of northern Igboland, the town of Akwa became an important center for trade and manufacturing. This was also a fertile area for the cultivation of both grains and root crops, which encouraged growing population densities. Many communities also grew up along the creeks of the Niger delta. They had easy access by water to trade routes. Rich agricultural land in many Igbo and Ibibio areas led to town growth, such as at Orlu, Owerri, Ikot Ekpenne, and Abak.

As trade precipitated the movement of people as well as goods, towns devised means to deal with numerous and often diverse migrants and traders. In some cases, newcomers to an area, often referred to as strangers, would be adopted by members of the community and given communal land if they were going to settle permanently. In most cases, migrants from outside a region or from other nations would be housed in "stranger quarters." These ethnic wards were designated for people on the basis of language, culture, or occupation. One function of the wards was to maintain harmonious relationships among groups, but wards were also given considerable autonomy to run their own affairs. For instance, social control in each ward or quarter was typically in the hands of the residents. Families owned their own buildings and provided their own security. Ward leaders and officials, who represented the wards and carried out certain community functions, came from local families. The leaders from the wards met together to settle intergroup issues or personal disputes. If a problem transcended the ward, it went to the king or other town officials for resolution. Local officials also created new wards for new groups as the need arose by allocating land that was under their authority.

The ward system was one factor in the development of ethnic, and later religious, identities and loyalties. By concentrating people along these lines and giving them the responsibility to govern themselves, people came to have interests in common. In northern areas, after the cities and governments became more thoroughly Islamized in the 1800s, stranger quarters were segregated into those who were subject to Muslim rule and the authority of the emirs (local Muslim rulers) and those who were not. The non-Muslim area was called Sabon Gari (new town). In southern cities like Ibadan in Yorubaland, these areas were called Sabo. Many Hausa lived there. Although initially they were a means to ensure ethnic and religious harmony, currently many of Nigeria's violent ethnic and religious outbreaks are in or between these ethnically and religiously separated quarters.

Richard Hull provides a vivid description of early African towns before the colonial period that aptly describes urban life in Nigeria:

> Urban pre-colonial Africa was an exciting, civilized cosmopolitan arena which fired the imagination and enthusiasm of most foreign visitors. Most urbanites

were born, raised, married, reared children, grew old, and died within the confines of a given quarter or ward. If anything, family and lineage connections were strengthened by urban living. Towns and cities were not the abode of a faceless, anomic human mass. In their own quarters or wards, urban dwellers knew and respected each other's person and property and in turn each one respected the integrity of neighboring wards. When faced with problems involving the welfare of the entire community, everyone worked together. This identification was undoubtedly made possible because everyone's voice was heard, through a chain of representation extending from the family head to the lineage head to the ward leader to the urban chiefs to the king's council and to the king. (Hull 1976, 92–93)

Kano, Benin City, and Ibadan are examples of some of the variations in cities with stranger quarters. Kano was one of the earliest cities to establish stranger quarters or wards in Hausa towns. It had 127 wards, with more created by Fulani immigrants after 1450. In the early 1500s, the Yoruba were located in Ayugi, the Nupe in Tudun Nufawa, North African Arabs in Dandalin Turawa, and so on. After the Fulani jihads in the 1800s, more wards were added. In the southern town of Benin City, dominated by the Edo people, wards were organized by crafts rather than ethnicity. The local king, the oba, ruled over the entire area, which was administered by the trade guilds from each ward. After the civil wars among the Yoruba in the 1800s, many of their towns, such as Ibadan, became war camps. Armies under a warlord controlled the wards, rather than an oba or kinship/ethnic-based groups.

Generally, peaceful relationships among groups were encouraged by the mutual benefits and interdependence that trade offered among diverse groups. This was also true of groups other than those in the cities and towns. Pastoral and agricultural peoples in the north traded with each other. In the middle belt of the forest region, smaller ethnic groups along the trade routes were interdependent due to the craft specialization that developed among them. Groups specialized in such occupations as blacksmithing, cotton production, beer making, house building, or weaving. Peaceful interethnic relations were the norm, because they were essential to maintain the trade on which people's livelihoods depended.

On the other hand, ethnic relations could sometimes be characterized by mistrust, discrimination, and even violence. This occurred most often when drought, competition for control of trade routes or allies, or exploitative relationships (like slavery) were involved. Slavery became a major factor in conflicts once the Atlantic slave trade expanded and became the main source of commerce in Nigeria, a subject addressed in chapter 3. Conflict could be in-

A panoramic view of central Kano, one of the oldest and most famous Hausa cities. It is currently the capital of the northern state of Kano. (Paul Almasy/Corbis)

traethnic (if using present ethnic identities) or interethnic. This will be demonstrated in the following section of this chapter when the development of Yoruba, Hausa-Fulani, and Igbo culture and society are discussed, but at this time being discussed here, there was an absence of fixed identities and allegiances among the three groups. The foundation of contemporary ethnic, regional, and religious identities remained to be built at this point.

The Yoruba

The Yoruba in the past were a diverse and divided people who came to live in southwest Nigeria and to develop a common language. Their homeland now varies from swamps and lagoons along the coast to rainforests, bush, and woodland savannah in the interior to the bend of the Niger River. Much of

A young Yoruba woman in Benin
(Corel Corporation)

the land is fertile, with many rivers and streams. The Yoruba are a people of mixed origin resulting from numerous waves of migration into and out of the region. The main source of commonality in the past was the Yoruba language and certain cultural beliefs and practices. Before the eleventh century, the main cultural similarities were such things as patrilineal descent, a preference for living in towns, and farming as a way of life. The Yoruba were, in fact, the most urbanized people in Africa. Most lived in towns even though their farms might be located miles outside of the urban area.

By the eleventh century, the formation of city-states was under way. Subordinate towns were subject to a dynastic chief from a stronger town. Artistic developments flourished under these more centralized kingdoms, especially at Ife. Some of the most acclaimed bronze sculptural art in Africa using the lost wax method comes from Ife (and also Benin). Many trace the artistic tradition found in the area to the Nok culture of 2,500 years ago. Regional and long-distance trade across the Sahara also promoted the growth, power, and prosperity of the region and affected the cultures that developed there.

The Oduduwa origin myth provided a unifying, divinity-oriented explanation for the development of the new system of rule based on the supremacy of kings and for the demise of the previously more decentralized system of clan rule. The Oduduwa myth was not enough, however, to create an ethnic Yoruba identity. This has only developed recently, mainly in the twentieth century. In earlier times, most Yoruba-speakers' main focus for collective identity was associated with their town. Intense rivalries among towns were common, and such rivalries among the Yoruba are still common today. These rivalries are similar to those of the Italian city-states before Italy became unified in the nineteenth and twentieth centuries; only then did an ethno-national identity develop.

Some loose centralization did exist due to the system of kingship (oba-ship) that developed in Yorubaland. Ife was the senior and most prestigious Yoruba town. Its oba, the oni, exerted some control over the other city-states, but even Ife was subordinate to the kingdom of Oyo (and later to that of Ibadan). By the fourteenth century, the kingdom of Oyo had some control over an area of more than 10,000 square miles. Oyo was located at the extreme edge of Yorubaland, near Borgu to the north and west and the Nupe kingdom to the northeast. Oyo was in the savannah rather than forest belt, which allowed the Oyo military to develop a formidable cavalry. The kingdom was also well situated to take advantage of the lucrative trade along the Sahel. Both trade and warfare brought power as well as new technology, ideas, and goods to Oyo and, through Oyo, to other parts of Yorubaland.

The words *some control* were used above when describing states among the Yoruba for good reason. Centralization of power and unification of the Yoruba has always been an elusive goal. Most towns, even if part of a larger kingdom, remained largely sovereign entities, and the power of rulers was limited. The main ruler in the Oyo kingdom was the alafin, who was regarded as a divine king. Kingdoms and towns subject to Oyo were ruled indirectly through local political representatives and were given much independence.

Each major town had its own local leaders, female as well as male. The oba was typically a male, but not always. As Yoruba society was patrilineal, the right to rule usually passed to men. However, in Ife, Oyo, Dassa, Ondo, and Ilesha, women also served as obas. Women had other important positions of leadership as well. For instance, in most towns, women were represented by a female chief, who coordinated women's activities. These women chiefs also participated in the political direction of the state. They were chosen by the oba and his chiefs and sat in their council. In Ilesha and Ondo, where female rulers and some bilateral descent (that is, descent determined through both the mother and the father's families) existed, women chiefs had a great deal of political influence. Another area in which women exercised power was in various town associations. In Oyo, for example, people were organized into social or professional associations, in which women played an important role. Women were also highly active in trade, crafts, and religious activities as well as in government.

The main obligation subordinates had to the oba was to pay tribute. The power of the alafin and other obas was limited by custom, which amounted to an informal "constitution." The alafin, for example, had to get approval for his decisions from a council of notables (the Oyo Mesi). As the ultimate limit on abuse of power by the alafin or other obas, if the council repudiated an oba, he could be required to commit suicide. Rule would then pass to a selected member of the royal family. Thus, an elaborate system of checks and balances, limited government, and local autonomy were early influences on Yoruba political sensibilities. They remain, as will be shown in later chapters, influential components of Yoruba politics today, even to the point of calls to decentralize Nigeria's current system of government.

The major Yoruba state of Oyo fought with its neighbors, such as the Ijebu and Ekiti, as well as with other Yoruba states. Until about 1600, however, Oyo was a minor state unable to extend its control into neighboring areas outside of Yorubaland. Its power was partly limited by the powerful Edo kingdom of Benin. Earlier, in the fourteenth century, Benin had been a dependency of Ife, but by the fifteenth century it had asserted its independence. Benin was now a major trading power with control over important trade routes to the coast. The territory of the Egba and Egbado peoples did come under Oyo control, which gave Oyo access to trade routes to the coast.

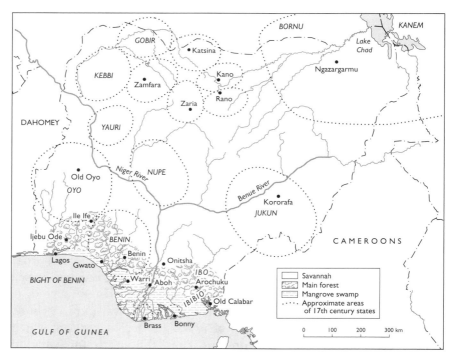

Map 2.1
Seventeenth-Century Nigeria

In the eighteenth century, at the height of the Atlantic slave trade, the kingdom of Oyo reached its zenith but also experienced its decline. In the first half of the century, imperial control was exerted as far away as the Fon kingdom in Dahomey, but this was increasingly challenged. In 1783, the Oyo army was defeated by Borgu, and in 1789 and 1790, the Nupe defeated them as well. By the end of the century, the Egba revolted, and other areas also claimed their independence. Other threats came from Dahomey and the Fulani jihad from Hausaland: In 1824, the Fulani captured Ilorin only twenty miles from Oyo, and in the 1830s, the Oyo capital at old Oyo was conquered by jihad forces. This resulted in most of the population of northern Yorubaland fleeing south for refuge in other Yoruba towns.

This period of instability had considerable consequences throughout Yorubaland. For one, new towns were created, the most important of which was Ibadan. Towns under Hausa-Fulani control, such as Ilorin, now were influenced by Islam, which introduced a new religiously based culture and a set of religious conflicts not present before. Some groups in the region were replaced by the Oyo refugees or lost power as a result of these migrants moving south. For example, the local Egba people in the Ibadan area were forced to move southwest, where they founded the small kingdom of Abeokuta. They had ended up fighting with each other rather than uniting to prevent the refugees from displacing them. Various towns began quarreling and fighting among themselves. Economic and physical security was breaking down, which was manifested in growing banditry by the Borgu, slave raiding along northern Oyo roads, and destructive warfare. Another consequence of the breakdown of law and order in Yorubaland was that towns, and loyalty to town leaders, became even more important to citizens. The town had become the only effective political unit, and only town officials could ensure survival. As a result, loyalty based on culture or kinship declined in importance.

Violence, warfare, and chaos so gripped the area that this period of history is still remembered today by the Yoruba, and suitable lessons were derived from it. Ibadan, Abeokuta under the Egba, and the Ijaye states struggled against each other for power in the Sixteen Years' War. Western Yorubaland came under the control of Dahomey and later under French rule (in the late 1800s). Northern and western Yorubaland were invaded by the Fulani and Dahomeans, and the eastern states were struggling against the westward expansion of Benin. The Nupe, now under Fulani rule, became a threat in the northeast until stopped by the British Royal Niger Company in 1896. In fact, it was the British, not the warring forces, that finally put an end to the warfare.

The disintegration of a functioning and stable state system in Yoruba-land was not simply a reflection of internal struggles for power among competing rulers and armies. The conflict was not related to long-standing ethnic, regional, or religious identities or enmities. After all, much of the fighting was among various Yoruba groups and states. Only the Islamic jihads were inspired by religion, as will be shown in the following section of this chapter. Much of the rivalry and violence were connected to the Atlantic slave trade and to the new and destructive forces it introduced into much of West Africa. What is important for understanding contemporary ethnic, regional, and religious identities and relationships is the meaning given to these earlier events in the current social, political, and economic dynamics of Nigeria.

The Hausa-Fulani

Hausa-Fulani society and culture are closely tied to the introduction and eventual triumph of Islam in northern Nigeria. Therefore, this discussion will center on developments beginning in the thirteenth to fourteenth centuries, when Islam became a growing influence on northern societies.

The Hausa built a distinctive urban culture in such cities as Kano and Katsina. These walled cities were called biranes or birni. Before the 1200s, the Hausa had lived in hamlets, which were based on common origins or kinship. The biranes, by contrast, contained a diversity of peoples from many different regions and lands who lacked such bonds. The leader of the dominant town in the city-state was the sarki. The sarki surrounded himself with an elaborate court and rituals to display his power. The sarki also presided over his own court outside his palace, where he also heard appeals from lower courts. The cities were walled for protection, with an army, which included cavalry, located in and around the city. Each city had its wards, and each ward had its own local vigilante group to maintain law and order. After the introduction of Islam, cities had a central mosque and a market; each ward had its own mosque, school, and market as well.

The Hausa were one of the few African cultures to have a written history. Each city-state among the Hausa had its own chronicle in which to record its history. The best known of these is the Kano Chronicle. It records the conversion of the sarki and ruling dynasty to Islam by clerics and traders from Mali and significant events and conversations from that time forward. The excerpt below, from one of the chronicles, provides some insight into the importance of warfare and the role of the sarki as a warrior. It also reveals the

A Benin rectangular bronze plaque (Christie's Images/Corbis)

existence of domestic slavery in West Africa from early times, a factor of significance in the Atlantic slave trade that developed after the early 1500s.

Kanajeji, son of Yaji (1390–1410)
The thirteenth Sarki was Kanajeji. His father's name was Yaji. His mother's name was Aunaka. He was a Sarki who engaged in many wars. He hardly lived in Kano at all, but scoured the country round and conquered the towns. He lived for some time near the rock of Gija. He sent to the Kwararafa and asked why they did not pay him tribute. They gave him two hundred slaves. Then he returned to Kano and kept sending the Kwararafa horses while they continued to send him slaves. Kanajeji was the first Hausa Sarki to introduce "Lifidi" (quilted armor) and iron helmets and coats of mail for battle. They were introduced because in the war at Umbatu the losses had been so heavy. He visited Kano and returned to Umbatu the next year, but he had no success in the war. He returned a second time to Kano, and again went out the following year. He again failed, but said, "I will not return home, if Allah wills, until I conquer the enemy." He remained at Betu two years. The inhabitants, unable to till their fields, were at length starved out, and had to give in to him. They gave him a thousand male, and a thousand female slaves, their own children. They also gave him another two thousand slaves. Then peace was made. (Collins 1990, 51)

Like the Yoruba, the Hausa are a mixture of diverse peoples who have used origin myths to create a sense of common identity through descent from a common ancestor at a fixed point in the past. As with the Yoruba, religion was important to the legitimacy of the rulers, who were expected to supervise the local religious cult. This was so important that gaining control over the local cult was often the focus of political conflict. It is also notable that women as well as men were rulers among the Hausa. The most famous of these is Queen Amina, a warrior who ruled in Katsina during the first half of the 1400s. Another renowned woman ruler was Bazao-Turunku, who led a warrior tribe in the area of Zaria.

The Hausa city-states prospered from trade and from fighting with each other and neighboring states, usually over trade routes. As an example of intra-Hausa warfare, Katsina and Kano were at war with each other for eighty years from 1570 to 1650. The Hausa never formed more centralized political units than the city-state. Apparently, there was little interest in political unity, or conditions were not conducive to any state gaining such control over other states. Instead, the Hausa preferred to maintain their own separate identities, economies, and independence.

The early impact of Islam on the Hausa was significant but limited. It was mostly the rulers and urban dwellers that adopted the new religion and the cultural practices associated with it, such as prayer five times a day and the veiling of women. Rural villagers typically maintained their local cultures and religions. One impact of Islam was to justify the growing slave raiding against the south because they were "pagans." This did not prevent raids against other Muslims, however. For instance, Kano raided the Jukun and the Nupe, but they also took slaves from the Hausa state of Zaria.

Trans-Saharan trade was facilitated by the adoption of Islam, because it provided a common cultural base all across the Sahel and between the Sahel and the Mediterranean Muslim world. Islam helped to lay the foundation for flourishing intellectual and cultural growth in Hausaland. By the 1600s, for instance, Kano had become an Islamic city of international repute comparable to Fez in Morocco and Cairo in Egypt. It not only produced renowned scholars but also attracted students from great distances throughout the Muslim world. As a result, the cities of the caliphate became centers of a multiethnic society.

Slavery in Hausaland was to assume a harsher form than was typical in Africa. Slave raids became frequent as the demand for slaves increased. Slaves were sometimes settled in slave villages around Hausa towns and made to work in agriculture or crafts, often producing goods for local consumption as well as for export markets. Slaves were important commodities in their own right and could be readily purchased in local markets throughout the region. After the Fulani gained power in the 1800s, the Hausa states became virtual fiefdoms for their new Fulani rulers, who depended on the work of slaves in agriculture but also within their households and the government. Slavery became the economic base of these states and led to growing dependence on a large and ever-expanding pool of slaves to meet local demand, not to mention demand from the overseas slave market. (The relationship between domestic slavery and the Atlantic slave trade will be discussed in the next chapter.)

The role of the Fulani in shaping society and culture in Hausaland goes back to the thirteenth century. It is around this time that the pastoral Fulani, who had originated in the Senegambia, entered the area. Some remained pastoral, but others settled in the cities and married into Hausa families. Some became members of the educated elite that served the sarki. During the sixteenth and seventeenth centuries, the empires of Songhai and Borno controlled most of northern Nigeria. In the mid-eighteenth century, Borno's control weakened, and the Hausa came to increasingly fight among themselves. Drought led both to Borno's decline and to the growing influx of the Fulani into Hausaland to escape a growing threat of famine due to drought.

All of this set the stage for the Fulani jihads (literally, holy wars) from 1804 to 1812 that resulted in the Fulani becoming the rulers of Hausaland. The jihads began in 1804 in Gobir. They were led by a Fulani cleric, Uthman dan Fodio, along with his brother, Abdullah, and his son, Muhammed Bello. The Hausa ruler of Gobir found dan Fodio and his followers a threat to his rule and tried to eliminate them. Dan Fodio was now able to attract even more Fulani support for his cause, which was to rid the Hausa states (which were at least nominally Muslim) of un-Islamic practices and pagan influences. The jihads also had the support of the Hausa masses, who had suffered from oppression and exploitation by the Hausa aristocracy. The jihads promised them liberation. By 1810, all of the Hausa states were conquered by the Fulani and converted into Islamic states. The Hausa rulers had been unable to unite against their common Fulani enemy after so many years of distrust and fighting against each other. The Kano Chronicles discuss this period; the following is part of an account of the Sarki Mohamma Alwali, who ruled from 1781 to 1807.

> The forty-third Sarki was Mohamma Alwali, son of Yaji. His mother's name was Baiwa. In Alwali's time the Fulani conquered the seven Hausa States on the plea of reviving the Muhammadan religion. The Fulani attacked Alwali and drove him from Kano, whence he fled to Zaria. The men of Zaria said, "Why have you left Kano?" He said, "The same cause which drove me out of Kano will probably drive you out of Zaria." He said, "I saw the truth with my eyes. I left because I was afraid of my life, not to save my wives and property." The men of Zaria drove him out with curses. So he fled to Rano, but the Fulani followed him to Burum-Burum and killed them there. He ruled Kano twenty-seven years, three of which were spent in fighting the Fulani. (ibid., 52–53)

The Sokoto Caliphate was established as the center of the new Islamic empire. The caliphate was divided into emirates, each governed by an emir, who owed allegiance to the sultan of Sokoto. Hausa rulers were replaced by Fulani emirs, and dan Fodio's son, Muhammed Bello, became the sultan of Sokoto. Islamic law (*shari'a*) was implemented throughout the caliphate. Islam was now the main force for cultural change affecting politics, personal conduct, and family life, as well as politics and the law.

Through peaceful means and the jihads, Islam was extended into many Yoruba areas, notably Ilorin, where a southern caliphate was established. Badagri, Epe, and Lagos were other cities where many Muslims could be found. Despite such successes, Islam remained a minority religion outside the north. Notably, there was peaceful coexistence between Islam and the in-

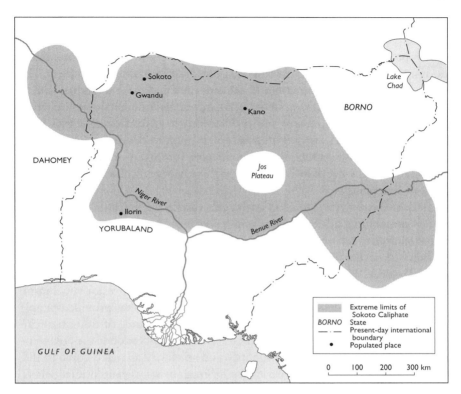

Map 2.2
The Sokoto Caliphate, Mid-Nineteenth Century

digenous Yoruba religion (and later with Christianity). Local Muslims outside the north created a moderate form of the faith that did not demand jihad against local rulers or the imposition of shari'a over local laws. This climate of religious tolerance for the most part still characterizes Yorubaland,
whereas in the north, where Islam became more monolithic and linked to a
theocratic state, the foundation was laid for eventual conflict with non-Muslims, especially Christians.

Even before the triumph of the Fulani jihad, Hausaland was a stratified society of rulers and of people with numerous other status rankings. Over time
and after the jihad, Hausa-Fulani society became increasingly feudal, authoritarian, and bureaucratic. Hereditary rulers and family dynasties occupied
a privileged position in society, and slaves and peasants provided most of the
labor. Stratification increased as ordinary people became organized into
hereditary occupational classes. Intricate patron-client relationships linked

together people who had previously had unequal status and unequal access to resources. Being a patron and having many clients was a major basis for self-respect as well as the respect of others. One's position in this hierarchical system clearly identified one's social position in Hausa-Fulani society. The rank of one's occupation was another important indicator of status. Ruling was clearly the most highly ranked occupation. Next in status was being an Islamic scholar or successful trader. The lowest-ranked occupations were butcher, praise singer, blacksmith, servant, hunter, or drummer. These characteristics of Hausa society would prove to be important in influencing developments in the north during the period of European colonialism and subsequent independence.

Despite the effort of the jihad leaders to create a total Islamic society, most of the population in Hausaland, especially those living outside the towns, found their lives relatively unchanged. Although most people in this area now embrace Islam, the jihads and subsequent efforts to erase pagan practices have not been successful. Pre-Islamic cults, such as the bori cult, continue to attract followers, and indigenous beliefs, such as witchcraft and ancestor veneration, persist even among Muslims. On the other hand, Islam has provided people of the north with a common religious identity and source of unity that can transcend ethnic differences. Similarly, the Islamic brotherhoods the Fulani introduced are a major source of identity and solidarity as well. People of different ethnicity, place, or class travel to pilgrimage centers, share similar beliefs, and observe similar practices that bind them to each other even today.

The jihads came to an end by the late 1800s, although Muslims today continue their efforts to spread their religion through peaceful means. Successful southern efforts to halt northern military expansion, the introduction of Christianity by Europeans and Christianity's rivalry with Islam for converts, and growing British colonial intervention are all factors that coalesced in the nineteenth century to limit northern influence on the south.

The Igbo

The Igbo are a diverse people of more than 200 groups. Their origins are uncertain, but archeological evidence from the Igbo Ukwu site shows that the Igbo had developed a rich material culture by the ninth century C.E. The Nri kingdom that flourished before the seventh century indicates that at least some small, centralized societies were established by the Igbo. Oral tradition says that Nri was the cradle of Igbo culture. For the most part, the Igbo lived in separate societies of one to thirty or more (usually small) villages rather than in centralized states. Each of these villages had its own government, and there was little sense of common ethnic identity among the Igbo until recent times. Among the Igbo, loyalty to one's kinship group and village was primary. It was also common for groups to maintain distinctive identities from each other, although some intermarriage occurred. Religion more than ethnicity played a unifying role among the Igbo. Although there were many cults and deities (each community tended to have its own), some gods attracted widespread devotion. The earth mother god, Ala, for example, was worshipped throughout Igboland. The authority of the oracle at Arochuku also provided a basis for loyalties across many groups.

The Igbo have a long history of local political autonomy and decentralized government, of popular participation in decision making, and a tradition of resistance to what they perceive as autocratic rule. Most Igbo societies were acephalous societies. That is, they had a decentralized system of government in which decisions were made through the consensus of a council of elders. The council of elders was made up of family leaders who were answerable to their villages and kinship groups. There were no chiefs or kings. At the village level, the traditional governing body was based on the men's age grade groups. The middle age grade was responsible for law making and had much judicial authority. The senior age grade was an advisory body. The junior age grade acted as messengers, collected fines, summoned offenders to be judged, and policed the central market. Checks and balances prevented the abuse of power by any group or individuals. For instance, village assemblies allowed most of the people the right to participate in decision making and to express their views.

Other important groups were the secret societies, which played a significant role in upholding community norms. Secret societies existed for both men and women, and acquiring honorific titles in these societies was a major source of status and authority in Igbo communities. The ekwe title for women, associated with the goddess Idemili, is an example. The most powerful of these women, the agba ekwe, was reputedly the most powerful political figure among her people.

The Igbo shared their territory and traditions with several other groups, such as the Ijo, Ndoni, Ogoni, Ibibio, and Yako. The Igbo had long been a trading people, and almost all towns of any size had their own markets. Some men were full-time professional traders who traveled to various towns bringing rare and costly goods for sale from long distances. They traded salt, fish, yams, cocoyams, palm oil, plantains, and other commodities with each other and developed a similar culture that was mostly based on farming. There were many skilled craftsmen and artisans, slaves, and unskilled laborers among the Igbo, as well as many farmers. To maintain valuable trade, communities had to maintain peaceful relationships with each other, and traders forged these relationships with households and communities along their trade routes. Water transport, mainly along the Niger delta and the Niger and Cross Rivers, facilitated the movement of bulk goods. Otherwise, goods had to be carried on foot. In the eighteenth and nineteenth centuries, during the peak of the Atlantic slave trade and before British colonial rule, many traders migrated into the area.

Many communities along the trade routes from the coast to the interior specialized in certain crafts or occupations. These included blacksmiths, wood carvers, potters, and healers. Others were nonspecialist farmers or fishermen. The people of Kalabari specialized in carrying the produce of the Niger delta up the New Calabar and Imo Rivers to sell; then they moved goods from there back to the delta. In Arochuku, the center of the oracle for a famous local god, Chuku (or "the Long Juju"), people were ritual specialists who produced no food but purchased it from poor groups around them. These patterns of economic activity developed over hundreds of years, long before trade patterns were altered by European contact and the Atlantic slave trade.

Trade and cultural practices that promoted the pursuit of titles and other forms of individual distinction have had significant consequences for the Igbo up to the present. These practices encouraged the pursuit of rank and wealth differences and personal advancement. Such cultural practices have been compatible with the spread of capitalism into Nigeria, and the Igbo are widely known throughout the country for their pursuit of economic advancement, education, and business success. In other ethnic traditions, a greater emphasis was placed on individuals using their success to promote the interests of their ethnic groups, communities, or kin.

Conclusion

Terence Ranger has written that in Africa, ethnicity was a "precolonial possibility." During the period of time discussed in this book so far, this certainly applies to Nigeria. One notices that Nigeria has tremendous diversity, based on the existence of hundreds of distinctive cultural groups. The Yoruba, Hausa-Fulani, and Igbo are among them. But at this time they were not unified ethnic groups that were the basis of a primordial ethnic identity or loyalty; all of these groups were diverse mixtures of peoples, whose loyalties shifted due to changing political circumstances or as a result of new configurations of people mixing in their cultures and languages or religions. In many cases, they fought with and exploited each other and had little sense of commonality. There were regional loyalties typically to village-level communities (the Igbo) or to a city (the Yoruba and Hausa-Fulani). However, regional loyalties and identities never encompassed the entire language or cultural community that is now called Yoruba, Hausa-Fulani, or Igbo. Certain social, political, and economic foundations for these more recent identities are being laid, however. For one, the possibility for divisions between an Islamic north and a non-Islamic south had its beginning here with the jihads of the 1800s. The Sokoto Caliphate provided the basis for a more homogeneous Hausa-Fulani identity, one largely based on shared religion, which transcended differences based on ethnicity. The south, for the most part, remained non-Islamic, a collection of divided and culturally heterogeneous groups and loyalties. This fact, too, will be seen to have important repercussions once European contact and colonialism are discussed in subsequent chapters.

The next chapter will begin to show more of the foundation for current identities and intergroup relationships. The peoples of Nigeria will be forever changed by their contact with a new group of strangers, the Europeans. The Europeans, mainly in the form of traders, explorers, and missionaries, were looking for financial gain, knowledge and adventure, and the salvation of souls, respectively. They introduced or accelerated far-reaching economic, political, and sociocultural changes in many other parts of Africa as well as Nigeria. In the process, they helped to create many of the issues of diversity Nigeria must deal with today.

Timeline

1000	Trade develops with North Africa and the Middle East
1000–1100s	Yoruba and Hausa states are established
1200s	The Fulani enter Hausaland
1300s	The Oyo kingdom is established
1400s	Islam is introduced to Hausaland
1570–1650	The Eighty Years' War between Katsina and Kano occurs
Early 1700s	The peak of the Oyo kingdom's power
Late 1700s	Oyo power declines
1804–1812	Uthman dan Fodio leads the Fulani jihads in Hausaland
Mid-1800s	The Oyo empire collapses
1877–1893	The Sixteen Years' War (the Yoruba Wars)

Significant People, Places, and Events

AGE GRADE SYSTEMS/GROUPS In many African societies, including among the Yoruba and the Igbo, males and females can be grouped together based on age. At each age, members of the age grade group take on new responsibilities or activities. This system of age grades reinforces social bonds among the society's members throughout life.

ANCIENT KINGDOMS AND EMPIRES IN THE SAHEL Most of West Africa's states were located along the Sahel from the Nile valley to the Atlantic Ocean. Among the greatest and most famous were Ghana, Songhay (Songhai), and Mali. Mali at its peak of power in the fourteenth century was the largest empire in the world and was internationally famous for the wealth of its ruler, Mansa Musa.

BENIN Benin was a major trading power and rival of Oyo and Ife. It shared many cultural similarities with them, including rule by an oba and a spectacular artistic tradition in bronze casting using the lost wax method. Benin reached the height of its power in the sixteenth and seventeenth centuries.

BORI CULTS These spirit possession cults have their origins in pagan Hausa religion but have incorporated elements of pre-Islamic Arabic beliefs as well as in spirit possession. Today, bori cults attract mostly women and low-ranking occupational groups in Hausaland.

DAHOMEY Dahomey was a rival kingdom of Oyo and subject to its control for part of the 1800s. Dahomey became famous for its brigade of women warriors, sometimes called Amazons. Dahomey came under French colonial control in the nineteenth century and is now part of the country of Benin, west of Nigeria.

IFE Little is known about Ife society, but it is famous, along with Benin, for its sculptural art using the lost wax method. Especially famous are Ife's life-size cast bronze and copper pieces. Ife remains important today in the Yoruba religion, political system, and culture (for example, in ideas of kingship and as the center of the veneration of various deities and the location of numerous shrines).

KANO CHRONICLE The Kano Chronicle was written in the late 1800s but was probably based on earlier accounts destroyed by the conquering Fulani. In their zeal to impose Islam and uproot paganism, they viewed the Hausa sarkis, who were the central actors in much of the Chronicle, as infidels who deserved to be destroyed along with all their works. Luckily, the records on which the Chronicle was based were not destroyed.

PATRILINEAL DESCENT In most African societies, family lineage ties are reckoned through the father's side of the family, that is, patrilineally. If the mother's side of the family is used to reckon lineage, it is called matrilineal descent. Descent systems that trace the family line from both the father and mother's sides of the family are called bilateral. One's lineage is the usual basis for assigning rights to land and other property in the family as well as many other kinship rights and obligations.

PRAISE SINGER Praise songs are a means of extolling the virtues and exploits of rulers and other important people. They also help to preserve family histories and are a source of oral tradition in nonliterate cultures. It is the job of the praise singer to preserve the reputations of important people and events in song and to sing these songs in appropriate ritual or other circumstances; for example, before a warrior goes into battle, the praise singer may sing of the exploits of the warrior's ancestors in order to embolden him for the conflict he is about to face.

Bibliography

Collins, Robert O. 1990. *Western African History.* Princeton, NJ: Markus Wiener.

Falola, Toyin. 1999. *The History of Nigeria.* Westport, CT: Greenwood.

———. 2001. *Culture and Customs of Nigeria.* Westport, CT: Greenwood.

Hull, Richard W. 1976. *African Cities and Towns before the European Conquest.* New York: W. W. Norton.

Jones, G. I. 1963. *The Trading States of the Oil Rivers: A Study of Political Development in Eastern Nigeria.* London: Oxford University Press.

Lloyd, P. C. 1965. "The Yoruba of Nigeria." Pp. 549–582 in *Peoples of Africa: Cultures of Africa South of the Sahara.* Edited by James Gibbs. Prospect Heights, IL: Waveland.

Morgan, W. B. 1972. "The Influence of European Contacts on the Landscape of Southern Nigeria." Pp. 193–207 in *People and Land in Africa South of the Sahara.* Edited by R. Mansell Prothero. New York: Oxford University Press.

Ottenberg, Phoebe. 1965. "The Afikpo Ibo of Eastern Nigeria." Pp. 1–39 in *Peoples of Africa: Cultures of Africa South of the Sahara.* Edited by James Gibbs. Prospect Heights, IL: Waveland.

Ranger, Terence. 1999. "Concluding Comments." Pp. 133–144 in *Ethnicity and Nationalism in Africa.* Edited by Paris Yeros. New York: St. Martin's.

Smith, Robert S. 1988. *Kingdoms of the Yoruba.* Madison: University of Wisconsin Press.

Uchendu, Victor C. 1977. "Slaves and Slavery in Igboland, Nigeria." Pp. 121–132 in *Slavery in Africa: Historical and Anthropological Perspectives.* Edited by Suzanne Miers and Igor Kopytoff. Madison: University of Wisconsin Press.

CHAPTER THREE

European Contact and the Atlantic Slave Trade

C HAPTER 2 DISCUSSED THE ROLE THAT TRADE PLAYED in the mixing of people and forging of mutually beneficial ties of interdependence in Nigeria's early history. It was observed that identities and loyalties were tied mainly to local villages, cities, or city-states. These ties did not typically extend to the entire ethnic group of those sharing a common language or cultural similarities. In fact, when conflict and war broke out, it was often intra-ethnic fighting as much as interethnic.

After contact with Europeans, new trading relationships developed ones based on the buying and selling of human beings in ever-increasing numbers. This Atlantic slave trade transformed Nigerians' relationships with the outside world and with each other. Trade was no longer based on mutually beneficial transactions but on an exchange system that endowed some societies with lavish new wealth and power but led to the downfall of others. Because the benefits of success and costs of failure in the slave trade became so great, relationships among Africans became increasingly predatory and violent as they moved into the seventeenth and eighteenth centuries.

Estimates vary as to the total number of African victims of the Atlantic slave trade. A rough estimate would be that approximately 10 million slaves reached the New World between 1500 to 1900. Perhaps 20 percent died en route. Many others died from the wars, from slave raids, or from the appalling conditions slaves suffered in transit to the coastal ports or while waiting in slave holding areas. The total number who died before transit may be nearly as great as the number actually sold and shipped overseas.

The period of the slave trade is one of major cultural, and especially religious, change in Nigeria. In the 1800s an expansionist Islamic movement from the north developed that was determined to save souls and install a new righteous leadership through *jihad* (holy war) but also through peaceful conversion. Islam eventually confronted an equally zealous European-inspired

Christian missionary movement dedicated not only to saving souls but also to ending slavery and introducing European values and institutions to Africans. A "clash of civilizations" was in the making.

Finally, as an industrializing Europe turned away from slavery in the 1800s, Great Britain assumed the preeminent role in shaping Nigeria's future. Once again, Nigerian societies and identities became transformed as new demands and pressures were placed on them. Societies formed and deformed by the slave trade had to now change to "legitimate trade" as they were absorbed into a newly emerging global capitalist economy dominated by a handful of European powers. By the dawn of the twentieth century, the steady encroachment of European government, traders, and missionaries had led to outright colonial control.

In exploring these themes, this chapter will first discuss the origins and development of the Atlantic slave trade and its impact on Nigeria. Then the focus will move to the efforts to end slavery and reform Nigerian society. The British government, business interests, and Christian missionaries joined forces in this effort, aided by a new class of Westernized African converts who sought to bring civilization to their brothers and sisters living in "darkness." Finally, this chapter will show the process by which the colony of Nigeria came into existence.

The Atlantic Slave Trade

It is important to note that the Atlantic slave trade did not introduce slavery to Africa or to Nigeria. Trade in slaves and domestic slavery had long existed. Chapter 2 discussed the trans-Saharan slave trade and its prominent role in commerce and trade networks within Nigeria, across the Sahel and North Africa, and all the way to the Middle East. There was also a flourishing East African slave trade. Slaves were also used in the north in Nigeria for domestic purposes. This domestic slavery intensified under the Sokoto Caliphate. Muslims were not allowed to enslave other Muslims, but they could enslave infidels (nonbelievers). So northerners felt free to supply commercial markets with slaves from the south or from pagan groups in the north.

West African slavery typically had little resemblance to the form of slavery that developed in North America, however. In North America, slavery involved far more people and became a permanent and hereditary condition for slaves and their offspring. Slaves were relegated mainly to menial agricultural or domestic tasks. None of this was true in Africa or in Nigeria. Ex-

Slaves in Africa carry firewood and cut rice; from an illustration by a European traveler in 1864. Domestic slavery existed in Africa before the Atlantic slave trade and persisted after British efforts to end the Atlantic slave trade in the early 1800s. (North Wind)

cept in Muslim states with a plantation-type agricultural system, or in Benin (in the south) where cheap labor was needed, slavery involved few people and took a variety of forms.

For example, the Yoruba system of domestic slavery had two forms: slavery and iwofa. In iwofa, people voluntarily pawned themselves or a child as a security for debt or to raise capital for trade or some other venture. Once the debt was repaid, the person was free again. In this system, slaves could come from within the particular Yoruba kingdom or from elsewhere in Yorubaland, or they could be non-Yorubas. They were commonly used for farm labor, in households, as bodyguards to chiefs, or as long-distance traders. Those who were royal slaves could have high and influential positions, such as ambassador. Some might also be used as ritual sacrifices. In general, though, slaves were well treated. They could own property and cultivate their own land, and they could be treated as subjects by their masters only. Slaves could not be treated as inferiors by others in the community. Most people became slaves as war captives, debtors, or criminals. Although the children of slaves remained the property of their masters, offspring of a freeman and a slave were free. Slaves could also purchase their own freedom by accumulating enough wealth.

Among the Igbo, slaves were traditionally acquired through capture, kid-napping, purchase, pawning, or dedication to the service of deities. In the latter case, the poor sought mercy at a religious shrine. By dedicating themselves to the shrine, they and their descendants became osu and thereby permanent outcasts. Serious crime could also lead to a sentence of slavery. A slave could not be purchased without the consent of the slave's kinsmen. The main reasons a family would agree to such a purchase of a family member were delinquency, abnormality, or persistent debt. Pawning was a last resort to pay a debt or raise money (for example, for bridewealth). In the case of a loan, a child was typically pawned as security for the loan. If the debt was not repaid, the pawn remained a slave. In intra-Igbo slave dealings, young girls were preferred, and boys were purchased for two-thirds of a girl's price. Boys were seen as less valuable and more likely to run away.

Although slaves owed total obedience to their Igbo masters, they were usually well treated, although abuses sometimes occurred. Masters were required to feed and clothe their slaves. Slaves were incorporated into their master's household. Under the supervision of the women of the household, slaves worked, ate, and carried on their activities. Living conditions of most slaves were much the same as that of ordinary people. When slave boys became adults, they established independent households and were provided with wives by their masters. Females would be married out of the household or become the wives of their masters. Slaves were able to earn their own income to support their families.

There were several ways for slaves to gain their freedom. In one scenario, slaves were incorporated into the families of their owners over time and thus became free. This could take more than one generation. In another scenario, slaves who worked and accumulated wealth (for example, by hiring themselves out or investing in livestock or trade) acquired social status, which often led to their freedom. Also if a female slave married a freeman (including her master), she became free.

The Atlantic slave trade was readily adapted to the earlier forms of the slave trade and domestic slavery, although it transformed African slavery in significant ways, a point to which this discussion will return. However, this chapter will first examine the development of the Atlantic slave trade. (Refer to map 2.2)

The Portuguese were the first Europeans to have direct contact with Nigeria, at the end of the 1400s and in the early 1500s. As an extension of their exploration of the Gold Coast and their search for the legendary gold mines of Africa, they began to travel along the Nigerian coast. The *Esmer-aldo de Situ Orbio* is an account of these early contacts. It describes an estuary (the Niger delta area) that the Portuguese called the Rio Real. Living there in a large village were about 2,000 warlike Ijo people, described as naked except for copper necklaces, who made salt from salt water. The Portuguese were impressed with their large canoes, which carried up to eighty people. These canoes were used to travel upriver where salt was exchanged for yams, slaves, cows, goats, and sheep for local villages. The Portuguese discovered that they could acquire a slave for the cost of eight to ten copper bracelets, an item highly prized by the Ijo. Over time (from about 1450 to 1550), the Portuguese engaged in a growing trade in slaves with Bonny and other villages in the area.

In the late 1500s, Portuguese traders came in contact with the Edo kingdom of Benin. Initially trade was limited because Benin had no gold, which was the commodity the Portuguese first sought. Trade with Benin was mainly in peppers and a few slaves. The slaves were sold to the Gold Coast, where the Portuguese needed them to carry goods into the interior. In exchange, Benin received guns, copper, and beads. Benin grew in power and wealth as a result of its expanding trade in slaves with the Portuguese. By the seventeenth century the demand for slaves had increased sharply. The Portuguese and other European colonial powers were developing sugar plantations, such as at São Tomé, off the coast of west Africa, and in the West Indies. As the Europeans expanded their overseas colonies, the demand for slave labor grew as well. At the port of Gwato the Portuguese bought slaves for São Tomé. By the seventeenth century the French, Dutch, and English had joined the Portuguese in trading with Benin for slaves.

In order to monopolize this trade, beginning in the late fifteenth century Benin's armies sought to control as much of the coastline as possible. Benin wanted to deny access to its major rival, the Yoruba state of Oyo, by controlling the port of Lagos, which was the first permanent break in miles of beach to the east of the Volta estuary in what is now Ghana. In 1603, Lagos became a military camp of soldiers of the king of Benin and, by 1760, it was a major slave port. Benin's political influence extended into Yoruba territory. The ruling dynasties of Lagos (which was originally a Yoruba settlement), Ijebu, and Ondo are said to have descended from Benin princes or warriors. Benin also began advancing eastward through the Niger delta to Bonny. In the interior of Nigeria, Benin's control extended into the territories of the Igbo. At the Igbo towns of Aboh and Onitsha, the Benin systems of centralized rule by obas replaced traditional decentralized political systems. Benin's influence eventually extended as far north as Idah.

For Benin, maintaining control over its far-flung empire and a monopoly over the slave trade proved impossible in the long run. Local rulers on the coast began dealing directly with the Europeans and sought their independence from Benin's control. During the eighteenth century, these rebellious provinces broke away from Benin's control. Civil war broke out, which conveniently added to the supply of war captives for the growing slave trade. South of Benin, new states emerged to challenge Benin. Among these were the Itsekiri state of Warri, and, in the eastern Niger delta area, Brass, New Calabar (or Kalabari), and Bonny became thriving Ijo city-states. Farther east, the Efik created another trading city, Old Calabar. These various coastal towns had previously been small fishing and salt-producing areas but now expanded to accommodate the lucrative commerce in slaves. As its empire declined, Benin also found itself losing out in the slave trade as it faced growing competition with merchants from Dahomey (now the country of Benin) and Oyo.

Oyo was another state whose development after the fifteenth century was influenced largely by the slave trade. With Benin controlling the coast as far as the Niger delta and the delta city-states controlling the area from the Delta to Calabar, Oyo was left with no coastal outlet for trade with the Europeans. This led Oyo to begin expanding to the west into the kingdom of Dahomey. Oyo's advances were aided by its acquisition of horses and the development of cavalry. By the end of the seventeenth century, Oyo had gained its outlet to the sea via the Dahomean seaport at Porto Novo, and Dahomey was eventually defeated by the armies of Oyo around 1747. Oyo came to control the main slave trade routes from the Niger River to the coast of Badagri and Whydah, and kingdoms in the area were controlled as vassals to the alafin, who was the ruler of Oyo. The seventeenth and eighteenth centuries were to be the zenith of Oyo's power, which was made possible by the slave trade. But Oyo's dominance was not to last.

For both Benin and Oyo in the eighteenth century, the slave trade proved to be a curse after the initial boom. Civil war, outside war, and internal elite rivalries resulted in the demise of Benin as a regional power by the nineteenth century. Similarly, Oyo's power declined in the nineteenth century and eventually collapsed. The chief Yoruba ruler of Oyo, the alafin, was unable to control the conquered states or to prevent internal rivalries among the various Yoruba city-states. The *fon* (king) of Dahomey and the Egba asserted these states' independence by the mid-1800s. Another crisis was the loss of the northern Yoruba city of Ilorin. The northern areas of Oyo were already weakened by the movement of trade to the south as the result of the slave trade and rivalries among the Yoruba. Ilorin's leaders asked the Fulani, who now ruled northern Nigeria, to help them gain their independence from Oyo. After defeating the alafin's armies, the Fulani added Ilorin to their empire in

1822. They eventually took over other major Oyo towns as well. By this time, the alafin effectively ruled only the city of Oyo and its hinterland.

The Fulani control of Ilorin accelerated the breakdown of Oyo. For one, Yoruba access to slaves from the north was now blocked. As a result, the Yoruba turned on each other as sources for slaves. Yorubaland was reduced during a period of eighty years to a state of almost continuous warfare. Never more than loosely united, the Yoruba were now unable to cooperate against the Fulani threat or the loss of Ilorin. In fact, Ilorin managed to gain allies against the alafin from some other Yoruba towns. By 1835, Ilorin had become even more powerful than Oyo. Recognizing its precarious situation, Oyo tried to ally itself with its former enemy, Borgu, but their combined armies were defeated by Ilorin. Oyo was then attacked and destroyed. A mass flight of refugees from Oyo to the south occurred. New Oyo was established on the edge of the forest. Other towns also were established by the refugees and, in the process, Oyo-Yoruba culture and institutions were spread among the local groups with whom the Yoruba mixed.

The Fulani advance south into Yorubaland was finally halted. One factor in this was the tsetse fly, which killed the Fulani's horses and rendered their formidable cavalry ineffective in battle. Another factor was that the Yoruba were able to buy guns by selling slaves acquired through almost constant warfare. The Fulani and Hausa, by contrast, did not learn to use guns until about 1900. A final factor was the growing strength of the Yoruba town of Ibadan. Ibadan had become a large town when Yoruba refugees moved there in 1829 to escape the Fulani advance into Yorubaland. The alafin, now residing in New Oyo, assigned the ruler of Ibadan the duty of defending the remaining Yoruba towns against the Fulani. In 1840, the Ibadan army defeated the Fulani forces from Ilorin. This marked the end of Fulani expansion in Yorubaland.

War, especially civil war, was the ultimate undoing of the Yoruba. By the end of the eighteenth century, the Oyo army had been defeated by Borgu and by the Nupe. Next, the Egba and other Yoruba groups asserted their independence. Then came the revolt in Ilorin and the outbreak of more intra-Yoruba warfare that lasted almost to the twentieth century. Between 1830 and 1855, intense rivalries and war among Yoruba towns resulted from the power vacuum left by the decline of Oyo. Warlords effectively ruled the towns. The escalating demand for slaves was at the center of the cycle of endemic warfare that lasted throughout most of the nineteenth century. To get slaves, captives from warfare were needed. To wage war and get war captives to trade as slaves, guns were needed. To get guns, one needed to trade slaves. And so the tragic cycle continued to its destructive end.

The great demand for slaves occurred because of the huge markets for slaves in Brazil, the Caribbean, and the United States. The intensifying violence and lethal conflict among the African slave traders in Nigeria that accompanied this growing demand affected places other than Benin and Oyo. As was true for Benin and Oyo, so in other states and regions wealth and power were tied to involvement in the slave trade. The commerce in slaves gradually eclipsed every other form of trade, including the traditional trade in gold, ivory, crafts, and so on. Not only was the slave trade lucrative, but it was also the main means by which Africans could acquire European-made firearms. Possession of guns became critical to a group's ability to ward off aggression from others or to wage war.

As was outlined above, a vicious cycle was set in place. As states or groups sought to acquire slaves, firearms were needed to attack other groups, because war captives and slave raiding were the main sources of slaves. Even groups that just wanted to protect themselves from being victims of these wars and slave raids could do so only if they had firearms, and the only way they could buy such weapons was to purchase them from Europeans or traders in exchange for slaves. Thus, groups and rulers who opposed the slave trade were forced to enter the trade themselves and to engage in the predatory and cruel behavior that the acquisition of slaves required. Widespread violence resulted from the competition to control access to Europeans and to the coastal ports where the Europeans were located, for as more and more firearms found their way into African hands, wars and slave raids grew in number and became more deadly and destructive. Whole villages and crops were destroyed and looted. Productive African industries declined or disappeared as cheap European imports of textiles, metals, beads, and weapons replaced those made locally. The climate of violence and the dominance of rulers and states based on violence led to a general coarsening and brutalizing in African states and cultures.

The slave trade also shifted patterns of trade in Nigeria. Traditional trading networks and directions of trade were altered. As already mentioned, slavery eclipsed other kinds of commerce and led to the decline of peaceful and productive trade in traditional goods and services. The direction of trade also changed; the coast rather than the savannah was now the center of trade. European traders were restricted to their local bases, and coastal states and merchants became the middlemen actually supplying them with the slaves. Local rulers jealously limited Europeans to these coastal enclaves and charged the Europeans rent, as well.

Class formation was another aspect of Nigerian society affected by the slave trade. Not everyone was a victim; indeed, many of the victimizers—the

African traders and local rulers—grew rich. Many new political rulers emerged as a result of profits from the slave trade. Especially on the coast, ambitious and enterprising Africans found the slave trade to be the primary avenue for economic and political advancement. Even slaves could gain wealth and power this way.

The Ijo, mentioned by the Portuguese in their early writings about the coastal people of Nigeria, provide a good example of how slavery affected societies along the coastal city-states. Traditionally, the small communities of the Ijo were divided into wards or houses headed by an elder. Age grade and dancing societies promoted unity among the wards. As the slave trade expanded, these communities became major trading states, among them Bonny, New Calabar, Okrika, and Brass (or Nembe). The Efik established Old Calabar as a trading city-state on the Cross River. These new states grew in population from a few hundred to thousands. The slave trade became the basis for new and unprecedented economic and political inequality. The elder's status changed from ritual leader to political leader. To be a head of a ward depended now on wealth gained from the trade in slaves. The ward became a "canoe house," a trading organization whose leader was wealthy and powerful. Each house had numerous slaves, and there was intense competition among houses to control the slave trade and thereby have power in the town. The large canoes that had so impressed the Portuguese in their early contacts with the Ijo were the namesakes of the canoe houses. Long used to transport goods from the interior of Nigeria to the coast, these canoes were now used for slave trading. They had been converted into huge ships armed with cannons.

European writings from the 1600s indicate that at that time most of the slaves sold along the eastern coastal states came from the interior and were purchased in markets there. They were not war captives. Europeans remained on the coast, often sequestered on board their own ships, while Africans acted as their brokers. These Africans took European goods to the interior slave markets and purchased slaves with them. This period appears to have been a time of peace in the area. Canoes full of armed men (with shields and short, spear-like weapons called assegais) were for defensive purposes, not war. Europeans described having a pleasant stay in Calabar and Bonny.

The peace was short-lived, however. As firearms became more common in the late 1600s, violence and warfare increased. During the eighteenth century, the vicious cycle of violence that had proved so destructive in western Nigeria was having similar effects in the east. Trade rivalries increased, followed by a growing demand for firearms. More firearms led to more warfare.

All of the ethnic groups in the Niger delta (for example, the Itsikiri, the Ijo, and the Efik) came to adopt the canoe house form of social organization. Canoes from the various houses went into the interior to get slaves via a variety of rivers and waterways that flow into the Niger River and delta. Thousands of mostly Igbo slaves were kept as domestic slaves, to be pullers on the canoes. Slaves were members of the house and part of the extended family. The canoe teams elected the head of the house, who was called the father. Capable slaves were loaned trade goods and allowed to trade independently and to keep a percentage of their profits. In this way they could accumulate property and wealth and purchase their freedom. Slaves could even become heads of their own canoe houses. This system, which allowed slaves to advance themselves by cooperating with their owners, worked to prevent slave rebellions. Slaves who became wealthy came to support the slave trade because they bought slaves themselves and benefited from the trade. All was not equal, however. In the delta, status was based on being "freeborn" or, if a wealthy slave, a "gentleman." The main limit on a slave was that he could not become a king, a new position of political power previously unknown among delta societies before the slave trade. Despite these inequalities, by absorbing large numbers of slaves into the indigenous population, the canoe house system produced an ethnically mixed and cosmopolitan urban population in the delta towns. In most towns, three languages were spoken—Ijo, Efik, and Igbo—along with pidgin English, the trade language used with Europeans.

In the late seventeenth century, Hugh Crow, an English sea captain and slave trader, described life at Bonny, one of the main Niger delta city-states. In the following excerpt from his memoirs, Crow refers to the locals as "Eboes," although he acknowledges that they are a mixture of local peoples. Crow notes the positive attributes of the Eboes. He then goes on to describe the large numbers of Eboe slaves acquired and how the slaves were procured by the canoes described earlier in this chapter.

> The Eboes have already been spoken of as a superior race, and the inhabitants, generally are a fair dealing people, and much inclined to a friendly traffic with Europeans, who humour their peculiarities. The king of New Calabar and Pepple, king of Bonny, were both of Eboe descent, of which also are the mass of the natives; and the number of the slaves from the Eboe country, which throughout the existence of the British trade were taken from Bonny, amounted to perhaps three-fourths of the whole export. It is calculated that no fewer than 16,000 of these people alone were annually exported from Bonny within the twenty years ending in 1820; so that, including 50,000 taken within the same

period from New and Old Calabar, the aggregate export of Eboes alone was not short of 370,000. Bonny has long been celebrated for the size and construction of her canoes. They are formed out of a single log of the capok, a species of cotton tree. The slaves are procured from the interior, and much bustle takes place when the inhabitants are preparing their canoes for the trade. These vessels, which are large of the kind, are stored for the voyage with merchandise and provisions. Evening is the period chosen for the time of departure, when they proceed in a body accompanied by the noise of drums, horns, and gongs. At the expiration of the sixth day they generally return, bringing with them 1500 or 2000 slaves, who are sold to Europeans the evening after their arrival, and taken on board the ships. (Collins 1990, 199, 201–202)

The Igbo are now the largest group in the southeastern part of Nigeria. Although they were often victims of the slave trade, some, such as the Aboh, had more centralized political systems and became major slave traders. The Aboh live on the Niger River about 130 miles from the coast. Aboh merchants controlled much of the trade in European goods from the coast, as well as dominating local trade. They also brought slaves, palm oil, ivory, and produce to the coast. Some slaves were taken through warfare or slave raids, but most were purchased, sometimes from northern markets. Many of these slaves had Hausa-Fulani names, which indicates the slaves' origins as captives from wars or raids in the emirates (after the jihads in the early 1800s). The Aboh traded slaves for cowry shells, guns, beads, cloth, and liquor from Europe.

As was traditional among the Igbo, the Aboh incorporated slaves into the household as quasi-family members, and there were opportunities for personal advancement. Some slaves served as the armed forces for local chiefs. Others became involved in trading and were able to purchase their own canoes and slaves. Eventually, a successful slave could build his own house and become head of a large compound and trading company. Slaves were not allowed, however, to have full equality with the freeborn in ritual matters or political power. A wealthy slave and his descendants remained second-class citizens.

Just as the slave trade led to the transformation and adaptation of local institutions, it also encouraged the corruption of others. One example is the ritual center of the Arochuku oracle, mentioned in chapter 2. The oracle served the god Chuku (sometimes called the Great Juju), who lived in a cave near Aro, a town about forty miles from the coast. The oracle had many followers among the Igbo, Efik, Ibibio, and Ijo. The oracle acted as a supreme court judge, settling difficult disputes. In the eighteenth century, the people of Aro helped to make the slave trade organized and peaceful along the trade routes in the interior of Igboland. The Aro began to exploit their position by establishing settlements along the trade routes, where they began to instigate disputes and then to encourage the participants in the case to go to the oracle for resolution. Targeted for this scam were important men who were accompanied by hundreds of followers. They were made to wait outside of Aro, often for months, where the Aro merchants sold them food and other provisions at exorbitant prices. Once the oracle heard the case, the god would deliver his verdict from his cave. The losers had to enter the cave to be eaten alive by the god. In reality, the losers were clubbed, bound, packed in canoes, and shipped down the river to be sold as slaves. Through these and other exploitative means, the Aro came to dominate the slave trade in the area interior to Calabar.

Ending the Slave Trade

The Atlantic slave trade lasted for about four centuries, and a large proportion of its victims were from Nigeria. In the eighteenth century, more slaves came from the Nigerian coast than from anywhere else in Africa. In the nineteenth century, almost one-third of the slaves came from Nigeria. During the entire period of the slave trade, an estimated 3.5 million people from Nigeria were shipped to the New World. Most were Igbo and Yoruba, although a significant number were Hausa, Ibibio, and others. In the eighteenth century, Oyo and Aro provided most of the slaves from Nigeria. In the nineteenth century, most slaves were Yoruba victims of the Yoruba civil wars. From the mid-1500s to the 1700s, Portugal was the dominant European country involved. In the 1700s, the Dutch, French, and British became more deeply involved as their colonial empires and demand for slave labor both increased. The French and British were the major slavers in the eighteenth century, with Portugal now at number three. In the seventeenth and eighteenth centuries, however, a new trade commodity began to emerge, palm oil and palm kernels. This new trade was destined to challenge and then virtually replace the slave trade in the nineteenth century.

The gradual eclipse of the slave trade was initiated by Great Britain, which in the 1800s had become the greatest power in Europe and the major foreign influence in Nigeria. In 1807, the British unilaterally outlawed the slave trade and began a naval patrol of the West African coast to intercept its own slave trading ships and relieve them of their cargo. Increasingly, the ships of other countries were subject to the same treatment. The British already had established the colony of Sierra Leone in 1787 as a place to which the freed slaves would be sent.

What led to this dramatic change in policy? There were two mutually reinforcing forces at work. One was the rise of evangelical Protestantism in Great Britain in the late eighteenth century. Churches began to send missionaries to convert black slaves in the West Indies to Christianity. Once there, the missionaries realized that they could not make good Christians of Africans as long as there was slavery. How could Africans be good Christian spouses or parents if they could be sold or bred by their owners as though they were animals? The missionaries also turned their attention to Africa as the source of the slave trade. It was missionaries like Dr. David Livingstone who helped to promote a greater British interest in Africa and to promote the dominant view of Africa as the "dark continent," full of nakedness, polygamy, disease, heathen beliefs, and other abominations. As with the West Indies slaves, much of the blame for Africa's pathologies was placed on the dehumanizing and degrading trade in slaves. In 1772, the Quakers managed to pressure the British government to pass a law that effectively freed all African slaves in Great Britain. This was followed by a plan to create the colony of Sierra Leone, where freed slaves in West Africa could be sent and where slavery and the slave trade would be outlawed. Then, in 1807, the British slave trade was completely banned.

The other force ending slavery was the Industrial Revolution. As long as the British depended on a plantation economy for much of their wealth, religious arguments against slavery had little effect. As industrial capitalism spread, however, the principle of "free labor" came into vogue. Labor was now seen as a commodity in a system of free trade, and industrial capitalism was regarded as the means to national wealth. Slaves were an anachronism; they made poor customers for British manufactured goods and were poor candidates for an industrial labor force. With economic self-interest as a motivator, there was growing support among the business class, not just the religious reformers, for an end to slavery.

The goal became to end slavery in Africa by replacing it with a new form of trade— "legitimate commerce." Religious and business aims were combined in the belief that slavery would only end when Africans were converted to Christianity and to legitimate trade. The philosophy underlying British policy toward West Africa could be summarized as "Christianity, Commerce, and Civilization." Implementing this ideal would require the support of good African rulers, that is, those who supported legitimate commerce and Christian missionary activities among African people. By contrast, rulers who continued in the slave trade and were hostile to missionaries were to be opposed by force, if necessary.

The British began to aggressively promote the two legs of its new policies in Nigeria. The first leg was legitimate commerce. To break African dependence on the slave trade, the British had to find new African commodities to substitute for slaves. Palm oil and palm kernels became a major alternative. Not only did oil palm trees grow abundantly and wild in West Africa, but palm products also were highly marketable in industrializing Europe. In Nigeria in the nineteenth century, the main export from the eastern delta quickly became palm oil. So important was this commodity in Africa's trade with England that the Niger River came to be called the Oil River. The states in the area, which had once grown rich on the slave trade but were now enriching themselves by trading in palm oil, became known as the Oil River States. The delta states did not embrace legitimate commerce immediately, however. At first, cities like Bonny and Brass traded palm oil with the British while continuing to sell slaves to the Brazilians. By 1830, the oil trade was so profitable that many African traders abandoned the slave trade on their own volition.

The economy of the north was also to be transformed in order to achieve the switch to legitimate commerce. The British saw cotton as a good raw material export for the Muslim states there. Already the British had developed a bias toward the north. Because of its centralized states, Islamic culture, and aristocratic leadership, the British saw the Muslim states as more civilized than the less centralized (and at that time often war-torn) southern states. Visions of exporting manufactured goods to the north, including British-made cotton robes made from northern-grown cotton, seemed to be an ideal economic arrangement.

To facilitate the expansion of trade in legitimate commodities, it was necessary to determine trade routes, make trade agreements with local rulers, and evaluate infrastructure needs. With this in mind, interest in the interior of Nigeria increased after 1790. Especially important was mapping the Niger River and other major river courses. Before the 1850s, malaria made this effort extremely dangerous. Most early attempts by Europeans to explore the Niger River area led to death from the disease (or in some cases from lethal encounters with local people).

The semi-arid north was another matter. Here, travel was healthier and safer. In the 1820s, British explorers Dixon Denham and Hugh Clapperton visited Sokoto to discuss trade with the sultan, Muhammed Bello. Clapperton's writings, excerpted below, provide valuable information about the emirates at this time and reveal the sultan's interest in learning in general and about the Europeans in particular.

> At noon we arrived at Sokoto where a great multitude of people was assembled to look at me, and I entered the city amid the hearty welcome of young and old. After breakfast, the sultan sent for me. He asked me a great many questions about Europe and our religious distinctions. I bluntly replied we were called Protestants. "What are Protestants?" says he. He continued to ask several other theological questions, until I was obliged to confess myself not sufficiently versed in religious subtleties to resolve these knotty points. [On a second visit to Sokoto, Clapperton writes about his audience with the sultan.] Saw the sultan this morning, who was sitting in the inner apartment of his house, with the Arabic copy of Euclid before him that I had given him as a present. He said that his family had a copy of Euclid brought by one of their relations, who had procured it at Mecca; that it was destroyed when part of his house was burnt down last year; and he observed that he could not feel but very much obliged to the king of England for sending him so valuable a present. (Davidson 1991, 381–382)

The conversations the sultan had with Clapperton and his companions had the unintended consequence of encouraging the Fulani expansions into the south that helped to promote the disintegration of Oyo and the outbreak of war in the area. It had already been a goal of the Muslim jihadists "to dip the Quran into the Atlantic," and the prospects of wealth from expanded trade made this goal even more compelling. The north had no outlets to the coast and was, therefore, at a disadvantage with regard to access to trade with the Europeans. The Fulani hoped to change this situation by expansion into the south. They first advanced into Nupe and from there into Yorubaland, but they were ultimately unsuccessful in gaining access to the coast.

Ironically, British efforts to end the slave trade by substituting legitimate trade sometimes had the opposite effect on African domestic slavery. In Yorubaland, for example, warfare led to a growing demand for slaves to meet domestic needs for labor. Much of this demand for labor was for the production of palm oil and palm kernels. The sale of palm products was then used to buy firearms for more war and more slaves and to maintain the luxurious lifestyle of the warlords. The Ijebu and Egba who lived close to ports on the coast became the middlemen in this trade. Competition to control trade routes for legitimate trade became a major cause of political instability and war. Another reason the demand for domestic slaves increased in the south was because slaves were used to carry trade goods and commodities like palm oil between markets in the interior and the coast. In northeastern

Igboland, another use for domestic slaves was for defense purposes. Whole communities of slaves were established to serve as militias in areas where territorial defense forces were needed. Slaves also served as cheap farm labor.

As was mentioned previously, few Europeans left the coast of West Africa before the 1850s to venture into the interior because of the threat of disease, especially malaria. Those who did spend any time there usually succumbed quickly to the disease and died. (Clapperton, for example, died on his second trip to Sokoto in the late 1820s.) In Nigeria, fear of malaria kept any European designs for imperial expansion at bay and allowed African traders, rulers, and societies to maintain a position of equality in relations with the Europeans.

All of this began to change after 1850 with the discovery of quinine, which provided treatment for malaria. Great Britain was now in a far more favorable position to implement its vision of "Christianity, Commerce, and Civilization." European explorers and traders began to enter the Niger River interior for the first time. Christian missionaries also now had access to people in the interior, and mission activity increased as a result. In the 1840s, missions could be found in various towns in the south, and, in 1857, a chain of mission stations was established for the first time along the Niger River. As the penetration of the interior increased, it set the stage for the steady march toward Nigeria's eventual colonization.

The Christian missionary movement was to have a profound impact on Nigeria in the nineteenth century, but its progress before that was slow and limited. Initial efforts to introduce Christianity to Nigeria began with the Portuguese in the 1500s. Some Africans from Benin and Gold Coast were taken to Portugal and educated for the priesthood, and the Portuguese hoped to convert the oba of Benin so that he would bring his people to the Christian faith. The oba did have some of his chiefs become Christian, and he built a church. Missionaries from Portugal were welcomed. The missionaries had their greatest success at the port city of Warri (south of Benin), where Christianity survived for almost two centuries before it died out. One reason Christianity failed to sustain itself was that over time missionaries died or left and were not replaced, thus leaving local Christians with no leadership. The neglect of the faith was due to the fact that the Portuguese lost interest in West Africa in the 1600s and shifted their focus to India and the East, where trade was more lucrative. When the Dutch, French, and British succeeded the Portuguese in the 1700s, they were interested in buying slaves, not saving souls.

A major difference between the earlier, largely failed, attempts to convert Nigerians to Christianity and the missionary movement of the nineteenth century is that the nineteenth century missionary movement included African missionaries, many of them from Nigeria. After the British outlawed slave trading along the West African coast, many freed slaves, including many returning to Africa from the Americas, went to Sierra Leone. (Others went to Liberia, which was a colony established by the United States.) Although the ex-slaves came from many places in Africa, a large number were Yoruba from Nigeria. Many of them or their children were educated in missionary schools in Sierra Leone. They had learned English and the value of literacy and had received a European-style education. In the 1840s they began to return to their homeland, bringing with them their new Christian faith.

Under the auspices of the Christian Missionary Society, eager Nigerian missionaries spearheaded the mission effort. The mission stations along the Niger River in 1857 were established by Nigeria's most famous missionary, Bishop Samuel Ajayi Crowther, a Yoruba supported by the Christian Missionary Society (CMS). The stations were staffed entirely by African missionaries, most of them trained in Sierra Leone. Other areas where the missionaries settled were Gbebe and Lokoja (towns on the Niger-Benue River confluence). Another well-known African missionary was James Thomas, who was of Eki-Bunu origin. He was stationed at Gbebe. His hometown of Ikudon was a community three to four days from Gbebe. Thomas and many of his fellow missionaries saw their purpose as teaching and preaching to their "benighted countrymen who are still worshipping the gods of wood and stone." Another missionary was T. C. John, a second-generation Hausa, who returned to Nigeria from Sierra Leone. John was highly Westernized; he even dressed as an Englishman in order not to be mistaken for one of his Muslim Hausa countrymen.

An important characteristic of the African missionaries was their lack of ethnic consciousness, an attitude they hoped to transmit to their fellow Africans. For instance, Crowther and his clergy worked equally with the Igbo, Ijo, Igala, and Nupe. The missionaries envisioned a new nation without ethnic boundaries and with the Niger River as its center. They saw the Christian church as a training ground for self-government and citizenship in a new, progressive African society. More ominously, they also concluded that their goals would need British intervention if they were to become a reality.

The missionaries made only slow progress in their conversion efforts. In some places, the Christian message had its main appeal among marginal, low-status groups in society. In other areas, religious pluralism robbed Christianity of its exclusivity; that is, Christianity was viewed as one of a variety of religions of roughly equal merit. In areas like Gbebe and Lokoja, for example, the population was ethnically and religiously heterogeneous.

This encouraged an inclusive and tolerant attitude toward religion, with none treated as being the only true faith with the only true god. Everyone was welcome to participate in common ceremonies for household and group deities. Worshippers of particular deities often consulted and worshipped other deities as well. Christianity was viewed by most of the locals in the same light; it was simply another way to worship. Local Ifa priests might go to Sunday services at the mission and participate in Christian prayers. Muslims attended Christian services, and Muslim clerics would visit with the missionaries. In cosmopolitan towns like Lagos or Abeokuta, African missionaries received a similar reception. They were not special but were one of several immigrant groups residing in the towns in large numbers. These groups included Muslims, secularists, and pagans as well as Christians. The Christians were mainly regarded as special for their Western education and skills.

Even though the locals failed to respond to Christianity as the missionaries had hoped, the African missionaries themselves were often well received and respected as returning kinsmen. Many of the missionaries in Gbebe and Lokoja had been born in the area and still had relatives there. They fit easily into the indigenous cultures and societies rather than treating the locals as barbarous inferiors. Many, in fact, spoke local languages. James Thomas, for instance, spoke Eki, Nupe, and Bassa.

In the Yoruba towns, the situation was quite different. The religious culture and the ethnic makeup of the population were more homogeneous, and there was less acceptance of Christianity. There were also fewer ethnic and kinship ties among the locals and the missionaries than was the case in Gbebe and Lokoja. The Ijebu, for example, refused to welcome the Sierra Leonean missionaries. They saw them as a threat to the stability of their communities. Most of the Yoruba remained true to their own religion and used the missionaries as a tool in local political struggles. Another problem for the missionaries was European rather than African control of the Yoruba missions. Unlike the Africans, the Europeans were often ethnocentric and prejudiced toward local people and their cultural practices. At one point, white missionaries were actually kicked out of Abeokuta.

The African Christians gained influence in many areas because their roles were not strictly religious. The returnees were of many professions and had valuable skills and resources to offer local communities. Among these valued resources was access to highly desired foreign manufactured goods and to ties with the British. Josiah and Samuel Crowther, Bishop Crowther's sons, are good examples. They were traders as well as missionaries. Some of the Yoruba returnees brought their own ships with them and traded along the

coast in such places as Lagos. By 1830, there were many African Christian settlers in the interior in Abeokuta, while others established themselves along
the coast in Badagri and Lagos. Some of the African Christians earned a place
in their communities by becoming military advisors to local rulers.

The Egba of Abeokuta called the freedmen from Sierra Leone "Saro"
and saw it as advantageous to welcome them as friends of the white man.
The Saro were responsible for requesting that Sierra Leone send missionaries to Lagos. The man who responded to the call was Thomas Birch
Freeman, who was of mixed African-English descent. Freeman established Wesleyan missions in Badagri and Abeokuta in 1842. Samuel Ajayi
Crowther and two European missionaries were sent by the CMS to
Abeokuta in 1843. After a problematic start, the missionaries eventually
gained acceptance and influence as the chief military advisors to the Egba
state when Dahomey invaded in 1851. Thanks to the missionaries, the
British sent weapons and other military supplies, which enabled the Egba
to defeat the invaders.

Many Protestant denominations were to become active in Nigeria in the
1800s. The Presbyterians established themselves at Calabar in 1846. Their
leader was Hope Waddell, whose staff was made up of Africans from Jamaica.
The missionaries became politically influential and gained support among
ex-slaves and local rulers, who now feared the growing threat of a slave revolt. In areas where local communities received direct and practical benefits
from the Christian missionaries, missionary influence was greater. In Gbebe
and Lokoja, for instance, missionaries built churches, but also schools and
houses. They spent a great deal of money and hired many local workers, both
men and women. The local economy greatly benefited from this. Indeed,
apart from the slave trade, income generated by missionary activity was the
most important source of local income. The missionaries also bought some
slaves their freedom from local owners at a high price. This also was profitable for the local economy. As many missionaries (like the Crowther brothers) were also traders, they encouraged local export production and legitimate trade. Local farmers benefited from the expanding market for their
cotton and palm oil production.

On the other hand, in areas where locals were less dependent on missionaries as a source of economic gain, the missionaries typically had less
influence. In much of southern Nigeria, the most important merchants
were not missionaries. They were chiefs, obas, other nobles, and private
traders (for example, nonmissionary Sierra Leoneans and ex-slaves from
Brazil). People in the south had ways to gain wealth independently of the
missionaries. Under these circumstances, the missionaries had no exclusive

or major advantage to give them status or influence. This was the situation in most Yoruba, Niger delta, and Igbo towns.

For much of the 1800s, Nigerians had the freedom to choose whether to accept the missionaries and on what terms. People could accept, reject, or incorporate the missionaries and their message as they saw fit. As long as communities had their independence and power, Christianity as a religion had limited impact. To have an influence, Christian missionaries had to treat Africans with equality and mutual respect. However, growing British power and colonization eventually changed the situation decisively. Once the missionaries gained the backing of British colonial authorities, they became much more authoritarian and treated Africans, even Christian converts, as inferiors. As the colonial missionary effort expanded, it also became dominated by whites. At that point, Christian missionaries became more racist and determined to destroy those aspects of African cultures they judged to be objectionable. This led to growing resistance toward the missionaries in areas such as Igboland, for example. The conflict between the missionaries and Igbo villagers is eloquently described in Nigerian writer Chinua Achebe's famous novel, *Things Fall Apart*.

Christianity was not the only religion competing for the allegiance of Nigerians in the 1800s. Islam was extending its influence outside of the north into Nupe and Yorubaland in the 1800s. Although the jihads were stopped, traders and preachers from Ilorin went to other parts of Yorubaland peacefully seeking converts. They eventually found themselves competing with Christian missionaries. In such Yoruba cities as Lagos, Badagri, Epe, and even Ilorin, Islam was a minority religion appealing mainly to slaves, traders, and merchants, especially those from the north. When confronted with the choice of Islam or Christianity, most Yoruba remained loyal to their indigenous religions. The southern Yoruba political elite especially avoided Islam, as much of their legitimacy was based on indigenous religious ideology. When Oyo fell in the 1830s, many Muslims fled with other refugees to Ibadan and Abeokuta. Muslims were not persecuted, and Islam even became attractive to some due to its focus on literacy and Muslim education. Moreover, Yoruba Muslims tended to be tolerant of indigenous rulers and local beliefs and practices. Christianity arrived in southern Yoruba towns at about the same time as Islam. It had an edge over Islam due to the appeal of European education, which was more economically advantageous than its Muslim rival. European education grew in importance as British economic and political influence expanded. The rivalry between the two religions was destined to intensify over time.

The March toward Colonialism

By 1840, the British blockade of the West African coast to intercept slave ships had much reduced the slave trade. The British navy then became an instrument for promoting the interests of British palm oil traders in the area. By 1849, the palm oil trade was so valuable that a British consul was stationed in West Africa to protect Britain's commercial interests. One of the consul's responsibilities was to regulate trade on the Oil Rivers through treaties with the various African governments in the area.

Making treaties soon gave way to political interference, the use of force, and colonial control. The first consul, John Beecroft, imposed himself as the final legal arbiter in area affairs. When he became unhappy with King William Pepple of Bonny, the local African ruler, he had him deposed. He also imposed his choice of a successor to be the ruler in Calabar. Then, in 1845, in a dispute between King Akitoye of Lagos, who had been overthrown by his nephew Kosoko, Beecroft interceded on behalf of the king. Kosoko was deposed, and Akitoye was restored to power but as a virtual puppet of the British, to whom he owed his rule. In 1861, Docemo, Akitoye's son and successor, was "persuaded" by the British to cede Lagos to British control. Lagos thus became Great Britain's first colony in Nigeria.

At this time, the British were reluctant to embark on a policy of wholesale colonization in West Africa. In 1865, the British Select Committee of Parliament had decided on a policy of making Sierra Leone the only permanent British settlement in the region. Despite such decisions, local British officials were becoming more interventionist. In the Oil Rivers areas, trade disputes handled by Courts of Equity regularly favored British traders over Africans. After Lagos was annexed, the British governor became involved in stopping the Yoruba wars in order to expand trade in Yorubaland and into the lands of the Nupe and the Muslim north. British interventions almost led to war with the Egba in Abeokuta and helped to provoke the expulsion of all white missionaries from the town.

In the 1880s, British policy changed in favor of greater control over Africans as a result of competition with the French, who were seeking to expand their trade along the lower Niger River. This placed the French in direct competition with the British United Africa Company (which became the National Africa Company in 1882). The British feared a French challenge to their dominance in Yorubaland, the Oil Rivers area, and even Igboland in the east. To prevent this from happening, the British government in 1882 abandoned its noninterference policy and established a "protectorate" over the Oil Rivers area and Cameroon. In Cameroon, the British failed to act quickly enough to establish their control. This allowed the Germans to step in and seize Cameroon as a colony in 1884. The British did succeed, however, in establishing a protectorate over the Oil Rivers area in 1884, which became the Niger Coast Protectorate in 1894.

European competition for colonies in Africa intensified in the 1880s. To prevent a possible war, the European powers met at the Berlin Conference of 1884–1885 to lay out clear ground rules for the various European countries active in Africa. In effect, spheres of influence were agreed upon, but it became necessary to establish each country's claims to territory on the ground. This set off a "scramble for Africa," in which such countries as France and Britain began to gobble up territory and establish their control by any necessary means. The result was outright colonization all over Africa. Needless to say, none of Africa's people were consulted in the matter, nor did they realize while the conference was taking place that their days as sovereign peoples were quickly coming to an end.

In Nigeria, initial moves were made by the National Africa Company (formerly the British United Africa Company) to bring African states under their control in the interests of trade along the Niger. Their right to a monopoly over trade along the river had been established at the Berlin Conference. Renamed the Royal Niger Company in 1886, the company had been given a charter by the British government to administer the area. The company asserted its claim to vast territories on the basis of duplicitous treaties it had made with local rulers of such groups as the Igala, the Igbo, and the Ijo. The company then sought control over the entire Hausa-Fulani empire and began to administer large areas of the Sokoto Caliphate. To gain dominion over the Oil Rivers area territories, British traders in league with the local British consul used treachery to get rid of King JaJa of Opobo, who was an obstacle to their goal of monopolizing the palm oil markets on the coast.

Control over Yorubaland was completed in the 1890s. Since 1886, the British had been the main power there, but internecine war was a constant threat, especially between the Ijebu and Abeokuta. In 1892, the Ijebu government was overthrown by the British governor of Lagos. The governor then began to make treaties with other Yoruba rulers, which effectively gave the British authority over almost all of Yorubaland. As of 1896, only Ilorin was outside of British control. One positive result of Britain's power over the Yoruba territories was that the Yoruba wars were finally brought to an end.

The British then began to tighten their grip on what remained of independent Nigeria. Benin, Ilorin, and Nupe were conquered in 1897. Between 1900 and 1903, the Protectorate of Northern Nigeria was established, with Frederick Lugard as High Commissioner. From 1900 to 1906, Lugard launched military campaigns against the Hausa-Fulani until all northern resistance was

FRENCH WEST AFRICA
(France, 1902)

Lake
Chad

• Sokoto

Kano •

NORTHERN NIGERIA (1900)

DAHOMEY
(France, 1893)

• Kaduna

Part of German
Cameroon
(1906–1914)

CAMEROON
(Germany, 1906)

Niger River

• Ilorin

Benue River

• Oyo

Lokoja

• Ibadan

SOUTHERN NIGERIA (1906)

Benin •

CAMEROON
(Germany, 1884)

Lagos
(1861)

Lagos Colony and
Protectorate (1886)*

Calabar

Oil Rivers Protectorate (1887),
Niger Coast Protectorate (1894)

ATLANTIC
OCEAN

Fernando Po
(Spain, 1778)

— · — Present international boundary
——— Colonial boundary, 1914
- - - - Protectorate boundary, pre-1914
· · · · · · Approximate limits of effective
        administration by Royal
        Niger Company, 1885
•   Populated place
▨   Gradual expansion of British
        protectorate in Southern
        Nigeria, 1887–1906

0   100   200   300 km

* Part of West African settlements (1866–1876)
  Gold Coast colony (1876–1886)

Map 3.1
British Presence in the Niger Region, 1861–1914

crushed. Only the Igbo (and Ibibio) remained to be "pacified." Their small, de-centralized communities put up much resistance and proved difficult to defeat. In 1902, the British attacked Arochuku, the site of the notorious oracle. The cave of the god Chuku was destroyed, but not Igbo resistance. The British campaign against the Igbo lasted from 1900 to 1911, when it finally ended with the British being left in control of the entire territory of Nigeria.

Conclusion

Little did anyone imagine that the initial contact in the 1500s between the peoples of Nigeria and the Europeans would lead from trade in commodities to trade in slaves and, finally, to the subjugation of the entire area to European colonial domination. Moreover, no one could have foreseen the enormous consequences both the slave trade and colonialism would have on Nigeria, effects that would last into the present.

The impact of the Atlantic slave trade on Nigerian society was both profound and multifaceted. Concentrating trade on the coast irreversibly altered the population distribution; the rise and fall of states; and economic, political, and social life. Coastal ports became a magnet for people and trade at the expense of interior regions. This promoted new prosperity for some (such as the delta states) and the decline of others (such as Oyo). Populations were raided and depopulated as a result of the slave trade. The Egba, Ibibio, and Igbo were among the groups that suffered the most. Slaves became the main commodity traded by Nigerians, while manufactured goods were increasingly imported. Local skills and industry languished as a result. British cottons, salt, and tools were among the products replacing those of local manufacture. Many of the manufactured goods purchased through the sale of human beings such as firearms, tobacco, and liquor were detrimental to the people of the region rather than beneficial.

Later, as legitimate commerce replaced slavery, settlement patterns changed once again. New land was settled and brought under cultivation to produce crops for export. Areas that were able to profit from the new trade benefited while others remained poor and marginalized. Coastal port cities thrived as entrepots for global trade, whereas previously great trading cities of the old trans-Saharan trade were now largely backward, medieval curiosities.

Class relations were altered as well. Some Africans became rich and powerful from the slave trade. Kings and dynasties were created among groups where none had existed before. Warlords and those who traded in human beings rose to the top of the status hierarchy, but genuinely productive activity went largely unrewarded. The wealthy classes during and after the slavery era were dependent on trade with Europeans for their prosperity. Many sent their children to Europe for education. Those who used their wealth for productive activity, that is, for legitimate commerce, usually owned many slaves to produce their wealth and maintain their households in lavish comfort and style. The foundation was being laid during this time for Nigeria's (and Africa's) role in the global economy as a producer of cheap labor and raw materials. By contrast, while Nigeria was cannibalizing itself through the slave trade, Europe was using its wealth from the slave trade and legitimate commerce to industrialize and mold a global economy that would mainly enrich it and other industrial nations.

The slave trade was responsible for unspeakable violence, inhumanity, and waste of human life. When the British condemned African societies for being barbarous and disordered, they usually blamed the Africans themselves rather than the demand for slaves in the Western world for the evils that they saw. The slave trade had been initiated by Europeans and maintained by them to meet their insatiable demand for slave labor without regard for the human and social cost. By the mid-1800s, the conditions the British decried but helped to create would be used to justify colonial domination.

With colonialism, Nigerians lost their independence and control over their future, and their societies were placed under Great Britain's "guidance" so that they could be "civilized." In reality, Nigeria, along with Britain's other African colonies, was to be turned into a source of valuable commodities, cheap labor, and markets primarily for the benefit of Great Britain. The next chapter will examine the impact of colonialism on Nigeria, with an emphasis on how different regions and ethnic groups were affected. As will also be shown, colonialism over time generated a nationalist movement for independence and played a major role in shaping today's Nigerian identities.

Timeline

Late 1400s–1500s	Portuguese contact with Ijo, trade begins with Benin, expansion of Benin begins
1500s–1600s	Oyo expands its territory
1500s–1700s	The Portuguese dominate the slave trade with Nigeria
1700s–1800s	The slave trade is dominated by the Dutch, then the British and French
Late 1700s	The Christian antislavery movement begins in Great Britain
1700s–1800s	The gradual decline of Benin and Oyo occurs
1800s	The Yoruba civil wars ensue until 1896
1807	Great Britain bans the slave trade
1822	Ilorin, with the help of the Fulani, defeats Oyo; Oyo collapses
1829	Oyo refugees flee to Ibadan
1830	The Egba move to Abeokuta; the palm oil trade is replacing the slave trade
1840s	Christian missionaries are arriving in Nigeria; Fulani expansion ends
1850	Quinine is discovered for the treatment of malaria

1861	The British consulate is established in Lagos; Lagos becomes the first British colony in Nigeria
1884–1885	The Berlin Conference is held
1894	The Niger Coast Protectorate is established
1897	Benin, Yorubaland, and Nupe come under British control
1900–1903	The Protectorate of Northern Nigeria is established
1911	Igbo resistance to the British is defeated

Significant People, Places, and Events

BERLIN CONFERENCE OF 1884–1885 Fourteen European nations met at this conference in Berlin. The participants agreed to end slavery and manage the imperialist expansion that threatened the peace. At this time, it was slavery by the Arabs rather than the Atlantic slave trade that was at issue. The major colonial powers in Africa at this time were Great Britain, France, Germany, Portugal, and Belgium.

BRIDEWEALTH In many African societies, parents arrange the marriages of their children. Bridewealth is a form of compensation to the family of the bride for the loss of their daughter. The amount of the bridewealth indicates the value of the girl and the status of the families; it does not mean the girl is being sold.

CHRISTIAN MISSIONARY SOCIETY (CMS) The CMS is a British mission agency established in 1799 to spread Christianity to every part of the world. It currently remains active in Africa, Asia, the Middle East, and Europe.

COWRY SHELLS On the West African coast, the use of cowry shells as money dates to the sixteenth century. The shells were imported from the Indian Ocean by way of Egypt.

CROWTHER, BISHOP SAMUEL AJAYI In 1864 Crowther, an African missionary, became the first African Anglican bishop.

EAST AFRICAN SLAVE TRADE The slave trade affected East Africa to a lesser extent than West Africa. Most of its slaves went to Arabia and Persia, although some went to French sugar plantations in the Indies. A few even found their way into the Atlantic slave trade.

GOLD COAST The center of the Gold Coast is now the modern-day country of Ghana. In 1481, the first European fort, Elmina, was built here by the Portuguese. It became a major port for the African gold trade until the slave trade replaced gold as the major commodity on the coast in the 1600s. The area eventually became a British colony.

INFIDEL Muslims consider themselves, Christians, and Jews to be part of the same religious tradition and to be "people of the book" (that is, possessors of sacred scriptures). Although all non-Muslims are sometimes considered infidels (unbelievers), the term is often reserved for pagans, who are not "people of the book."

KING JAJA OF OPOBO JaJa was the only slave to become a king in a Niger delta state. Because of his efforts to maintain African independence from the British and due to his betrayal and exile by them, JaJa is considered a national martyr in Nigeria.

LAGOS The name of Nigeria's largest city came from the Portuguese name "Lago de Curama." Lago means lagoon, or lake. Lagos was named for an inlet on the great lagoon where the city is located.

LUGARD, FREDERICK Before being appointed to govern the protectorates and then the colony of Nigeria, Lugard had been the first British administrator in the British East Africa colony, which is now Uganda.

NIGER COAST PROTECTORATE This protectorate, established in 1894, stretched from the Niger delta east to Calabar.

OIL RIVERS The British thought that the Oil Rivers were distinct rivers. In reality, they are numerous delta outlets of the Niger River.

PALM OIL Palm oil is used as a lubricant for machinery and in soaps and cosmetics. It is also commonly used in West Africa for cooking.

PORTUGUESE The Portuguese first bought slaves on the coast of Mauritania from the caravan trade across the Sahara. The Portuguese continued to be active in the slave trade well into the nineteenth century in order to supply Brazil and other colonies with slaves.

RULERS WHO OPPOSED THE SLAVE TRADE Not all African rulers embraced the slave trade or did so willingly. One of these rulers was King Affonso of Congo. In 1526, he appealed to the king of Portugal to forbid Portuguese merchants from trading with his people for slaves. In the early 1700s, the fon of Dahomey also opposed the slave trade, but Dahomey was eventually forced to enter into slave trading in order to buy the firearms needed to protect its people from slave raids, especially from Oyo.

SOKOTO CALIPHATE The Sokoto Caliphate was founded by Uthman dan Fodio during the Islamic jihads of the early 1800s. In 1860, the caliphate had more slaves than any other country at the time except for the United States.

THINGS FALL APART In Chinua Achebe's well-known novel, he tells about the destructive impact of Christian missionaries and British colonialism on traditional society in an Igbo village in the late 1800s.

TRADE GOODS Although guns were the main commodities Europeans traded for slaves, many other new goods also entered the African market, such as textiles, beads, and metals. New foods were also introduced, which greatly expanded the African diet. These included maize, cassava, groundnuts (peanuts), sweet potatoes, citrus fruits, pineapples, and tomatoes.

TRANS-SAHARAN SLAVE TRADE No one knows with any accuracy how many slaves were traded during the approximately 1,000 years of this trade. It only officially ended at the beginning of the twentieth century. Slavery still exists in some countries along the Sahel, such as Mauritania and Sudan.

UNITED AFRICA COMPANY The United African Company was started by George Taubman Goldie in 1879. It was a monopoly of all British firms trading on the Niger River. It became the National Africa Company in 1882. In 1886, the company was renamed the Royal Niger Company.

Bibliography

Achebe, Chinua. 1994. *Things Fall Apart.* Garden City, NY: Doubleday.

Collins, Robert O. 1990. *Western African History.* Princeton, NJ: Markus Wiener.

Davidson, Basil. 1991. *African Civilization Revisited.* Trenton, NJ: Africa World Press.

Falola, Toyin. 1998. *Violence in Nigeria: The Crisis of Religious Politics and Secular Ideologies.* Rochester, NY: University of Rochester Press.

————. 1999. *The History of Nigeria.* Westport, CT: Greenwood.

Flint, John E. 1966. *Nigeria and Ghana.* Englewood Cliffs, NJ: Prentice-Hall.

Freund, Bill. 1998. *The Making of Contemporary Africa: Development of African Society since 1800.* Boulder, CO: Lynne Rienner.

Jones, G. I. 1963. *The Trading States of the Oil Rivers: A Study of Political Development in Eastern Nigeria.* London: Oxford University Press.

Kolapo, Femi J. 2000. "CMS Missionaries of African Origin and Extra-Religious Encounters at the Niger-Benue Confluence, 1858–1880." *African Studies Review* 43 (September): 87–115.

Nwachuku-Ogedengbe, K. 1977. "Slavery in Nineteenth-Century Aboh." Pp. 133–154 in *Slavery in Africa: Historical and Anthropological Perspectives.* Edited by Suzanne Miers and Igor Kopytoff. Madison: University of Wisconsin Press.

Smith, Robert S. 1988. *Kingdoms of the Yoruba.* Madison: University of Wisconsin Press.

Uchendu, Victor C. 1977. "Slaves and Slavery in Igboland, Nigeria." Pp. 121–132 in *Slavery in Africa: Historical and Anthropological Perspectives.* Edited by Suzanne Miers and Igor Kopytoff. Madison: University of Wisconsin Press.

Colonialism and Nationalism

FTER HUNDREDS OF YEARS OF TRADING SLAVES with Africans along what came to be called the Slave Coast, the British initiated a change in policy in the early nineteenth century; "legitimate" commerce, accompanied by cultural and religious reform carried by Christian missionaries and Westernized Africans, was to be imposed. As the century progressed, the interest in trade led to imperialism on a global level. Industrialization in Europe had reduced the need for slaves but had multiplied the demand for raw materials, cheap labor, and markets for European manufactured goods.

In West Africa, the British came to realize that protecting their economic and geopolitical interests along the Niger River would require more intervention and control over African affairs. Exerting this control culminated in outright colonial domination of the territorial entity the British eventually named "Nigeria." After conquering all of Nigeria's major ethnic groups by 1911, the British appointed Frederick Lugard in 1912 to be governor of both the Northern and Southern Protectorates. In 1914, the two protectorates were united to become the Colony and Protectorate of Nigeria, with Lugard as the first governor-general.

In the process of ruling their new Nigerian domain, the British instituted policies that had unintended consequences. Among these consequences was the laying of the foundation for many of the current ethnic, regional, and religious identities and cleavages that Nigeria struggles with today. This chapter will examine that period of roughly sixty years of colonialism in Nigeria. This chapter will illustrate how British colonial rule operated and how it helped to change, or even create, group identities as well as influence intragroup and intergroup dynamics. The chapter will look first at the political and then economic impact of colonial rule, then it will illustrate the effects of demographic changes involving the movement and distribution of people. Finally, this chapter will investigate how colonialism set the stage for the growth of nationalism and ethnically based political parties.

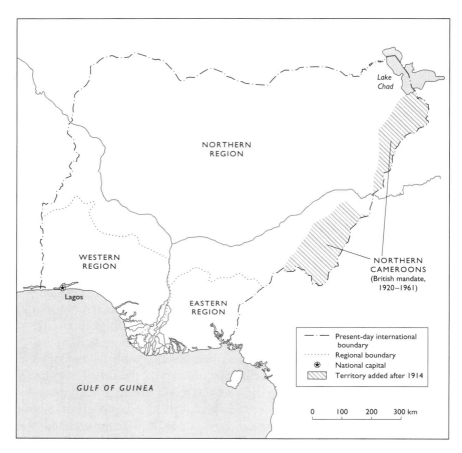

Map 4.1
Unification of Nigeria, 1914

Indirect Rule and the Shaping of Identities

To understand the impact of colonialism on Nigeria and its people, one must keep in mind the goals of colonialism. The main goal was to mold Nigeria into a society (or, more accurately, a collection of societies) that would produce cheap raw materials for export and would purchase British manufactured goods. This was necessary to promote the material standard of living desired by Great Britain's burgeoning population. Colonies were justified by the claim that only monopoly control established by colonial dominance could ensure that British national interests were met in this regard. At the same time, the "white man's burden" was invoked to justify colonialism as a service to native peoples, and not just a means to European enrichment at natives' expense. Below is an excerpt from Frederick Lugard's 1926 book, *The Dual Mandate in British Tropical Africa,* which explains and justifies colonialism and describes administrative policy in Nigeria. The "dual mandate" refers to the requirement of colonial administrators both to serve economic interests back in Great Britain and to promote the "progress" of the "native races" (in ways determined by British policymakers).

In this excerpt, Lugard justifies the economic necessity and benefits of colonialism:

> There is no doubt that the control of the tropics, so far from being a charge on the British taxpayer, is to him a source of great gain. The products of the tropics have raised the standard of comfort of the working man, added to the amenities of his life, and provided alike the raw materials on which the industry and wealth of the community depend, and the market for manufactures which ensure employment.
>
> Prior to the war [World War I] Nigeria was the latest addition to the Empire, and if against the original payment to the Chartered Company and all subsequent grants, be set the profit derived by the British Exchequer on the import of silver coin, and the contributions offered by Nigeria to the war, it will be found that the debit is on the other side, and the country, with all its potentialities and expanding markets, has cost the British taxpayer nothing. Its trade, the greater part of which is with the United Kingdom, is of the kind which is the most valuable possible to the workers of this country—raw materials and foodstuffs in exchange for textiles and hardware.
>
> Europe is in Africa for the mutual benefit of her own industrial classes, and of the native races in their progress to a higher plane; the benefit can be made reciprocal, and that is the aim and desire of civilized administration to fulfill this dual mandate. We are endeavouring to teach the native races to conduct their own affairs with justice and humanity, and to educate them alike in letters and in industry.
>
> As Roman imperialism laid the foundations of modern civilization, and led the wild barbarians of these islands along the path of progress, so in Africa today we are repaying debt, and bringing to the dark places of the earth, the abode of barbarism and cruelty, the torch of culture and progress, while ministering to the material needs of our own civilization. British methods have not perhaps in all cases produced ideal results, but I am profoundly convinced that there can be no question but that British rule has promoted the happiness and welfare of the primitive races. (Lugard 2002, 13–18)

A procession of emirs from northern Nigeria (Hulton-Deutsch Collection/Corbis)

If one can assume Lugard's sincerity in the above statements, it becomes apparent that colonialism in Nigeria was perceived to be for the good of the British as well as the Africans. Of course, it was the British who determined that colonialism was good and beneficial. Africans were, from Lugard's perspective, "barbarous" and incapable of advancement on their own terms and without British domination over them.

The first task of Nigeria's British rulers was to find the most effective way to rule their new territory, a territory composed of many unrelated cultural groups with very different political systems. One decision the British made, based in large part on Lugard's recommendations, was to interfere as little as possible in the daily life of the many peoples it ruled. It was determined that interference should be limited to what was necessary to meet the needs of the colonial administration and the economic exploitation of the colony or to eliminate cultural practices that were unacceptable to British morality. A policy of indirect rule was chosen. Indirect rule involved British rule through local traditional rulers, called native authorities. These local rulers would be responsible for taxation and for carrying out British policies among the people. This had the advantage of minimizing the need for

British administrators to directly tax the people or force colonial policy upon them. Ruling the colony through the Africans' own leaders would also lessen resistance to colonial rule by making it less visible. It would provide the illusion that African rulers were still largely in charge and that colonialism was not all that disruptive. Administrative costs would be lower as well if locals could be made to do most of the administrative work, under British supervision to be sure. In some areas, such as northern Nigeria, indirect rule would also insulate Islamic societies from European Christian influences that might threaten the social order and raise violent resistance to colonialism from local leaders. The goal of good administration was, after all, order and efficiency so that maximum profits could be made from colonial possessions.

Northern Nigeria with its centralized states, emirs, and established government bureaucracies was seen by Lugard as the most suitable candidate for indirect rule in Nigeria. Some had argued that the original Hausa leaders should be restored to power because they had a greater claim than the Fulani emirs to being the north's traditional rulers, but Lugard justified his decision to retain the Fulani ruling class and government on two basic grounds. One was that replacing the Fulani would be too disruptive. Second—and this was true of indirect rule in general—the Fulani rulers would be collaborators and partners with the British in maintaining colonial rule. In Lugard's words,

> There were indeed many who, with the picture of Fulani misrule fresh in their memory, regarded this system [of indirect rule] when it was first inaugurated with much misgiving. They thought that the Fulani as an alien race of conquerors, who had in turn been conquered, had not the same claims for consideration as those whom they had displaced [the Hausa], even though they had become so identified with the people that they could no longer be called aliens.
>
> But there can be no doubt that such races form an invaluable medium between the British staff and the native peasantry. Nor can the difficulty of finding any one capable of taking their place, or the danger they would constitute to the State if ousted from their positions, be ignored. Their traditions of rule, their monotheistic religion, and their intelligence enable them to appreciate more readily than the negro population the wider objects of British policy, while their close touch with the masses with whom they live in daily intercourse mark them out as destined to play an important part in the future, as they have done in the past, in the development of the tropics.
>
> The personal interests of the rulers must rapidly become identified with those of the controlling Power. The forces of disorder do not distinguish

between them, and the rulers soon recognize that any upheaval against the British would equally make an end of them. Once this community of interest is established, the Central Government cannot be taken by surprise, for it is impossible that the native rulers should not be aware of any disaffection. (ibid., 8)

Despite the ideology of mutual benefit and minimal disruption of local cultures, British interference was extensive and in many ways far more negative than Lugard's writings indicate. In the north, for example, the British undermined the stability of the political system in ways that made traditional rule far more oppressive than it had been in the past. For one thing, the British reduced the status of the sultan to that of an emir. They also made it quite clear that the emirs and other high officials would only maintain their positions as long as they did the bidding of their British masters. By the same token, faithful service to their foreign masters would ensure the rulers' power and high incomes. As an object lesson, most of the original emirs were deposed and replaced with leaders that the British felt would be more cooperative. The British also changed the judicial system to lessen the authority of Islamic law (*shari'a*) and courts. The fact that the emirs implemented this and other policies considered "un-Islamic" by their subjects demonstrated the impotence of the emirs to their people.

The changes indirect rule created had the effect of destroying the traditional patron-client system in the emirates that had created some accountability of the Hausa-Fulani elites to the people they ruled. In the precolonial system, patron-client relations linked people of different status and power to each other in a system of mutual benefit and responsibility. With the rulers now dependent for their positions on the British and not on the people they governed, even officials who wanted to rule responsibly had little ability to do so. Under the traditional system, patrons (that is, those who were more wealthy and powerful) had to protect their clients (that is, those lower in status, including the common people) from unfair treatment by government officials and promote their economic interests. Clients reciprocated by supporting their patrons' political interests against their rivals. Corruption and other abuses of power by patrons were kept under control because clients could switch their allegiance to another patron or freely move to another area outside of the patron's control. Under the new colonial system, the wealthy and privileged now had no reason to maintain any responsibility toward the common people.

Another way the British undermined the delicate relationship between patrons and clients was by appointing village and district heads, ostensibly to promote administrative efficiency. As these new heads owed their position to the British and not to the emirs, abuse of power by these officials became more difficult to control. Once the emirs lost control over lower-level officials, the only recourse the people had against unjust and corrupt officials was to migrate to areas outside of the officials' control. As an indication of how bad the situation had become, migration became so commonplace that in 1908 the British tried to restrict it.

Lugard had claimed that British rule would be just and efficient and that headmen would be effectively supervised by the British staff in order to prevent abuses of power. In reality, the British were often more interested in officials' loyalty to the British than in the quality of their service to their people. In 1907, for example, the district head of Zamfara was deposed for his "lack of enthusiasm in assisting the British administrators." By contrast, the district head of Tambawel was allowed to remain in office despite numerous complaints of serious offenses, such as extortion. In fact, almost all of the local officials became discredited for their corruption, abuse of power, and venality. The people quite rightly came to see their real rulers as the British and to depend on the British, not their own so-called traditional rulers, whose legitimacy was now much undermined.

In all fairness to the British, they had been responsive until the 1920s to complaints against corrupt officials. They thought this would help to legitimate British rule in the eyes of the people. In their own eyes, and Lugard's writings reflect this, British colonial authorities believed they were saving the Hausa peasantry from Fulani oppression and misrule. By the 1920s, however, the British changed their policy because they decided it was undermining their administration. They no longer allowed people to report district heads' abuses to the emir or to British officials except in the presence of representatives of the accused chief. With the likelihood of reprisals against the accuser quite high under these circumstances, complaints against officials dropped sharply. It became virtually impossible for people to complain of official wrongdoing. This led to unprecedented extortion and oppression on the part of local officials. Between 1900 and 1934, for instance, extortionate taxes that were imposed on peasant farmers by district chiefs had reduced the peasants to "miserable poverty." At the same time, officials exempted their friends and families from such taxes as the land tax. Peasants were often made to pay more on the land tax than the official assessment so that corrupt tax collectors could pocket the difference for themselves.

It was not just venality and lack of accountability that drove these abuses. Other reasons were low wages paid to officials by the British and the abolition of domestic slavery in the 1920s and 1930s. Before colonial rule and under the old patron-client system, the expectation in Hausa-Fulani society was for officials to be generous with their money. They were judged harshly if they were unwilling or unable to do so. Gift-giving and other forms of largesse were important to maintaining patron-client bonds. Under the changes imposed by the colonial system, many officials were unable to support their families or clients without official theft. The loss of domestic slaves encouraged officials to engage in another form of abuse—forced labor. Officials used their positions to make people work on their farms, for instance. In 1933, the British officially outlawed forced labor, but it continued into the 1940s. Many people were illiterate peasants and were unaware that what the district chiefs were doing was illegal, so they continued to work for them.

Despite their loss of independent authority, many of the northern traditional elite flourished under colonial rule. The emirs retained considerable authority and functions as native authorities, and they benefited economically from extortionate taxes on the poor. Lugard had accurately predicted that the emirs and other rulers would become complicit in maintaining the colonial system. They knew that the power and privileges they enjoyed were dependent on British power. Lower officials whose positions were retained in the new colonial administration were equally beholden to the British. In fact, the colonial system became a major source of jobs and economic rewards for those educated in traditional Islamic schools, who might otherwise have been candidates for Islamic opposition against foreign rule. All in all, the emirs and other officials, regardless of how oppressive and corrupt they were, could rest assured of protection against popular revolts by the peasants. Not only did indirect rule give the Hausa-Fulani rulers undisputed control over the north; in some cases they were now able to impose their rule on groups in the Middle Belt who were not Hausa, Fulani, or even Muslim. This was the antithesis of Lugard's original assertion that British rule in the north was to protect the people from the misrule of the emirs.

Outside the north, indirect rule proved more difficult to implement. In Benin and Yorubaland, the old empires were gone, but this did not stop the British from trying to reimpose them. The monarchy was reintroduced in 1916, and an unpopular effort to bring back the Oyo empire was also attempted. As in the north, the power and authority of the newly installed obas became distorted and corrupted when imposed by outsiders. One problem was that, consistent with the doctrine of indirect rule, the obas were given the function of collecting taxes. Obas had not had this power in the past. Another problem was that the power and wealth of the obas was no longer limited, as in the past, by societal checks and balances. The obas were now backed by the British, who expected the obas to serve them. Many obas became autocrats because there was no longer any established way for the people to eliminate those who abused their power. This did not prevent spontaneous resistance, however. In 1916, for instance, four officials of the Oyo native authority were killed at Iseyin. And, in 1918, after direct taxation was introduced by the native authority at Abeokuta, a rebellion broke out and the local ruler narrowly averted being killed.

In many places in the south, indirect rule was a problem because of the lack of powerful traditional rulers and centralized government. This failed to discourage the British from imposing indirect rule anyway. In such places as Igboland, where there were no kings or chiefs, the British appointed warrant chiefs and other local agents to collect taxes and enforce colonial policies. This was totally inconsistent with the premise of indirect rule, which was that native people should be ruled by their own traditional leaders and that there should be minimal disruption of the people's everyday life. In almost every case, the warrant chiefs had no legitimacy in the societies they administered and were deeply resented by the people. To make matters worse, almost all of these so-called native authorities were unscrupulous and corrupt. All over Nigeria, when British-imposed or British-protected traditional rulers served as intermediaries between the colonial authorities and the people, the result was usually misrule and corruption by local officials and, eventually, resistance from the people. In 1929, in Igboland, tax abuse and other forms of misrule by the warrant chiefs and native courts sparked one of the most famous outbreaks in colonial Nigeria, the Aba Riots, also called the Igbo Women's War because it was led by thousands of Igbo women. Although the revolt started in the town of Aba, it quickly spread to other areas of Igboland, a clear indication of the level of discontent felt by the local population. Native courts, set up by the British to administer justice in cases involving local customs, also were generally a fiasco, where justice hardly could be said to prevail.

One group that was especially hostile to the native authorities was the new class of educated Africans. These were the migrants from Sierra Leone and a group of other Westernized Africans, who lived mostly in the south. Many of them were traders and clergy, who had benefited from the British policy of replacing the slave trade with legitimate commerce. Most were educated in Christian mission schools. By the end of the nineteenth century, Christianity was firmly rooted in the south among mission-educated Africans, whereas the indigenous religions practiced by most of the people were regarded with contempt. As will be discussed in the section on demographic change, most of the new African elite were located in the expanding cities of the south, which were located along interior trade routes and on the coast.

The new class felt that their education and civilized ways qualified them for more power and influence over the development of their societies. Their ambitions increased after the British allowed them limited participation in the legislative council the government had created in Lagos.

The British failed to share the African elite's view of the role they should play in colonial Nigeria. They disliked these upstart Africans and tried to contain their political and economic aspirations. Although Africans initially played an important role in the British administration in Lagos, eventually the British restricted them to subordinate roles. Once full colonization was established, indirect rule was seen in part as a means to marginalize the Western-educated Africans. This was one reason that traditional rulers and native authorities were favored in the colonial system. The British position toward educated Africans might seem odd, as Lugard and other British apologists for colonialism professed a desire to bring education and civilization to Nigeria and to promote rulers who were progressive and Christian. If so, the educated Africans would seem the ideal group to back, rather than the native authorities. In fact, one of the justifications for colonialism was that African rulers were backward and unable to rule their societies adequately. How could the same argument be made against Africans who embraced European values and civilization? The reason for thwarting the educated Africans was that they were perceived by the British to be a greater challenge to British rule over Nigeria because of their qualifications.

Just as the existence of educated, "civilized" Africans challenged the legitimacy of colonialism, keeping most Africans "traditional" and limiting their exposure to education and modern institutions justified colonial domination into an indefinite future. Indirect rule was a means to more or less freeze African societies in an imagined unchanging existence. Traditional rulers, with a vested interest in the status quo, were kept in place or imposed, and undemocratic political institutions like the feudal emirates and discredited obaships were sanctioned rather than the Western-style democracy the educated Africans hoped to see established. The fact that the British were little interested in promoting African development was evident in the fact that very few Africans had access to even the most basic schooling or literacy. Supporting undemocratic monarchies and chiefs, while cutting back on such minor exercises in modern democratic governance as the legislative council in Lagos after 1914, indicates that the British had little interest in providing Africans with experience in running modern democratic institutions. That experience would be necessary if the British were at all interested in preparing Nigeria for self-government at some future date. And, despite the fact that there was a growing number of Africans trained in modern Western legal professions, native courts were created to administer justice on the basis of an often-contrived customary law relevant to each officially recognized ethnic group.

The native courts became part of a dual legal system in Nigeria. Native courts operated side by side with newly established European courts and a common law legal system. By assuming that Africans lived by undisputed and timeless customs, which now became codified into law, the British further entrenched the power of traditional leaders and practices that were not necessarily just, democratic, or compatible with development. And by institutionalizing different systems of law rather than promoting a single, universalistic legal system, an independent Nigeria would find it very difficult to create a governing structure or set of laws that could unify its people. These contradictory forms of government and legal systems, modern Western and traditional customary, continue to duel for authority today in much of Africa, including in Nigeria.

Anthropologists were brought in to give scientific support for British indirect rule policies. They spread the view that African societies were static as well as primitive. Africans were said to follow ancient traditions and ways of life that had remained unchanged over long periods of time. Native authorities and customary law were codified versions of what were claimed to be timeless practices that should be preserved or resurrected if necessary. Such ideas distorted the reality of Africa, where societies were dynamic and institutions subject to change and adaptation just like societies anywhere else. It should be clear from the discussion throughout this book thus far that Nigerian societies have undergone many changes throughout history, including in response to contact with Europeans.

Traditional African rulers were understandably hostile toward the educated Africans. They dismissed the new class as a bunch of low-status, foreign upstarts. Living in such cities as Lagos and embracing the white man's ways, the new class was considered to be unrepresentative of most Africans, who were illiterate and rural or village-based peasant farmers. The British largely agreed with that assessment, which is another reason the colonial government threw its support to the traditional rulers.

Ironically, both the claims of the new class to the right to replace traditional rulers and the British (both administrators and missionaries) preference for traditional rulers rested on a similar ideological foundation. Both groups viewed African society through European lenses. African societies were seen as backward, barbarous, and subject to tribal warfare. They needed tutelage from outside, more civilized people and were unable to govern themselves. Thus, both the British and the African elite believed that a period of colonial rule was necessary to alter African deficiencies. The British were viewed as benevolent rulers and peacemakers. Elements of racism entered the equation as well. Africans (the "natives") were viewed in a pejorative light in comparison with Europeans. From the standpoint of the educated Africans, however, Africans who had become more culturally European (like themselves) were superior to other Africans. The decisive difference between the British and the new class of educated Africans came to be over who should rule African societies.

Through their policies, the British are largely responsible for many of the divisions in Nigeria today, represented by the division between the north and the south. By supporting the feudalistic, theocratic Hausa-Fulani state in the north, the British created a huge cultural, political, and economic gap between the two regions. By agreeing to prohibit the activities of Christian missionaries in the north, the British also prevented all but a handful of northerners from having access to modern education. In the 1920s, of the 4,000 elementary schools in Nigeria, only 125 were in the north. Of the eighteen secondary schools in the colony, none were in the north. Also, restricting Christian missionaries to the south inadvertently helped the spread of Islam in areas of the north and the Middle Belt that had previously been non-Muslim. Northerners were well aware of British favoritism toward the Islamic political elite and system. This helped to spur conversion to Islam among those seeking to advance themselves in the colonial system. They believed that being a Muslim was necessary to achieve political or economic success. Muslim traders played a key role in spreading Islam to new areas, thanks to new colonial-built transportation and communications systems that made travel and proselytizing easier.

By perpetuating the feudal Islamic system in the north, the British were entrenching existing patterns of social inequality, including gender inequality. Little was done to address the inequality of women that was legitimated by a very conservative interpretation of Islam. The lack of education in the north was especially disadvantageous to women, as very few women had any access to schooling traditional or modern. In general, northern Muslim women had far less ability than men to escape narrow, culturally defined roles. Along with the conservatism of the north, its relative lack of economic development made it more difficult for ordinary men as well as women of the north to improve their status compared to people in the south.

Regional divisions were another product of the British separating Nigeria into four parts for administrative purposes rather than having a policy of unitary rule. The four parts were the colony of Lagos and the western, eastern, and northern regions. In the 1950s, when Nigeria's independence was being negotiated, these colonial administrative regions became the basis for the regions in the proposed federal system. This regional structure, as will become evident in following chapters, proved to be a source of tragic ethnic rivalry and conflict. It was problematic because it excluded any meaningful basis for political unification, as leaders from the regions never came together to deal with common concerns. In a political sense, it would be accurate to say that Nigeria was really four separate colonies rather than one.

One minor exception was the Nigerian Council that Lugard established in 1916. The council was a consultative body made up of six traditional rulers from different parts of the country. Included were the rulers of Sokoto, Kano, and Oyo, among others. They met together with British officials to represent their regions in some policy matters. In reality, little consultation or representation took place. The rulers were mainly expected to listen to their British overlords, who informed the rulers what policies would be in place.

Along with regional separation, ethnic groups in Nigeria were also divided into tribes. It was on this basis that Africans were to be ruled and resources to be distributed. One reason for this insistence on universal African tribalism was ideological. The British notion of African societies as primitive and adhering to age-old traditions included the view that the basic identity of Africans was fixed along tribal lines. Indirect rule worked on the premise that these tribes were unified, culturally similar groups with tribal rulers and fixed customary laws. These stereotypical ideas were applied regardless of how inaccurate they were. Before colonialism, chiefs or kings did not always rule over culturally similar groups, and many ethnically similar groups were governed by different rulers or had none at all. Moreover, after years of migration and living in cities, many Africans were only nominally connected to their rural-based groups. In reality, many Africans belonged to diverse and overlapping groups; they did not identify solely or primarily by ethnicity.

Over time, the tribal identities imposed on Africans in Nigeria became real in the eyes of the so-called tribes as well as in the eyes of the British. For one thing, once the British assigned a ruler over a community, the people of the community often came to see themselves as a people sharing common interests based on their mutual subjugation. Also, it was now on the basis of their assigned identity that government policies often affected them. It was not long before communities that had previously not identified as a people began to see themselves as tribes and to mobilize on this basis.

To understand how an ethnic group identity can be created and the power such social constructions can have, consider the Hausa. Of course, the Hausa existed as a historical group in northern Nigeria before the colonial period. This only provided a foundation, however, for additional social constructions of Hausa ethnicity. Once the British established their colonial control in various parts of their empire, they used natives to build colonial armies and police forces to assist them in ruling these territories. They recruited from specific groups that they stereotyped as "martial races." In the mid-nineteenth century they sought to replace soldiers of the West India Regiment in West Africa by recruiting runaway slaves in Lagos into the local constabulary. These recruits were called the Armed Hausa Police Force. Although only some of the recruits were Hausa speakers from the north, Hausa was used as the language of command. The name Hausa stuck and was applied to the troops regardless of their actual ethnicity. These "Hausa" troops were used in military campaigns to destroy resistance to British colonial rule in the Gold Coast and from the Ashante in 1873 and 1874, and they developed a reputation for the Hausa as being a martial people. The Hausa had now become an imagined "tribe" far removed from their basis in historical reality. Even though most of the troops were from mixed ethnic groups in Lagos, Ilorin, Bida, and other towns, they were all labeled as Hausa. Adding to the illusion, in order to join the Hausa army, some southerners pretended to be northerners. European writers added to the invention of Hausa ethnic identity; they began to portray the Hausa as superior to southern groups. Their origins were said to be in the north and separate from other African "races." Due to the high status accorded the Hausa, many migrants to the south from different ethnic groups began to call themselves Hausa while they were away from home. The label came to be attached to any trader from "upcountry."

Stereotyping had a distorting effect on Hausa identity in other ways. The Hausa were incorrectly identified as being Muslim, as were all people from the north. This stereotype was one reason the British agreed not to allow Christian missionaries there. In reality, most of the Hausa forces were not Muslim, and in northern Nigeria not everyone was a Muslim. In general, Islam was not deeply rooted among most of the common people in the north; most of the more orthodox Muslim faithful were urban dwellers and members of the higher social classes. The peasants, the large majority of the population, often followed indigenous (pagan) religions or were syncretic in their beliefs and practices, that is, combining elements of indigenous beliefs with Islam. One must remember that the Fulani jihads date only to the early 1800s. Before that, under Hausa rule, Islam was not widely espoused outside the cities and was not very strictly practiced even there. Stereotyping Muslims also overlooked the differences among Muslims. Most devout Muslims were divided into two branches (*tariqas*): the Tijaniyya or Qadiriyya. These groups have significant differences in their beliefs and practices.

The Economic Impact of Colonialism

Economic changes during the colonial period were another element in the formation of identities and divisions in Nigeria. In general, rather than colonialism being mutually beneficial to the British and the Africans as Lugard had claimed, most Nigerians mainly experienced economic hardship and exploitation. Nigeria and other colonies could only justify their existence to people back home in Great Britain if the colonies were profitable and self-supporting. To meet these expectations, Nigeria's mostly peasant farmers were induced (by the desire for profits but also in order to pay heavy colonial taxes) to orient their farming toward the production of export crops. As a result, food crop production declined. The British also set the price for crops through marketing boards that bought farmers' crops and sold them at a profit. Farmers typically were paid low prices, and most of the profits went to various non-African middlemen, traders, and exporters. The British also took over the tin mines at Jos and reduced Africans to low-paid workers who no longer controlled their own natural resources. A variety of taxes added to the economic burden on the Africans. Finally, the colonial economy made Nigeria's economy dependent on European demand for their few export products while also dependent on the importation of European manufactured goods. When European demand fell for palm products or cotton, for instance, Nigerian farmers could be plunged quickly into dire financial straits.

Because of hardships in the rural areas and because of new opportunities for jobs in cities such as Lagos and Calabar, many Africans (mostly males) began to migrate to the towns, where they became wage earners. Although there were some opportunities for African traders and other entrepreneurs, these were limited. Lebanese and Indian merchants dominated retail trade, and European (mostly British) companies dominated most large-scale enterprises. The African middle class was employed mainly in the lower rungs of the civil service and in the professions. If one adds in the traditional rulers to these other groups, one can begin to see the basic class structure of Nigerian society during the colonial period. Class as well as region, ethnicity, and religion played a significant role in Nigeria, as will become evident in later chapters.

An important point about the economic impact of colonialism is that, for the most part, Africans remained in control of their land and system of agricultural production based on smallholder, peasant production. By contrast, in colonies such as Kenya, Rhodesia, and South Africa, much of the best land was expropriated from Africans and taken by European settlers. In Nigeria, where there were few Europeans, the British retained indigenous land tenure and production practices under the control of traditional rulers. This avoided the destruction of peasant smallholders and the creation of a large-scale commercial farming or plantation economy found in many parts of the colonial world. This was a conscious decision on the part of the British government and was another element in the support for preserving traditional culture and rulers.

The British wanted to keep the rural areas stable. They feared that destroying peasant production would result in huge numbers of landless peasants (many of whom would flock to the cities and create unemployment problems there), mass poverty, and the ruin of a stable African social order. Too much disruptive social change could in turn produce mass popular opposition to British rule. If the African peasantry was to be relied upon to produce the palm oil, cocoa, and other export crops the British desired, stability had to be reinforced by keeping most Africans "traditional," that is, uneducated, poor, and locked into conservative social institutions. For this reason, very little investment was made in education, training, or modernizing conditions in the rural areas where most Africans lived. British policy also ensured the economic marginalization and dependency of Nigerians once colonialism ended.

The economic impact of colonialism was experienced differently in the north and the south, with consequences that continue to divide the country today. For one thing, the north lagged behind the south in many areas. Although the north benefited from its exports of cotton and peanuts, overall there was less economic development in the north than in the south. One reason was that the north was more geographically isolated and its towns more provincial. The dynamic, culturally diverse ports and cities that were the main hubs of economic activity were concentrated in the south, especially in Lagos. Urbanization, the mixing of peoples, and access to new goods and services stimulated considerable development and modernization in the south. The south was also the main beneficiary of modern schooling, which tended to go hand-in-hand with missionary activity. This resulted in literacy, the learning of English, and exposure to Western culture and technology being much more widespread in the south, whereas the north was much more backward in these areas. As a result of their greater access to education, many southerners began to enter such occupations as journalism, law, teaching, medicine, and the ministry. Consequently, the African middle class expanded mainly in the south. By the early 1900s, Lagos, Nigeria's largest city and major gateway to the world, became the symbol and center of activity for Westernized, multiethnic Nigerians, most of whom were southerners. These economic and cultural differences between north and south were to be other grounds for divisiveness.

Demographic Change

During the approximately six decades of colonial rule in Nigeria, major social changes occurred that altered the identities of Africans. One of these changes was the movement and relocation of people. As mentioned above, migration to such cities as Lagos became more widespread during the colonial period in response to the economic and administrative activities being concentrated there. Economic opportunities in the cities attracted many traders and migrants from the rural areas, who were looking for jobs or other means of earning a livelihood. Almost anyone with any education was located in the towns and cities. Although most of the urban expansion was occurring in the south, urbanization in the north grew as well. For example, Kaduna was a new city built by the British to be the capital of the Protectorate of Northern Nigeria, and Jos became the center of the tin mining industry. The British also created Enugu and Port Harcourt in the south as new administrative centers.

Urbanization resulted in the mixing of people from many different parts of Nigeria, as people did not necessarily restrict their movements to cities and towns of their own region. In the early twentieth century, many people moved from the east and the Middle Belt to the southwest and the north. Many Igbo, for example, moved to Lagos, a city dominated by the Yoruba. Many southerners moved to the north to trade or to find jobs. Many northern seasonal workers and small entrepreneurs went to the south. Fulani cattle producers also moved south into Yorubaland to supply urban markets in such cities as Ibadan and Lagos. In many cases, rural-based ethnic customs began to break down, and new, more cosmopolitan ones began to develop in response to life in the city. Both economic and social interactions were promoted by life in the cities as well.

Changes in agriculture also stimulated the movement and mixing of people. Within Yorubaland, for instance, many young males moved to the cocoa belt to seek work or land. Cocoa had become a major and profitable export crop. In the southeast, Igbo groups moved into new areas of the forest to establish new settlements and palm groves or farms. River valley areas also became more populated by different groups, which contributed to ethnic mixing.

Although people from different groups were being exposed to each other in the cities, sometimes for the first time, a degree of segregation was maintained. The precolonial urban practice of creating stranger quarters or wards for people from different areas was retained in most cases. Colonial cities had special residential areas for Europeans (with most of the modern amenities like paved streets, electricity, and running water), but traders and others who came from all over Nigeria were often in separate quarters established on the basis of ethnicity. In Yoruba towns, Hausa traders from the north (some of whom were not actually ethnic Hausa) were considered common and had their own quarters. One reason there were so many northern traders in the south was that colonial authorities had deliberately cut the trans-Saharan trade in order to force northerners to use the coastal ports that the authorities controlled. This compelled the northerners to move to cities all over West Africa as well as to cities within Nigeria. Igbo traders, who migrated to many Yoruba and northern cities, were also in separate quarters, as were southern Nigerians in general, who established settlements around the old northern cities.

Growing class solidarity among the educated Africans in the south was also promoted within the cities. Their common educational background, ability to speak English, and adoption of Western culture enabled them to transcend ethnoregionalism. They tended to dominate the civil service and other jobs requiring formal education; this gave them occupational interests in common. It was this group that was best able and motivated to lead the nationalist struggle as discontent with colonialism increased.

Nationalism: The Challenge to Colonial Rule

Colonialism created Nigeria and Nigerians; neither had existed before European boundaries and European rule were established by force. Nigeria was not an indigenous creation, nor was it a part of any Nigerian's historical conception of who he or she was. Nonetheless, as with any other socially constructed identity, the idea of Nigeria and of a Nigerian people was one that came to appeal to a growing number of Africans during the colonial period (although certainly not to most of them). From 1880 to 1900, colonialism was opposed by most traditional rulers; they had no interest in being subsumed into a larger territorial entity under British overlords. They preferred their societies the way they were. It was the Westernized, educated African elite who initially favored British colonialism as a means of transforming African societies into a nation of equal citizens rather than so-called tribes.

The first generation of educated Africans in Nigeria (for example, Samuel Ajayi Crowther) saw European intervention, even colonialism, as a temporary means to create the foundation for African unity. The resistance of African traditional rulers and societies to a new multiethnic African nation had to be broken down by an outside force, but they believed such change could be accomplished in decades rather than generations.

It was the educated Africans who had the most contact with the outside world, including with other people of African descent, both on the continent or living in other countries of the world as a result of the slave trade. Many of these educated Africans within Nigeria went beyond being nontribalist. They embraced the new ideology of pan-Africanism, which advocated the unity of all people of African descent in the common cause of struggling against white racism and for the development of all African people.

Although critical of African societies, the new African elite could be critical of their British "saviors" as well. For one thing, the Africans resented British racism, especially when it was directed against them, the Africans who had become educated and "civilized." They also came to be resentful of their exclusion from higher administrative positions in the colonial government. Between 1860 and 1880, educated Africans had attained high positions in the colonial system, and by the 1890s, the Legislative Council in Lagos had several African members (appointed, not elected). By the 1870s and 1890s, however, the belief in Negro racial inferiority had spread among the British, in part to justify curbing African competition with whites for high positions. After years of mixing with the Africans, white officials began to segregate themselves and limit the advancement of Africans. Exclusion and discrimination led many of the educated Africans to move into such professions as journalism and law. Once colonialism was established, these professionals became more inclined to criticize colonial rule and seek redress of their grievances. African resentment of European racism also was expressed religiously and culturally. As white missionaries began to block the advancement of the African clergy and take control of the mission movement, as early as the 1880s and 1890s, many breakaway, independent, African-led Christian churches began to form. These churches were more accepting of indigenous African culture. After trying to shed much of their "primitive" African culture to become more like Europeans, the educated Africans also began to assert a renewed pride in their culture. This included native African food, language, and religion.

After World War I, the African elite began to express greater opposition to indirect rule and to their exclusion from political power. For one, they believed more power should be given to legislative councils and that such councils should be established in the north as well as the south. In 1920, a new group, the National Congress of British West Africa, was formed. It was an international group made up of members of the African elite from several colonial areas. The congress proposed expanding the powers of the legislative councils to include taking control of taxation from native authorities and appointing chiefs, who could be dismissed by their people. The

British ignored the African elites and saw them as foreigners who were es-
tranged from their societies and people.

Not all of the British officials backed the perpetuation of indirect rule and
keeping Africa "traditional." Hugh Clifford, who succeeded Frederick Lugard
from 1919 to 1925 as governor of Nigeria, had a very different vision for
Nigeria. He wanted to introduce Westernization as quickly as possible, including in the north. He thought this would lead to a more representative
form of government. Clifford also favored African-controlled economic development rather than dependent development under British control. He
wanted to promote southern enterprises in the north and restrict European
capital-intensive enterprises that provided little employment to the people.
Emirs and their rule were seen as backward, and it was thought that their
power should be limited. In the south, Clifford favored the expansion of education as a means to build an educated African elite capable of building the
Nigeria of the future. Indirect rule was seen by Clifford as divisive influence
rather than a means to unify Nigeria. In fact, due to the radical differences
between the north and the south, Clifford proposed the creation of two
colonies rather than one. His ideas were laid out in 1922 in the Clifford Constitution. Most of Clifford's ideas were rejected by the British government,
but it is intriguing to imagine how Nigeria might have turned out differently
if Clifford's recommendations had been implemented.

Actually, some of Clifford's ideas were accepted, and they led to policy
changes. Although the administration of the north was left intact, two new
regional legislative councils were established in the south. They replaced the
Lagos Legislative Council and the ineffectual Nigerian Council. For the first
time, there were limited elections outside of Lagos. These small steps toward
democracy encouraged the growth of political parties and, eventually, the nationalist movement.

By the late 1930s, colonialism was generating more discontent with British
policies and more mass support for the educated elite and their challenges
to colonialism. One example of that discontent, mentioned earlier in this
chapter, was the mass revolt led by the women of Aba in 1929 against the
warrant chiefs and British tax policies. The 1930s was a time of global depression, and African farmers and workers suffered along with others. Prices
were low for farmers' crops, and workers were demanding higher wages and
the right to form unions. New groups representing farmers and workers were
significant because they indicated the early development of class interests and
identities in Nigeria that crossed ethnic, religious, and regional lines. At this
time, however, the African elite did not seek solidarity with these other
groups, because they did not think the masses were ready for political power.

Nnamdi Azikiwe, premier of East Nigeria, shown upon arrival at Idlewild Airport from London on July 5, 1959 (Bettmann/Corbis)

A break within the ranks of the educated elite would change this situation. In the early decades of the twentieth century, many young Nigerian and Gold Coast students began to enter colleges for black students in the United States. In the past, students seeking higher education had gone to British universities. Although the black colleges were not as educationally rigorous, they produced African graduates who were much less elitist and more willing to work for change with the African masses. The masses, too, were changing; more were now literate due to an expanding access to mission schools.

Some of the graduates from the American schools entered journalism and began publishing nationalist material. One such person was Nnamdi Azikiwe, who became popularly known as "Zik." In 1937, Azikiwe returned to Nigeria from school in the United States. In Lagos he began publishing the *West African Pilot*, the leading nationalist publication in the colony, and he also lent his support to the Nigerian Youth Movement (NYM), which started in 1936. In a notable example of transethnic cooperation among the African elite, Azikiwe gained the backing of the Igbo elite in Lagos for the NYM.

The NYM provides insights into the nonethnic focus of Nigeria's early nationalist struggle. The movement was started by students at Yaba College, the first institution of higher education in Nigeria (founded in 1934). The students began to complain that their education was inferior and would condemn the Nigerian educated class to permanent subordinate roles under the British. These protests culminated in the formation of the NYM which was the first national, multiethnic organization in Nigeria. The NYM expanded its agenda to protests against imperialism, inequality, and economic exploitation. Its objectives were the advancement of Nigerians and the transfer of power to them. Another demand was for universal suffrage for all Nigerians over the age of twenty-one. The NYM had branches all over the country, with a membership of about 20,000 people. Significantly, most of the NYM's members in the north were southerners. There was no demand at this time, however, for an end to colonialism, only its reform.

Another group that played an important role in the nationalist struggle was women. In many areas of the south, market women and women's associations had considerable autonomy over their own spheres of activity. Many of these women's groups became very active and effective in opposing colonial officials and their policies. They also became highly involved in supporting the nationalist movement and political parties. In the north, women had limited roles in the public sphere, and they were not allowed to have active political roles; therefore, their involvement in the nationalist struggle was less than that of southern women and less visible.

Urbanization, Western education, and modern transportation and communications all helped to spread nationalist sentiments. Urban life under colonialism was conducive to the spread of new ideas and transethnic identities. New identities developed, such as urbanite, worker, and citizen, which created new perspectives, interests, and relationships among people of diverse backgrounds. Nigeria's cities contained people from all parts of Nigeria and exposed them to new ideas, which they took back to the villages. Living in new areas outside their places of birth, members of such groups as the Yoruba and Igbo in the north began to develop new organizations, including political parties. Many of these organizations began to advocate for national unity and reforms in the colonial system. Among the reforms sought was an end to racism, discrimination, oppression, and corruption among the native authorities.

By the 1940s, conflicting tendencies were discernible in the nationalist movement. In the effort to achieve greater self-government, nationalist leaders sought to build ties with groups that transcended region, ethnicity, and religion. At the same time, however, there was also an increase in groups and appeals for unity along those very sectarian lines. For example, ethnic unions had emerged to represent hometowns and religions. Typically, these were to help rural migrants adjust to their new life in the city, and they were not political. However, they also reinforced ties and identities to ethnic groups and local areas, which many Nigerians still argue work against national identities and unity, an issue that will be discussed in chapter 9.

The British played a role in creating these conflicting tendencies. When the British created Nigeria, they divided it first into northern and southern regions and then into basically three regions (north, south, and east). The lines drawn for these regions concentrated the three largest ethnic groups into separate areas. Ethnic labels were attached to groups under the system of indirect rule, thereby creating, modifying, or reinforcing precolonial identities. Each region was ruled separately, and indirect rule had created a hodgepodge of native authorities, such as emirates in the north and chieftaincies and monarchies in the south. During World War II, the British decided that larger, more consolidated colonial entities were needed to facilitate the spread of capitalism in Africa. In East Africa, for example, the British wanted to unite the colonies of Southern and Northern Rhodesia and Nyasaland into a federation to be called British Central Africa. Nigeria posed a problem in this scheme. Although Nigeria was economically integrated, politically it was anything but integrated. The British needed to come up with a way to establish a central bureaucracy over the entire territory. They decided to transform Nigeria into a federal unitary state, that is, a single political entity with a central government but composed of distinct states or regions with some autonomy.

Creating a new political structure for Nigeria was a goal influenced by growing nationalist pressures, which were spreading from the African elite to the masses. The British realized that the colonial system needed reform if it was to avoid widespread and perhaps violent opposition. By this time, Nigeria had the most highly developed middle class of educated merchants and professionals in Africa. Many Nigerians had served in the British armed forces in the Far East in World War II. They were exposed to the ideology in support of the war—that is, to fight against Nazi racism and for the rights of all people to self-determination, as expressed in the Atlantic Charter for the newly created United Nations. Nigerian soldiers had seen the disparities between the living conditions of whites and other people of the world under European colonial control. Upon returning to Nigeria, many of these soldiers joined nationalist political parties, which began calling for an end to colonialism.

Economic woes after the war added to the discontent with the colonial order. During the war, many military camps, airports, and roads had been built in and around many of Nigeria's major cities to accommodate troop movements. These cities benefited economically from this construction. With the end of the war, the economic good times came to an end. Local resentment of the concentration of economic wealth and power in the hands of Europeans and Asian-Lebanese business interests intensified. Most Nigerian traders were excluded from the most lucrative business opportunities by the colonial government. Small businesses and farmers were suffering from low prices. Representing workers' grievances, trade unions grew and became more politically active. A general strike by government workers and some large, urban nationalist demonstrations in 1945 were clear indications of popular unrest from almost every segment of Nigerian society.

Numerous efforts at national unity were evident in the 1940s. In 1944, Nnamdi Azikiwe helped to found the National Council of Nigeria and the Cameroons (NCNC), which he hoped would be a nationally based mass party. For ten years, the NCNC was the leading nationalist organization, with branches in various towns throughout Nigeria. Azikiwe tried to link the NCNC with the labor movement. Many other political leaders at this time were forming political associations and groups that appealed to anticolonial sentiments without using parochial appeals to ethnicity or region to mobilize supporters. Political leaders hoped to build political parties that were countrywide in order to gain seats in legislative bodies and to seek constitutional reforms.

Contrary to the above efforts to create national unity, others were appealing to regional, ethnic, and religious identities to create support. Ethnic associations, such as the Igbo State Union and the Egbe Omo Oduduwa (EOO), were becoming more overtly political. Started as a cultural organization in the 1940s, the EOO was the creation of the Action Group (AG), led by Obafemi Awolowo. To mobilize Yoruba support, the EOO used the Yoruba creation myth and the idea of a common ancestral home of all Yoruba and descent from Oduduwa. The organization became a political party in 1951. Alarmed by these ethnic-based unions, the emirs in the north formed the Northern People's Congress (NPC). The NPC appealed to Islam and the memory of the nineteenth-century caliphate to attract northerners to its ranks.

The British response to the growing chorus of demands for self-government encouraged political leaders toward a greater use of appeals to parochial rather than national interests. In 1946 to 1947, the British promulgated the Richards Constitution, a revision of a 1923 constitution. The new constitution created a quasi-federal government with three regional houses of assembly and houses of chiefs (which would perpetuate the native authorities). There would also be a central legislative council in Lagos to bring the north and south together for the first time. Also for the first time, a majority of the legislative council would be Nigerians, but only four members would be directly elected. The European-controlled Executive Council would hold most of the power. The regional assemblies would have no legislative power, and the franchise would be extended only to Lagos and Calabar.

With the three regions corresponding to the locations of Nigeria's three largest ethnic groups, both regionalism and ethnicity became the overlapping bases for political identities, interests, and competition. Some politicians were threatened by the idea of a central government and preferred to maintain the separate regional political structure. Powerful local and regional leaders and networks had been created by colonialism, and these leaders were determined to protect their interests and preserve their power. They feared losing power to the center in a new federal system. Especially in the north, where merchants and rulers had benefited greatly from indirect rule, the fear was that they would lose power if a new central government were created.

Not surprisingly, there was widespread opposition to the Richards Constitution and support for regional autonomy. There was, however, considerable disagreement along regional and ethnic lines about the specifics. Disagreements and rivalries between the Yoruba and Igbo led to most Yoruba withdrawing from the NCNC. This left the NCNC as mainly an Igbo party. The NCNC, reflecting the Igbo's position as the smallest of the Big Three ethnic groups, advocated a strong central government and many regions rather than just three. The Action Group, which was mostly a Yoruba party (under Awolowo), and the NPC (the mostly Hausa-Fulani party) wanted to concentrate their influence by having only a few regions and keeping their own ethnically dominated regions intact. In this jockeying for power among the politicians, such lofty principles as pan-Africanism and national unity were being pushed aside by the ethnic and regional politics that would come to characterize modern Nigeria once colonialism was ended.

Why was it so difficult to create and maintain alliances based on interests and identities other than region and ethnicity? The most common explanation offered is that tribalism (ethnicity) and region are primordial identities and have always been the primary source of African loyalties. Throughout this book, it has been shown, on the contrary, that the Nigerian ethnic identities Hausa-Fulani, Yoruba, and Igbo have changed over time and have not been a source of unity or primary identification. Certainly, the concept of being a northerner, southerner, or easterner did not exist before the colonial period. Indeed, it took a great effort among Nigeria's nationalist politicians to incite their ethnic group members to mobilize along those lines. Ethnic associations, such as the Igbo State Union and the Egbe Omo Oduduwa, claim that their ethnic groups have always been self-conscious, identifiable groups, but this is an ideological distortion designed to achieve this unity. It did not exist in the past and still remains an elusive goal. As a case in point, an Igbo leader who toured Igboland from 1947 to 1951 admitted that an Igbo identity at that time was virtually nonexistent. He had a difficult time trying to convince Igbo villagers that they were all Igbo, that is, members of a common group. The villagers could not imagine such an entity as "all Igbo." In the 1930s, the people of Aro and Onitsha actually rejected identification as Igbo. They saw themselves as separate from and superior to others.

There are other explanations for why ethnoregional politics came to supercede a more inclusive national focus. One is that regional disparities created or maintained by the colonial government made national unity virtually impossible. These include the differences in governance, education, and economic and social development between the north and the south discussed earlier in the chapter. Another explanation is that the appeal to ethnicity and regionalism proved to be the easiest and fastest way for political leaders from each region to mobilize support. Politicians created or refashioned ethnic myths to suit the political context of the Nigeria that was emerging in the last years of colonialism. Leaders found that such myths as the primordial existence of their ethnic group and its distinctiveness from other groups assured them of ethnic domains of influence. The more such sentiments were exploited for political purposes, the more divided along ethnic lines Nigeria became.

The politics of region and ethnicity became further entrenched in the 1950s. Not only would Nigeria be divided into three regions dominated by the three biggest ethnic groups, but the regions also had other population disparities as well. The northern region was created so that it was more populous than the two other regions of the south combined. This raised the obvious concern that the Hausa-Fulani would control their own region, the north, and the north would control the central government. Another problem was that minority ethnic groups had no region of their own; they were divided among three regions and could be dominated by the biggest group in the region. As a result of the way the regions were created, these and other issues that still are unresolved came to dominate the political scene:

- The north feared domination by the more economically developed south. The north was determined to balance southern economic dominance with political dominance.
- The south feared domination by the north. The north's population size advantage would allow it to control the federal government and use its power to support northern interests.
- Minorities would be dominated by the biggest ethnic group in their region. Only by creating more regions, in which minorities could become majorities, could they be assured a fair deal.

The Lyttleton Constitution of 1954 replaced the Richards Constitution. It provided the basic framework for a new, independent Nigeria and attempted to resolve some of the above concerns by creating a federal system with a fairly weak central government and considerable powers for the three regional governments. In 1957, the west and east assumed internal self-government. In 1958, a final constitution was approved. The north became self-governing in 1959. Elections also were held in 1959, and Nigerian nationalists achieved their goal. On October 1, 1960, Nigeria became independent, and British colonialism was finally at an end. Anticolonial struggles were occurring all over the world after World War II, including Africa. The European powers for the most part realized they must abandon their colonial empires or face increasing armed resistance. They began at this late date to prepare their colonies for eventual self-government.

Conclusion

Over the approximately six decades of colonial rule, Nigeria was transformed. New boundaries, regions, and ethnic identities were created or modified as the British sought to consolidate their control and administer this huge territory and its many diverse peoples. Christianity and Islam spread during this period, both helped by colonialism. Each religion was dominant in a different part of the country—Islam in the north, Christianity in the south.

Economic, political, and cultural changes were also introduced. Some groups were affected by these changes more than others and were affected in different ways. Western culture, religion, education, urbanization, technology, and economic influences had more impact in the south than in the north. In the north, indirect rule policies had allowed a conservative Islamic ruling elite to exercise power and minimize those modern and Western influences that could threaten their dominant class position. In the south primarily, a new educated class of Africans emerged to challenge traditional rulers and eventually colonialism itself. Joining with other elements of the population who had become discontented with the colonial system, the new elite defined and led the nationalist struggle and brought the country to independence.

Nigerian political leaders, however, were unable to sustain a politics of national unity that could overcome the stronger tendencies toward ethnoregional and religious divisiveness. These tendencies were destined to grow stronger after independence. The next chapter will examine the development of Nigeria's political culture in order to see what role it has played in shaping ethnoregional and religious identities and politics. This can make it easier to understand why, within a few years of Nigeria's independence, Nigeria became a society so fraught with sectarian divisions that its ability to remain a unified, democratic nation would be very much at issue and remains so today.

Timeline

1914	The Northern and Southern Protectorates are combined to create the colony of Nigeria
1920	The National Congress of British West Africa is founded
1920s–1930s	Domestic slavery is abolished
1929	The Igbo Women's War occurs
1936	The Nigerian Youth Movement begins
1937	Azikiwe establishes the *West African Pilot*
1940s–early 1950s	The NCNC, AG, and NPC political parties are created
1946–1947	The Richards Constitution is introduced and rejected
1954	The Lyttleton Constitution becomes the basis for an independent Nigeria
October 1, 1960	Nigeria becomes independent

Significant People, Places, and Events

ASHANTE (ASHANTI) The Ashante were a major African power in what is now Ghana but was in the 1800s known as the Gold Coast. They had to be forcibly subdued by the British after the Gold Coast became a protectorate in the 1870s. Ashanteland was invaded by the British in 1874, 1895 to 1896, and in 1900 before the Ashante were finally defeated and the Gold Coast colony was established.

CAMEROONS Cameroon was a colony first controlled by Germany in the 1880s until after World War I. After the war, Germany's colonies in Africa were divided between the French and the British. Cameroon was divided so that the part next to Nigeria was under British control; the rest of the territory was controlled by France. The Cameroons became the unified country of Cameroon in 1972.

CUSTOMARY LAW Most African societies did not have a codified system of laws. Disputes were often handled informally or in a nonstandardized way by various authoritative persons and groups. These decisions were often not uniform or undisputed. When the British decided to codify African practices, they relied on the opinions of elder males in the community in question, whose rendering of what African customs were could be self-serving, partial, or inaccurate.

GOLD COAST The Gold Coast was colonized by the British around 1900. At independence, Gold Coast changed its name to Ghana in honor of the ancient empire of Ghana.

IGBO WOMEN'S WAR In 1929, thousands of Igbo women demonstrated against the native administration, including ridiculing the warrant chiefs. As the revolt spread, British troops were called in. The women were fired upon, leaving more than fifty dead and fifty wounded. The British tried to deemphasize the fact that the incident was a reaction by unarmed women to colonial abuses by referring to it as the Aba Riots.

NORTHERN RHODESIA Named for South African British imperialist Cecil Rhodes, Northern Rhodesia became a British colony in the 1890s and the independent country of Zambia in 1964.

NYASALAND The British colony of Nyasaland in southern Africa became the country of Malawi in 1964.

PAN-AFRICANISM The pan-Africanist movement is closely associated with Marcus Garvey of Jamaica. Garvey's movement called for all blacks to unite for freedom and against colonialism. In 1920, a branch of the movement was started in Lagos. It influenced such Nigerian nationalist leaders as Nnamdi Azikiwe.

QADIRIYYA The Sufi, or mystical branch, of Islam is popular in West Africa, including Nigeria. Within Sufism, brotherhoods (*tariqas*) developed as a means of providing believers with an intimate religious experience of God (Allah) and a distinctive understanding of the faith. Each brotherhood follows a specific religious leader and his teachings. The Qadiriyya brotherhood originated in eleventh-century Baghdad. It is the largest brotherhood in the Islamic world. Because of its tolerance of local beliefs and laxity on enforcing strict Muslim law, the Qadiriyya gained wide acceptance in Nigeria and other parts of West Africa.

SOUTHERN RHODESIA Named for South African British imperialist Cecil Rhodes, Southern Rhodesia became the independent country of Zimbabwe in 1980. Zimbabwe's blacks had to fight a brutal war with white settlers who controlled the colony before it could achieve its independence.

TIJANIYYA In the mystical, or Sufi, branch of Islam, believers commonly belong to brotherhoods (*tariqas*). Each brotherhood follows a specific leader and his teachings. The Tijaniyya brotherhood was founded in North Africa in the 1800s. Its founder was Sheikh Umar Tal. By the time of his death in 1864, Sheikh Umar and his followers had established a large Islamic empire in West Africa, which included the states of Kaarta and Segu. The Tijaniyya brotherhood has many followers among Muslims in Nigeria.

Bibliography

Ekeh, Peter P. 1998. "Colonialism and the Two Publics in Africa: A Theoretical Statement." Pp. 87–109 in *Africa: Dilemmas of Development and Change.* Edited by Peter Lewis. Boulder, CO: Westview.

Falola, Toyin. 1999. *The History of Nigeria.* Westport, CT: Greenwood.

Flint, John E. 1966. *Nigeria and Ghana.* Englewood Cliffs, NJ: Prentice-Hall.

Freund, Bill. 1998. *The Making of Contemporary Africa: The Development of African Society since 1800.* Boulder, CO: Lynne Rienner.

Jones, G. I. 1963. *The Trading States of the Oil Rivers: A Study of Political Development in Eastern Nigeria.* London: Oxford University Press.

Killingray, David. 2000. "Imagining Martial Communities: Recruiting for the Military and Police in Colonial Ghana, 1860–1960." Pp. 119–136 in *Ethnicity in Ghana: The Limits of Invention.* Edited by Carola Lentz and Paul Nugent. New York: St. Martin's.

Lugard, Frederick. "The Dual Mandate in British Tropical Africa, 1926." http://www.swarthmore.edu (accessed June 30, 2002).

Metz, Helen Chapin, ed. 1992. *Nigeria: A Country Study.* Washington, DC: Library of Congress.

Morgan, W. B. 1972. "The Influence of European Contacts on the Landscape of Southern Nigeria." Pp. 193–207 in *People and Land in Africa South of the Sahara.* Edited by R. Mansell Prothero. New York: Oxford University Press.

Tibenderana, Peter K. 1989. "British Administration and the Decline of the Patronage-Clientage System in Northwestern Nigeria." *African Studies Review* 32 (1): 71–95.

CHAPTER FIVE

The Legacy of Colonialism and Postindependence Political Culture

S INCE GAINING ITS INDEPENDENCE, Nigeria has become a country rent by ethnic, regional, and religious conflict. Threats of secession by major regions of the country have occurred in the present day and in the past, and an actual secession by the east led to civil war in the late 1960s. The country has stumbled repeatedly from civilian rule to military rule and back again. Nigeria's government is dubiously renowned for its incompetence, greed, and corruption. Its citizens as well as its leaders appear incapable of transcending their parochial loyalties in the interests of the nation and the public good. Economic, political, and social decay are mystifying when considered alongside Nigeria's many assets: enormous oil wealth and abundant agricultural and natural resources; a well-educated middle class that has produced such internationally respected intellectuals as Wole Soyinka and Chinua Achebe; and many large, dynamic urban centers (which suggest a fairly well-balanced pattern of development in many parts of the country).

It is tempting to point the finger of blame at such easy targets as "tribalism," "primordial loyalties," and other concepts that imply cultural backwardness and traditionalism as the reasons Nigeria has failed to create a stable, modern democratic nation. But this chapter will look elsewhere to understand Nigeria's current problems. It will turn partly to the precolonial past, but mainly to the more recent colonial period, to find the foundations for Nigeria's current divisive political culture. The main focus will be on two interrelated areas of Nigeria's political culture that have become pervasive in the postindependence period. The first is the dominant role of ethnicity, regionalism, and religion in Nigerian political life. The second involves the role of patron-client relationships in creating official corruption, mismanagement, and a seeming lack of civic responsibility in many parts of society. Nigerian political culture needs to be understood within the context of contemporary economic, social, and political forces rather than as an inherent or inevitable outcome of the diversity of its people.

The Colonial Legacy

This book has already discussed the fact that Nigeria is an artificial creation resulting from British imperialism and colonialism. Until shortly before its independence in 1960, Nigeria's colonial rulers did little to create conditions for a viable, modern nation-state. Under the British policy of indirect rule, African cultures were to be left largely undisturbed unless such disruption was deemed necessary to promote the goals of colonial rule and the extraction of profits. Authoritarian traditional rulers and institutions were favored, and Western-educated modernizers were sidelined. Ethnic identities and regionalism were fostered for administrative purposes and by the relative isolation of groups from one another, especially northerners from southerners and Christians from Muslims. As a result, cultural differences became greater and became harder to reconcile. Southerners gained most of the advantages of Western education and access to modern technology, skills, and contact with the outside world. The north was largely insulated from such influences. Thus was created the basis for the overlapping clashes of ethnicity, region, and religion seen in the country today.

The division of the colony of Nigeria into three regions (east, west, and north) is the source of the major ethnic and regional divides of the postindependence period. By intentionally separating the three largest ethnic groups into different political units, ethnically and regionally based identities and interests were created where they had not existed before. These units and the majority ethnic groups within them found themselves competing with each other for resources from the colonial government; this pattern was reproduced in the post-independence period. Because access to political resources was based on which ethnic groups had the most power, ethnic group competition intensified, along with fears of domination if one group gained more power than another group. Ethnic solidarity was presented as the only way to prevent such domination.

Minority ethnic groups within each region were in a disadvantageous position in this system. If the dominant ethnic group was united, minority groups faced domination by them within the region. Indeed, at both the regional and federal levels of government, the big three ethnic groups were assured of control of the government. The British were aware of the inherent problems of the system of government they were creating in Nigeria.

A crowd applauds election results posted at the Lagos racetrack during the Nigerian general election in September 1948. Abubakar Tafawa Balewa was reappointed Prime Minister of the Federation of Nigeria, which achieved independence from Great Britain on October 1, 1960. (Bettmann/Corbis)

Nonetheless, when they were framing the structure of the postindependence government, they stuck with the three-region system despite minority group appeals for separate states for themselves.

One can only speculate how Nigeria might have developed differently with a different regional structure—for example, one that broke up the major ethnic groups into different regions or that created regions for minorities in order to counterbalance the power of the majority ethnic groups. In 1958, the Willinks Minority Report anticipated the problems Nigeria would face. It called for multiple states to ensure a more even allocation of state resources and to protect the interests of minority groups. The report pointed out that such a structure would be more likely to promote interethnic and other forms of group coalitions.

As early as the 1940s, the British had begun to promote regional government in Nigeria (with the Richards Constitution of 1946). This was followed by calls for greater regional autonomy by politicians who hoped to gain power in the new regional governments. To mobilize support, the politicians understandably appealed to both regional and ethnic identities. For example, Yoruba politicians in the western region tried to gain support for their party, the Action Group, by using the Yoruba creation myth to urge all Yoruba to stick together as the descendants of Oduduwa. In the north, Islam and the memory of the caliphate were invoked to promote ethnoregional political identification. In the east, the initial effort had been to create a truly national party. This eventually failed, and the dominant regional party became a largely Igbo party.

In the 1940s and 1950s, regionalism was a popular idea among aspiring businessmen as well as politicians. The British had begun to support greater Nigerianization of the political system and the economy and to invest more heavily in education, industry, and infrastructure throughout the three regions. Regional governments created many opportunities for politicians to gain public office and other high-status political positions. Regionalism also provided opportunities for Nigerian businessmen, who mostly operated locally or regionally, to gain access to government and bank loans and contracts. Politicians also tended to favor a regional political structure.

In the 1950s, the constitutional framework for an independent Nigeria was gradually created. The 1951 Macpherson Constitution provided for three regions, but the north was made larger so that it had representation equal to the other two regions combined (effectively creating a bipolar system of north and south). Early on in the process of creating the new government, there were problems that did not bode well for national unity. In 1953, southern politician Anthony Enahoro proposed Nigerian independence for 1956. This proposal was rejected by the north because it feared domination by the more economically developed south. Also, as southerners were more educated, they were seen as being likely to dominate the civil service. Southern immigrants to the north, especially the Igbo, were already seen as dominating both clerical jobs and many areas of trade in the north. The north went so far as to threaten secession if the balance of power was not tilted more toward northern interests. Equally apprehensive, the south feared that the north would use its huge size and population to dominate the south. Southerners saw the north as backward and as a threat to southern goals of promoting education and development throughout the country.

In an effort to maintain the unity of Nigeria, a new constitutional conference was called. The constitution was revised to give more power to the regions at the expense of the federal government. In 1957, the western and eastern regions of the south received the right of internal self-government. In 1959, the north became self-governing. General elections for the national government in Lagos were held in 1959. Independence was declared on October 1, 1960.

The result of all of this constitutional tinkering before independence was a political system that guaranteed future ethnoregional and religious tensions. From the colonial period to the present, political representation in regions/states and at the federal level have coincided with ethnic group locations, thus making ethnoregional politics almost inevitable. Northern Muslims would almost certainly control the federal government due to their larger population size. This, in turn, would ensure the resentment of the more educated, cosmopolitan, largely Christian southern political class, who would be effectively denied political power at the center. In the north, the insistence on regional autonomy protected the power of the conservative ruling class and allowed them to block (often using Islam for legitimacy) progressive reforms or reformers who challenged their control. Minority groups in every region felt insecure and marginalized and clamored for more rights (or felt that their rights were being denied). Over time, ethnic minorities began to demand regions and states of their own. Control of regional governments became the prize among rising politicians, due to the resources and opportunities for personal gain that regional government positions made available. Rather than eliminating ethnoregional discontents, however, the creation of additional ethnically based states resulted in the assertion of other ethnic group identities and demands for even more states, because claiming to be a distinct ethnic group provided justification for groups to have states of their own. Unfortunately, ethnic sensitivities and perceived ethnic favoritism and competition were heightened by the imbalance between the number of aspirants to the fruits of government office and the actual scarcity of rewards and resources. (These rewards included jobs, development funds, trade licenses, scholarships for higher education, and government contracts.)

The new democratic government of Nigeria's First Republic (1960–1966) was a federal system that reflected many of the characteristics of Nigeria's history under colonialism. In form, it was largely Western, but it also reflected elements of indirect rule and concerns related to ethnic, regional, and religious diversity. At the federal level, there were three branches of government: the legislative, executive, and judicial. The legislative branch had a House of

Representatives and a Senate. The House had members from the north, the east, the west, and Lagos (corresponding to colonial administrative areas). Northern dominance was reflected in northern control of 174 seats versus 73 for the east, 62 for the west, and 3 for Lagos (a total of 312). The Senate had fifty-six members, also from the regions and Lagos. Senators were selected by regional legislatures from a list submitted by the governor. Senators were not selected on the basis of population size, in order to ensure that minority group interests were represented. This was similar to the U.S. Senate, in which each state has two senators regardless of the population of the state.

Each regional government also had a legislative, executive, and judicial branch. The legislative branch had two houses: a House of Assembly (elected like the House of Representatives) and a nonelected House of Chiefs (a holdover from indirect rule through traditional rulers). The dominant officials in the executive branch were the premier, who was chosen by the House of Assembly (except in the north), and the governor. In the north the premier was selected by the House of Chiefs, which would ensure control of this key office by the emirs. The governor was appointed by the president of Nigeria with the advice of the regional premier. Regional ministers were appointed by the governor on the advice of the premier. Two ministers had to be from the House of Chiefs. At the judicial level (both national and regional), there was a High Court and more than one Court of Appeal. In the north, however, alongside Western-style common law and courts of appeal, there was also a shari'a court of appeal, that is, one based on Islamic law. The inclusion of religious law and courts and disputes about their place and jurisdiction in Nigeria's constitutionally mandated secular, democratic state would prove to have explosive consequences later.

Subsequent governments have repeatedly altered the constitution, the framework of government, and the number of states and political parties. These changes were made in order to lessen ethnic, regional, and religious tensions. Nonetheless, conflicts along these lines have continually plagued the country from the beginning.

Nigeria inherited other governance problems from the colonial system. These include a tendency toward authoritarianism and heavy state intervention in the economy. Both of these tendencies have been used to explain Nigeria's authoritarian rule under the military and economic mismanagement, and to explain corruption by both military and civilian governments. Such tendencies have characterized many African governments since their independence, not just Nigeria's. There is an erroneous assumption that Africa's European colonizers brought democracy and free market capitalism to Africa, which Africans were unable to maintain. In reality, though, democratic institutions were not used to govern Nigeria. Colonial governments were highly authoritarian, hierarchical, and repressive. They were designed mainly for political control and economic exploitation of the colony and its people. Such quasi-democratic institutions as legislative councils were unrepresentative and involved very few Africans. It was only within a few years before independence that any real experience in self-government was allowed in Nigeria. Most scholars agree that this was far too little time to develop a democratic political culture and stable, functioning democratic institutions.

One consequence of the failure to establish a stable democratic political culture is that civilian rule in Nigeria has a history of failure and replacement with dictatorial military rule. Studies of authoritarian governments, which are common throughout the developing world, indicate that autocratic personal rule by a strongman (typically from the military) tends to result from three factors: the newness of the state, the lack of an institutional tradition of democracy, and the absence of a shared political culture. All of these problems existed in Nigeria at the end of colonialism and have made a unified, democratic system very difficult to sustain since independence was achieved.

The colonial system also failed to establish the basis for a capitalist economy with autonomy from the state. This has resulted both in private businesspeople often being dependent on the state for economic opportunities and in state officials using their government positions to secure opportunities for private economic gain. For one, the colonial model was one of significant intervention in the economy by political authorities. For example, infrastructure and other investments were biased toward urban areas and commercial export crops. Another example is the much-criticized marketing boards that African governments used to set prices and compel farmers to sell their crops to the government. Marketing boards were originally established by colonial governments. Colonial governments also owned business enterprises, a practice handed down to African governments. These enterprises included a cotton ginnery and a rice hulling factory. These state-owned enterprises expanded under successive Nigerian governments, but colonial governments provided the initial model for the practice. The central role of the colonial state in allocating resources, often for political reasons rather than to maximize economic efficiency, was another lesson in governance Nigerian rulers learned from their British masters.

On the other hand, there were some positive aspects of the colonial period for Nigerian political culture that deserve mentioning. Most Nigerians have a strong commitment to individual liberties and to democracy as a desirable political system. There is a vibrant intellectual community, a well-established tradition of independent newspapers, and many civil society groups, such as labor unions, religions, ethnic associations, and women's groups. Much of this began to develop in the colonial system and is essential to a healthy democratic system. So strong is the democratic ethos that even the most brutal, repressive military governments in Nigeria have felt compelled to justify their rule as temporary and to promise a return to democratic civilian government.

Another positive legacy of colonialism is the English language. Making English the official language has allowed the Nigerian government to avoid the problem of selecting one of the indigenous languages as the official one. Given ethnic sensitivities, there would be no politically acceptable choice from among Nigeria's hundreds of ethnolinguistic communities. Although most Nigerians speak one or more indigenous languages, learning English at school and using it as a lingua franca creates a commonly accepted means to transcend the linguistic divide. English also has advantages for Nigerians in dealing with the outside world, where, increasingly, English is the global language.

Within Nigeria, Hausa is spoken by more people than any other language. It has been spread widely by Hausa traders as well as being the major language of the north. Hausa is also widely spoken among Nigeria's political class, allowing them to speak to each other regardless of ethnicity. As an indication of how sensitive an issue language is, efforts by some to make Hausa an official language are fiercely rejected by the Yoruba and Igbo because they fear it is a step toward "northern domination," a theme that will reemerge in later chapters of this book.

Ethnicity, Region, and Religion in Nigeria's Political Culture

Before the 1950s, most of Nigeria's nationalist leaders envisioned a unified nation of Nigerians who could work together and transcend the parochial boundaries of ethnicity, region, and religion. Yet, within a short period of time, appeals to ethnicity, region, and religion, and political organization along those very lines, came to dominate Nigeria's political culture. Nigeria is not alone in facing the predicament of trying to create or maintain national identities in states with ethnically and religiously diverse peoples. Many nation-states all over the world are turning out to be quite fragile, and irredentism, civil war, and secessionism have emerged as major components of conflict and warfare in recent decades.

Clearly, such conflict is not restricted to Africa or to developing countries. Examples are plentiful from all over the world. For instance, although the breakup of the Soviet Union was mostly peaceful, Russian efforts to crush the Chechen rebels have been anything but peaceful. Violence also resulted when Bosnia and Croatia sought to establish independent ethnic states out of the former Yugoslavia (still a fragile situation). The war for independence of Kosovo from Serbia and the secessionist struggles of the Tamil in Sri Lanka, the Kurds in the Middle East, and the Aceh rebels in Indonesia are other recent examples of ethnic conflict. Ethnicity was expected to wane as a political force as people of the modern world were absorbed into nation-states and as global capitalism promoted migration, travel, urbanization, and industrialization. Instead of ethnicity, class and class-based interests were predicted to become more central to people's lives. Contrary to such expectations, not only have ethnic attachments and conflicts not declined, but in many cases they have become resurgent or have emerged where not present before.

Are there any common denominators that can help one understand why identities such as ethnicity and religion are in many places becoming so highly politicized? Although specific conditions and causes vary, some common factors appear to be present. One is that politicized ethnic and religious identities and conflicts usually have recent, not ancient, causes. For developing countries such as Nigeria, these causes are often rooted in colonialism but then carry over to the postindependence society. In both the colonial and postindependence periods, group differences like ethnicity and religion become salient and volatile under conditions of intense competition for political power, economic resources, social status, and access to social services. People believe that only by organizing as a group can they make themselves heard or avoid being disadvantaged in relation to those groups who are organized. Ethnicity and religion are most likely to become primary in places where social classes are weakly developed and where political leaders contending for power have no other effective base of mass support. Another factor is the ethnic and religious makeup of the society. Diversity is a necessary but not a sufficient cause of "identity politics." Where there are few ethnic groups or a relative balance of power or balanced number of groups, there is usually little tension. However, if there are several large, geographically distinct ethnoregional groups, as in Nigeria, diversity is more likely to create instability, particularly if the impact of economic change under colonialism was unequal and if the colonial and postindependence governments promoted local identities and focused attention on group differences in their policies and treatment of various groups. In Nigeria, tensions were great from the beginning of independence, and little has been done to share power equitably among groups of disproportionate power and numbers.

The presence of ethnic, regional, and religious conflict does not mean that these are the only loyalties or identities people have. Although Nigeria, for example, is still largely a rural, nonindustrial society, social classes and class interests have developed. The presence of labor unions and a multitude of professional, business, religious, and women's groups sometimes cut across ethnic and regional lines. Nonetheless, it remains true that the prevalence of communal land tenure and low levels (and recency) of development and industrialization have limited class formation and have functioned to maintain most people's attachment to rural areas and communal groups. For most Nigerians there is little reason to feel any attachment to their government or to an abstract entity called Nigeria. As we will see, the national government in particular has done little to promote development or to serve the interests of most of its citizens.

In most contemporary societies, citizens have an influence on government by organizing into special interest groups. In the United States, for instance, these groups range from regional, ethnic, religious, and racial interest groups to those promoting single issues (such as pro-choice or antiabortion groups) or class, business, or professional interests. In Nigeria, such interest groups are weaker. It is mainly by affiliating along ethnic or regional (or sometimes religious) lines that groups and individuals can effectively make claims on the government and get access to government positions and resources. In fact, as political and economic conditions worsened over the years after independence, citizens have had to rely primarily on regional, local, or communal-kinship groups for support. Competition for scarce resources is so intense that any perceived favoritism in the treatment of other groups by the government is magnified, as are efforts to promote one's own group while excluding those defined as "other."

One result is an intensification of the social construction of identities, such as ethnicity, for political purposes. In the 1960s, for instance, there was a major campaign by Yoruba leaders to create a Yoruba identity among the Yoruba-speaking populace. These leaders, mostly from the educated upper classes, sought to promote cultural uniformity among all Yoruba. They went so far as creating legislation designed to define a traditional social or political structure common to all Yoruba. At festivals, the Yoruba began to emphasize their past by chanting praises to past *obas* (kings) and relating past events to the present. This effort at creating a Yoruba identity was intended to counter the factionalism and competition for power among the Yoruba. Chief Awolowo, one of the most powerful Yoruba politicians, was highly successful in building linkages among rival groups by organizing the Pan-Yoruba Society of the Descendants of Oduduwa, which evolved into the Action Group political party in 1951. Other ethnic groups were engaged in the same process of creating ethnic group identities. In the process, sharp boundaries between groups and a sense of ethnic group distinctiveness were created that had not existed in the past.

The strength of parochial identities is more complex than one ethnic group or region against another. Internal divisions within these groups are also widespread and reflect the same divisive forces described above. Political and economic problems; competition for scarce jobs, development assistance, and educational opportunities; and intergroup conflict have led many people to identify with subethnic groups such as people from their hometown. Even when migrants move to cities away from their home areas, they often join ethnic and hometown associations that maintain local attachments and networks of affiliation. Formal and informal hometown associations can isolate ethnic groups from each other but also can pit one ethnic subgroup against another in the competition for regional as well as national government resources.

This remains a significant problem for Yoruba-speaking groups. It is ironic that at the same time as Yoruba leaders call for Yoruba unity, Yoruba subgroups are competing among themselves and are mutually distrusting of each other. Towns compete against towns, making it doubly important that the town's sons and daughters, even if they live in Lagos or other cities, maintain close ties and support their hometown people against a wide range of rivals they face in Nigerian society. Class and rural-urban cleavages further complicate ethnic and subethnic tensions. For example, Yoruba who live in major towns see themselves as more civilized than those who live in the "bush" (the rural areas). "Bush people" are seen as uneducated and uninformed. Those in large towns also look down on those from small towns. Some subethnic Yoruba groups see themselves as superior to other Yoruba groups. Subethnic groups readily perceive discrimination or ill treatment from their subethnic rivals. For example, one Yoruba group may claim that a rival group will not help members of other groups when they are in government office and that they work to deny others government jobs or benefits. All of this tends to fuel a clamor for group autonomy and the desire for more separate government administrative areas based on ethnicity or subethnicity.

Religion has become a growing element of divisiveness in Nigeria. Most of this involves the politicization of Islam and Christianity, both of which cut across lines of region and ethnicity. At independence, religious tensions were to be minimized by stating in the constitution that Nigeria was a secular state. In the 1960s, it appeared that Nigeria's Muslims and Christians were largely

Islam is now the majority religion in Nigeria. (Liz Gilbert/Corbis Sygma)

satisfied with this arrangement. But as the secular state began to fail and social problems intensified, Nigerians began to turn more to religion to solve
their social, political, and economic problems. Religion, along with ethnicity and region, became a focal point for the frustrations and hardships people were experiencing. Resentment, distrust, and intolerance have led to
many clashes, nonviolent as well as violent.

Take Islam to begin with. In the 1960s, Nigeria's Muslims accepted the secular arrangement of Nigerian society, and religious pluralism and tolerance
were the norm. Northern Muslim politicians in power were accepted by
Christians, and vice versa. Muslims became more receptive to Western education for their children. Both Christian and Muslim leaders in the 1960s and
1970s made efforts to promote dialogue and mutual understanding. Among
some groups, especially the Yoruba, some were Muslim and others were
Christian. In these cases, tolerance and ethnocultural identities were stressed
to minimize religious conflict.

On the other hand, there were countertendencies. In the north, politicians
often combined appeals to ethnicity and Islam to create political unity
against the south. The north's foremost political leader, Ahmadu Bello, for
example, was determined to spread Islam in Nigeria and to further integrate
Nigeria into the larger Muslim world. In 1973, the Islamic Council of Nige-

ria was founded. It included representatives from every region of Nigeria. Its purpose was to present a united front to the government on matters affecting Islam. In central Nigeria, some groups converted to Christianity as a means to strengthen their identity and resist domination by Islam under the Hausa-Fulani political elite. Between 1940 and 1960, for example, minorities in the Adamawa area (bordering Cameroon) converted to Christianity in order to unite and build two political parties—the United Middle Belt Congress and the Middle Zone League. Christians also engaged in politics by turning their churches into political parties and creating cultures of resistance politics both before and since independence.

Relationships among religious groups have been on a downward spiral since the late 1970s. North-south political and economic rivalries helped to politicize both Islam and Christianity. Many of the issues that have sparked conflict had their origins in the colonial period: tensions involving secular education and Christian missionaries in the north; the influx of southerners (mostly Christian) into the north who compete with locals (Muslims) for jobs, trade, and land while maintaining cultural and physical separation from the locals; and unresolved issues about the role of religion and religious laws in a religiously diverse state. Other issues are of more recent origin, such as competition along religious lines as a factor in the distribution of political appointments, contracts, and other government resources. In addition, some religious conflicts are intrareligious. For instance, in the north, beginning in the 1980s, official corruption, the lack of economic development, and class inequality have incited intra-Muslim tensions and violence. There are also tensions among various Christian denominations, although this has not had the political ramifications of Muslim versus Christian and Muslim versus Muslim conflict.

A fundamental political issue dividing more militant Muslims from Christians is that many Muslims are questioning the foundations of the secular state Nigeria inherited from the colonial period. These Muslims believe that the institutions of secular society in general have failed. For instance, they believe that democratic governments have degenerated into ruthless military dictatorships, and both have been led by venal, corrupt politicians. Muslims regard Nigeria's adoption of the Western world's values and economic system as the cause of selfish individualism, materialism, and immorality. Crime and disrespect for authority and the rights of others are seen as other symptoms of a misbegotten adherence to Western secularism rather than fidelity to god (Allah) and his laws. Muslim critics of Nigerian society seek instead to build a unified and stable community of Muslim believers (the *umma*). Much of what is wrong with Nigeria from the standpoint of

Muslim reformers is related to Westernization, which is perceived by many Muslims as basically Christian culture that has been imposed on Nigeria by outsiders (that is, European colonialists).

Many Muslims now believe that an Islamic society is the solution to the ills facing the country. Adherence to Islam, they say, is the way to get moral leaders who will work for the welfare of the people rather than abuse power and line their own pockets. There is a growing demand for the expansion of shari'a law and other Islamic institutions, at least in the north, in order to achieve this transformation of society. Ironically, modern education is a driving force behind the politicizing of Islam. It is often young, more educated Muslims who are the leaders of new Muslim interest groups that are challenging the government and demanding reforms.

Christians have reacted with alarm and hostility to these efforts. To Christians, the secular state is a neutral guarantor of religious freedom and political stability. If Nigeria became too closely identified with Islam, Christians believe, it would quickly find itself broken into two countries or shattered by a religious civil war. Christians reject the imposing of religion as a basis of law and insist that only Western-based common law is acceptable in a democratic society. Christians retort that if Muslims in the north are allowed to govern themselves by Muslim law, should Christians in the south impose Christian law? Should indigenous and other religious communities all have their own separate legal systems as well? Christians already perceive that Nigeria's largely northern Muslim political class has favored Muslims over Christians and other non-Muslims, and relationships between the religious communities and the state are likely to continue to deteriorate if shari'a and other moves to "Islamize" Nigeria continue to be political issues.

Muslims counter Christian arguments with claims that Nigeria mainly has British colonial, Christian institutions even though one-half or more of its citizens are Muslims. Christians, they charge, are being hypocritical when they claim that it is Muslims who are the threat to religious pluralism. Muslims point out as examples that Nigeria is largely a Christian country now. The dominant legal system is common law, a product of European Christian culture that has been given priority over shari'a, which existed in Nigeria long before colonialism. Muslims also ask why Sunday, the Christian Sabbath, should be the official weekend, or why the Christian New Year and other Christian holidays should be celebrated while there is no official allowance for Muslim prayer at school or work. The doctrine of separation of church and state is also a product of Christian culture and is antithetical to the Islamic belief that Islam is the way to organize a just, godly society. The Muslims believe that such a society requires the unity of religion and the state, which is prohibited now under "Christian domination" of Nigeria.

Not only have religious debates such as these become common in Nigerian politics, but violence has been growing as well, mainly beginning in the 1980s. Although most of the violence represents Muslim-Christian clashes, some of the worst violence has been Muslim violence by jihadist elements who want to purify Muslim society and the government of the north. The Maitatsine movement and riots led by Muslim radical Mohammadu Marwa from 1980 to 1985 in Kano and other northern cities were an expression of economic hardships and political discontent, largely among the urban poor against the north's Muslim elite, who have failed to bring good governance or development to the people.

Religion and politics, including the Maitatsine movement, will be discussed in greater detail in the chapter on civil society. What is important at this point is to note that religion is becoming a key area of concern in Nigeria's contentious and sometimes violent political culture. Both Christians and Muslims are becoming more radical and fundamentalist. Christian fundamentalism is closely associated with the influx of American Pentecostal and other evangelical churches, which are pouring money and personnel into Nigeria (and elsewhere in Africa). Islamic fundamentalism is being promoted by the efforts and inspiration of outsiders such as Saudi Arabia, Libya, and Iran. Both Christian and Muslim radicalism are fueled by the negative stereotypes each group has of the other. Each sees the other as intolerant and as the instigator of problems and violence. The radicals are also critical of the moderate, mainstream elements in their own faiths. In many places, in the north especially, the atmosphere has become so hostile that efforts to promote peaceful coexistence, tolerance, or understanding are becoming very difficult.

Although religion is a divisive force, it also can be a force for transcending as well as reinforcing such identities as regionalism and ethnicity. This is because religion is an identity that has some contradictions as it intersects with these other identities. In some ways, for instance, religion reinforces regionalism along north-south lines, as most Muslims live in the north while most Christians are in the south. But there are many Muslims in the south and some Christians in the north (mostly migrants). The picture is even more complex with ethnicity. Both Islam and Christianity provide a basis for transethnic solidarities and interests. Although Islam is more associated with the Hausa-Fulani, about 40 percent of the Yoruba are Muslims, but the majority are Christians (some practice indigenous faiths). Many smaller ethnic groups in the Middle Belt are predominantly Muslim, but other Middle Belt groups are largely Christian. The Igbo are almost entirely Christian.

One must also remember that although ethnicity, region, and religion are the dominant elements shaping Nigeria's political culture, class elements are found as well. For instance, there is some unity among the political class, who share a common interest in controlling power and the spoils of power. This encourages alliances across the communal divide, even though the elite will also use patronage and appeals to parochial identities like religion or ethnicity when it suits their interests. By the same token, class elements are involved in many cases of political violence, such as the Maitatsine riots. Peasant revolts have also occurred. An example is the Agbekoya struggle, which took place in 1968 to 1969 in western Nigeria. This revolt was in opposition to unjust taxes. (In Yoruba, *Agbekoya* means "farmers who reject injustice.") Trade union activism is another class movement, one that often transcends parochial identities.

Patron-Client Relationships and the Culture of Corruption

It has been shown how the mobilization of ethnic, regional, and religious identities is a means for political leaders to get followers and for ordinary people to gain access to important resources for themselves and their communities. So-called tribalism is not an irrational expression of primordial passions or a reflection of the absence of modernity. It is a functional and rational response to combine with others on the basis of such ties in order to compete with like groups for scarce jobs and other necessities in underdeveloped political economies.

The competitive environment this produces promotes patron-client relationships among those of the same ethnicity, region, or religion. In such relationships, mutual obligations for the exchange of goods, services, and support are created and maintained. The result of such a system, however, is that modern, bureaucratic norms of impartiality and efficiency fail to operate in the transactions that take place between politicians/civil servants and constituents or service providers and clients. Instead, favoritism and parochial ties heavily influence exchanges. For instance, the more patron-client ties based on ethnicity influence the allocation of resources, the more ethnic clustering is encouraged. That is, individuals and groups feel they must combine and work together if they are to partake of the spoils of government office. The stronger the patronage system is, the more that members of society come to expect that the outcome of the competition for resources is based on ethnic or other parochial lines. This creates what is known as a self-fulfilling prophecy; that is, expectations and perceptions operate to reinforce and perpetuate the existing situation.

Gaining public office and control over the resources of office allows individuals to gain rewards for themselves and for their ethnic clients. In fact, it becomes expected that self-aggrandizement by those in positions of power will occur. Although this is not approved of by most people, such behavior becomes less objectionable as long as some of the gains are redistributed to clients ranging from political cronies, business associates, local community groups, and family and friends. Typically, ethnicity, religion, and regional identities play heavily in patronage decisions. However, among the most powerful and wealthy members of Nigerian society, mutual exchanges also occur to protect ruling class interests. These exchanges can occur along parochial lines but also can involve alliances with powerful members of other groups who share a common interest in maintaining control over wealth and power in Nigerian society. Readers will see in later chapters how this affects the political party system.

The use of public office for personal gain and the misuse of the resources of office to support clients is essentially corruption, and corruption has become endemic in Nigeria's political system. It has resulted in the virtual theft of billions of dollars of public money by political officeholders, an enormous waste of money and other resources on inefficient and substandard work for government contracts, and the neglect of vital social spending for education, health care, and development that would benefit the country. Despite its wealth in resources, especially oil, Nigeria is now one of the world's poorest countries as well as one of the most corrupt.

Corruption operates at all levels of society, not just at the top. It can be observed when dealing with low-level officials who expect a bribe for the delivery of services, the police officer who deliberately stops motorists and expects a payoff if the motorist wishes to continue on their way without further harassment. Corruption can also be seen with the government minister who receives kickbacks for government contracts from transnational corporations or local businesses. At all levels of public office, embezzling government funds or gaining favored treatment for oneself, family, or cronies is commonplace. This corruption is a major affliction in Nigeria, although such behavior is not a uniquely African or Nigerian problem. Even though corruption can be found in all societies, the dynamics and effects of corruption in poor countries such as Nigeria are worse, because the very scarcity of resources makes their misuse so costly to society's welfare.

With the stakes so high in the competition for office, politics takes on extremely high importance. Winning elections, for example, is everything, and losing is unthinkable. Losers have nowhere to go for resources and advancement, but winning means feasting from the "national cake." This intense competition makes identification with ethnic, religious, and regional groups essential and heightens the level of division and potential hostility among rival groups. Winning and losing do not just affect the politician, but the entire group they represent. There is also intense pressure on the wealthy and powerful (patrons) to use their office and wealth to assist the members of their ethnic, regional, and religious communities (clients). Essentially, public resources are now treated as though they are personal. In fact, the patron-client system and the identity politics and corruption it fosters have roots in precolonial society. African societies in general have a strong tradition of kinship and communal expectations of sharing resources and of reciprocity. To gather supporters and gain prestige as "Big Men," those with great resources would lavish them on their kin and communities. For ordinary people, attachment to a kinship or communal group and to a "Big Man" patron was the safest means to ensure survival.

Ironically, the competition for public office and resources is sometimes greatest among Nigeria's urban, educated middle classes, where "tribes" are fast disappearing. Indeed, manifestations of "tribalism" are greater in urban than in rural areas. For example, it is widespread among professors and students, many of whom seldom or never visit or live in their rural tribal areas or villages. The explanation for this is that tribalism arises due to conflicts over relative shares of public goods. It, therefore, can emerge in state universities as professors compete for jobs and promotions, using ethnic criteria rather than merit. Ethnic associations located in urban areas are mainly an invention of the urban, educated middle classes. These associations reflect the insecurity of the middle class, who find themselves in positions of authority and seek the support and reassurance of communal ties.

Recently emergent ethnicities, competition for state resources, the salience of patron-client relationships, and the expectations for Big Men are all evident in Lillian Trager's recent study of the hometown complex among the Yoruba. As the Yoruba become more mobile and leave their home places for new opportunities in cities, such as Lagos, efforts are intensifying for people to identify with a particular hometown, whether they live there or not. This is similar to being assigned or adopting an ethnic or subethnic identity. A hometown identity is not just emotional or cultural. The structure of Nigerian society is reinforcing such ties. For example, current political and economic problems are encouraging people to maintain hometown connections for mutual support. The hometown is the place people can go back to during hard times. At the same time, people are expected to contribute generously to helping their hometown. Another factor reinforcing hometown ties is that preferential acceptance to some schools is based on the father's hometown. Also, anyone with ambitions to political office at any level begins to build his or her base of support at the hometown level. Access to jobs can also depend on being from a particular area.

The important thing is that wherever a person considers his or her hometown to be, there are expectations to associate with the town, build a house, spend money there, and give the town leadership in the competition of communities for the resources of the state. The hometown is also the place where one expects to be buried. The most successful men and women are expected to do the most for their hometown. In return, these benefactors are given honor and prestige by hometown people.

Many observers thought that greater migration (including international migration) would mix different people together and lessen the strength of such communal ties as those to hometowns. In most cases in Nigeria, this has not been the case. Ties to ethnic groups and local communities remain strong among the Yoruba and other groups as well. This is likely to continue as long as communal discord, corrupt and inefficient government, and lack of economic opportunity leave most people little alternative.

Conclusion

This chapter has shown that Nigerian political culture is strongly influenced by identity politics. The main identities affecting perceived interests and the means of mobilizing political support are ethnicity, region, and religion. Class and other affiliations exist but are weaker bases for identification and political action. The intensity of competition for political power in the absence of other means to achieve advancement and acquire resources has led to considerable intergroup conflict and even violence. Patron-client relationships and corruption reinforce parochial ties while creating antagonisms among groups. They also undermine the economy and further weaken the legitimacy of government and the political class that controls the state.

There is disagreement as to the consequences of identity politics and patronage systems in Nigeria. Some observers have concluded that Nigerians have an undemocratic political culture due to the strength of parochial loyalties and an intolerance of others that undermines development and national unity. Others argue the most Nigerians do not have undemocratic values; they simply have an undemocratic state. Most Nigerians value democracy and want to see a democratic system work. As chapter 9 will show, Nigerians from many walks of life have been involved in prodemoc-racy and human rights activism often at great personal peril and cost, in-cluding losing their lives in the struggle. At the same time, it is important to recognize the disconnect between values and intolerant, violent, and unde-mocratic behavior on the part of many political leaders and their support-ers who use violence, intimidation, hate, and misrepresentation of facts to serve their political ends. It is also important to understand the economic, social, and political forces that drive some Nigerians to engage in behavior that undermines a viable democratic system.

The culture of patronage and corruption is one important factor that un-dermines democracy and national unity. Although social traditions of reci-procity and communal solidarity can provide identities and security for peo-ple, they can also undermine the fairness and efficient functioning of modern, rational-legal states and economies. The corruption, inefficiency, and mismanagement so pervasive in Nigeria are not caused simply by greedy and incompetent people, however. If they were, the cure could involve an ethics program for officeholders or the replacement of "bad apples" with "good apples." This will not solve the problem as long as conditions in Nige-ria (and most other African countries) do not favor the widespread embrace of universalistic, rational-legal norms. It is also true that many Africans ques-tion the superior ethics or morality of treating family, friends, and support-ers no differently than strangers or outsiders. The idea of a public good that encompasses "everyone in Nigeria" is an abstract concept that is hard to em-brace by people who in many cases still do not define themselves as Nigeri-ans and have little in common with most other Nigerians. Similarly, such ra-tional-legal norms as the impartial rule of law may seem impractical to politicians whose legitimacy and hold on power and income depend on what they can deliver through their patron-client networks.

Wole Soyinka, one of Nigeria's most celebrated intellectuals, recently wrote a book on the problems of Nigeria today. He has some noteworthy re-flections on the retreat to parochial identities in Nigeria. Soyinka blames the phenomenon on "a minority that constantly plays up innately innocuous dif-ferences, be they of ethnicity or religion, in order to set one section against another and thus assure itself of political control." As to why ordinary Nige-rians, including many former nationalists and pan-Africanists, are becom-ing more parochial in their focus, Soyinka adds, "There is so much work to do, and charity, it is said, begins at home." In reference to the many Nigeri-ans who have left the African continent, they are "desperate for a salvage op-eration of what is closest at hand." And finally, referring to religious ex-tremism, Soyinka caustically comments, "Fanaticism is not so much about religion, faith, or piety, but about power domination, and its complementary idiotization project unleashed on the rest of thinking humanity" (Soyinka 1996, 128, 141).

The next chapter will uncover how the centrifugal forces of region, ethnicity, and religion in Nigerian society nearly tore the country apart in a bloody civil war beginning in 1967. We will also see the impact the war has had on intergroup, especially ethnic, relationships and on changes in the political system since the war ended in 1970. Subsequent chapters will further explore the problematic elements of the political culture discussed in this chapter to reveal the destructive political and economic consequences they have had.

Timeline

1946	The Richards Constitution is proposed
1951	The Macpherson Constitution replaces the Richards Constitution
1953	Anthony Enahoro proposes independence, to take place in 1956
1957	The western and eastern regions become self-governing
1958	The Willinks Minority Report is issued
1959	The northern region becomes self-governing
October 1, 1960	Nigeria becomes independent

Significant People, Places, and Events

ACHEBE, CHINUA Achebe is one of Nigeria's most famous authors. His novels, which include the acclaimed *Things Fall Apart, A Man of the People,* and *Anthills of the Savannah,* are vivid portrayals of Nigeria's torturous path through colonialism and the modern independence period.

CIVIL SOCIETY The concept of civil society refers to groups and organizations outside of the control of government that represent diverse societal interests. This would include labor unions, women's groups, and business groups.

COMMUNAL LAND TENURE Most precolonial African land tenure systems were based on community rather than private ownership of land. Land was allocated to families for their use in order to ensure that all families had land to maintain themselves and their members over the generations.

FEDERAL SYSTEM (FEDERALISM) Federalism is a form of government in which a union of states agrees to delegate power to a central government, which handles common affairs such as defense and foreign affairs. The United States is a federal system.

IRREDENTISM This refers to the effort to join a region or regions to a related country from which it is currently separated. An example would be the failed effort to add the Ogaden region of Ethiopia to Somalia in the 1980s. Most of the people in the Ogaden were ethnic Somalis.

NIGERIANIZATION Shortly before independence, the British sought to promote greater Nigerian political and economic participation and control in order to facilitate self-government after years of colonial domination.

RATIONAL-LEGAL This is a concept associated with German sociologist Max Weber. It describes the way modern societies use impersonal rules and regulations, standardized procedures, and meritocratic standards to promote efficiency, accountability, and the attainment of organizational goals.

REGIONALISM This involves the division of a country into regions that have considerable autonomy to govern themselves. Regionalism also refers to the tendency to favor one's own region and its interests over others.

SHARI'A Islamic law, or shari'a, is based on the Qur'an and the hadith, the purported sayings of the prophet Muhammed. Many Muslims favor using shari'a as the basis of modern legal systems, including criminal law, as well as in family life and property issues.

SOYINKA, WOLE Soyinka is Africa's first winner of the Nobel Prize for Literature. His large body of literary work includes poetry, political analysis, and theatrical and screen plays. He was forced into exile during Nigeria's most recent military dictatorship under Gen. Sani Abacha.

Umma In Islam, the community of believers is the umma.

Bibliography

Bienen, Henry. 1993. "Leaders, Violence, and the Absence of Change in Africa." *Political Science Quarterly* 108 (summer): 271–282.

Brenner, Louis. 1993. "Muslim Representations of Unity and Difference in the African Discourse." Pp. 1–20 in *Muslim Identity and Social Change in Sub-Saharan Africa.* Edited by Louis Brenner. Bloomington: Indiana University Press.

Diamond, Larry. 1990. "Nigeria: Pluralism, Statism, and the Struggle for Democracy." Pp. 351–409 in *Politics in Developing Countries.* Edited by Larry Diamond. Boulder, CO: Lynne Rienner.

Ekeh, Peter P. 1998. "Colonialism and the Two Publics in Africa: A Theoretical Statement." Pp. 87–109 in *Africa: Dilemmas of Development and Change*. Edited by Peter Lewis. Boulder, CO: Westview.

Falola, Toyin. 1998. *Violence in Nigeria: The Crisis of Religious Politics and Secular Ideologies*. Rochester, NY: University of Rochester Press.

———. 1999. *The History of Nigeria*. Westport, CT: Greenwood.

Joseph, Richard G. 1998. "Class, State, and Prebendal Politics in Nigeria." Pp. 44–63 in *Africa: Dilemmas of Development and Change*. Edited by Peter Lewis. Boulder, CO: Westview.

Ottaway, Marina. 1999. "Ethnic Politics in Africa: Change and Continuity." Pp. 299–317 in *State, Conflict, and Democracy in Africa*. Edited by Richard Joseph. Boulder, CO: Lynne Rienner.

Soyinka, Wole. 1996: *The Open Sore of a Continent: A Personal Narrative of the Nigerian Crisis*. New York: Oxford University.

Trager, Lillian. 2001. *Yoruba Hometowns: Community, Identity, and Development in Nigeria*. Boulder, CO: Lynne Rienner.

CHAPTER SIX

The Biafra Civil War

O n May 30, 1967, less than seven years after Nigeria became an independent country, C. Odumegwu Ojukwu, the military commander in the east, declared that the eastern region of Nigeria was seceding and that it would now be the new nation of Biafra. The Nigerian government's response to this proclamation was to initiate Nigeria's first (and so far only) civil war. The war ended on January 15, 1970, with the defeat of Biafra. The causes of the civil war are complex, and its effects on Nigeria have been profound and long-lasting.

This chapter will examine the foundations of the civil war by looking at the dynamics of government and politics in the First Republic, which lasted from 1960 to 1966. Especially important is the structure of government at the time of independence and the destructive ethnoregional competition among the Nigerian political classes. Next discussed will be the end of the First Republic in a military coup in 1966. The failures of the First Republic precipitated efforts to reorganize the structure of the country and patterns of governance. These events took place in an atmosphere of growing ethnoregional distrust and calls for secession and the breakup of the country. The next part of the chapter will look at events leading to the secession of the east and at the war itself. The focus will be on the role of ethnic and regional issues before and during the war. Lastly, readers will see what the impact of the war has been, especially its political effects and its impact on ethnoregional relationships up to the present.

Ethnoregionalism in the First Republic

The first Nigerian national elections in 1959 were intended to determine which political party would rule Nigeria. The main party contenders were the Northern People's Congress (NPC), the Action Group (AG), and the National Council of Nigerian Citizens (NCNC), previously the National

Lieutenant Colonel Odumegwu Ojukwu, leader of secessionist Biafra, announces introduction of new currency and postage stamps, officially issued on January 29, 1967, at a meeting of his consultative assembly in Owerri. It was reported January 30 that, in an interview earlier that week, Ojukwu told United Press International that he would welcome U.S. intervention to end the bitter six-month-old civil war caused by Biafra's breakaway from Nigeria. (Bettmann/Corbis)

Council of Nigeria and the Cameroons. During the colonial period, the western part of Cameroon was part of British colonial holdings. Nigerians hoped British Cameroon would become part of an independent Nigeria. A referendum was held in British Cameroon, and they voted to become part of Cameroon instead, so the NCNC became a Nigeria-only party and changed its name. Political parties were mainly regional and identified with the major ethnic group in each of their respective regions: the NPC with the Hausa-Fulani and the north, the AG with the Yoruba and the west, and the NCNC with the Igbo and the east. None of the parties had succeeded in developing a national program or national following. They had come to see themselves as defenders of regional interests and were typically hostile and suspicious toward people from other regions. Each party was also inordinately sensitive to the potential threat of "domination" by other major ethnic groups. This led them to focus mainly on the distribution of power and resources by the government along ethnic and regional lines rather than for the purpose of government to serve all the people and to promote the interests of the country as a whole.

A major reason for the ascendance of ethnoregionalism in politics was the constitutional framework for the country that was created by the British in the last years of colonialism. The constitution stipulated that there would be three large regions, which coincided with the locations of the three major ethnic groups. The result was to heighten the importance of ethnic and regional identities and interests in comparison to other identities and interests. However, because the three regions also included many minority ethnic groups, tensions within regions were created between the dominant groups and the minorities. Leaders from the various groups contended with each other for power and government resources. Minority leaders in all three regions complained bitterly of discrimination and neglect of their interests by a government controlled by their rivals. These complaints were only partially addressed by the creation of a new state, the midwest region, out of the western region in 1963.

One of the most contention-ridden issues in the early 1960s was the national census of 1962. The census was the basis of determining representation in the national government and was thus a subject of great ethnic and regional concern. The census showed a large increase in population for all three regions since the last census. However, much to the consternation of the east and the west, the census results showed the north having the majority of the population. The other regions were concerned that this would ensure the dominance of the north and the NPC in the government. None of the political parties would accept the census results; therefore, a new census was taken in 1963.

The results were much the same and still showed the north's population to be greater than that of the other two regions combined.

Despite protests from the east and the west about the inadequacies of the census, the NPC-dominated national government used its clout to get official acceptance of the census results. This led to further ethnic and regional polarization. The Igbo and the NCNC were especially alienated by the census results, which resulted in growing hostility between the NCNC and the NPC. NCNC and NPC relations were already strained due to the unsatisfactory alliance they had established after the first national elections in 1959. At that time, the NCNC refused to join other southerners against the north. They hoped to get a better payoff by joining with the dominant party, the NPC. Unfortunately, the coalition failed to produce many benefits for the NCNC or its eastern supporters. Instead of sharing the spoils of office with its NCNC allies, the NPC made its constituents in the north the main beneficiaries of government spending. The disgruntled NCNC now turned to the west for support in an effort to undermine the NPC. This put the NCNC in competition with the AG, the dominant western party, and led to sporadic violent interparty clashes in the western region. The AG itself split as a result of leadership rivalries and poliy disagreements, and intraparty violence occurred as well.

The political situation became quite volatile and produced growing discontent among many elements in the country. It became obvious that the political parties and politicians were mainly interested in getting and keeping power in order for the politicians to enrich themselves and their cronies. Elections were fraught with violence and fraud. The bitter rivalries among the politicians led to constant disagreements over how to divide government revenues, distribute cabinet positions, or even do a census. In 1962 and again in 1964, the western regional government broke down as political rivalries and conflicts over elections led to violence, and intraethnic violence brought chaos among the Tiv; in both cases the military had to be called in to restore order.

In the competition for power, ethnic and regional hostilities were incited by the politicians and parties in order to attract supporters. This led to a worsening of relationships among various ethnic groups, many of them now moving to regions that were home to other groups. Negative stereotyping and perception of threats posed by the newcomers were common. One perception among the locals was that "strangers" practiced a "tribalism of aggression." That is, they despised and wanted to destroy the traditions and institutions of their hosts. Therefore, the host people had to counter with a "tribalism of defense" by mobilizing their people to repel the aggression of strangers. Northerners particularly felt threatened by the influx of educated southerners, many of them non-Muslims. Many Christians felt superior to their Muslim hosts and antagonized them by efforts at evangelizing and at spreading Christian churches, schools, and secular influences. The Igbo, and to some extent the Ibibio (both eastern groups), were also subject to negative perceptions. They were accused of living apart from their hosts and refusing to mix with them. It was said that they married girls from home and maintained their own culture and way of life rather than assimilating. At the same time, they tried to gain control of local councils in order to promote their interests. The locals felt compelled to protect their traditions against these hostile strangers. An example of the threat to local traditions was the alleged attack on traditional Yoruba kingship (the *oba*) by the Igbo, who were accustomed to decentralized government.

As the above discussion indicates, competition for jobs and political power, as well as cultural misunderstandings, were at the root of escalating ethnic tensions and clashes. Most of the conflict was occurring in cities throughout the country where migration and ethnic mixing were increasing.

The 1966 Coup and the End of the First Republic

One very important group that was becoming dismayed by the chaos and disarray in the civilian government was the Nigerian military. The military was alarmed by the seeming inability of the civilian politicians to govern the country or deal with its problems. The resulting political instability also threatened to discourage the foreign investment necessary to develop the economy. Only 10,000 strong at independence, the army was a colonial creation. Before World War II, recruits came mainly from among poor, politically marginalized minorities. After the war, other ethnic groups were recruited, including members of the Western-educated middle class from the south. Under the government of Prime Minister Tafawa Balewa, efforts were made to replace the British officer corps inherited at independence with Nigerian officers. University graduates were sought, which resulted in the recruitment of a disproportionate number of southerners, especially Igbo.

British military training was based on the principle that the military was subordinate to civilian rule and should not interfere in politics. Despite their training by the British, however, the Nigerian military was not above dabbling in politics. By 1962, most of the officers were southerners, because relatively few northerners had the requisite education. The elite of the military were also members of Nigeria's governing class. The main concern of many officers was to gain promotion for status purposes and to have the opportunity for alliances with the civilian political elite. Politicians sponsored their favorite candidates for military promotion, and ethnic group representatives lobbied for the appointment of officers from their ethnic group to major positions. Northern politicians were especially determined to see a greater recruitment and promotion of northern officers to counter the dominance of southerners. It appeared to many officers, particularly among the Igbo, that an ethnic and regional quota system favoring Hausa-Fulani northerners was replacing merit as the criterion for advancement.

It was the military's discontent with what was happening in the country and in the military that led to the first military coup in January 1966. The First Republic was brought to an ignoble end and replaced with a military government. The coup was carried out by about thirty mostly middle-ranking officers (out of a total of 500) and about 100 to 150 troops (out of 10,000). Most of the officers involved in the coup were Igbo. Their plan was to strike the capitals of the four regions, Ibadan in the west, Enugu in the east, Benin in the midwest, and Kaduna in the north, along with the capital, Lagos. The senior federal government officials, senior military officers, and the premiers of each region would all be killed. The coup leaders were convinced that such extreme measures were needed to save the country.

Things did not turn out for the coup plotters exactly as planned. Among those killed were Prime Minister Tafawa Balewa; Ahmadu Bello, the premier of the north (and also sardauna of Sokoto, an important political leader dating to the Sokoto Caliphate of the early 1800s), and Chief S. L. Akintola, the premier in the west. In the end, the coup failed, as loyal officers and troops rallied to the defense of the government. Major General Johnson Aguiyi Ironsi took control of the military and convinced the civilian government to turn control of the government over to him as well in order to prevent a civil war.

The 1966 coup was very controversial among Nigerians, and ethnicity tended to determine how the coup and subsequent takeover by the military was perceived. For many Nigerians at the time, the coup and the end of the First Republic was popular and seen as justified. Defenders of the coup accepted the military's explanation that their motive in seizing power was patriotism. The military claimed that they had to stop the corruption and ruin wrought by incompetent politicians who were threatening the unity of the country with their divisive tribalist politics. Opponents of the coup, particularly northerners, saw a more sinister motive at work. To them, the coup and seizure of power by Ironsi were motivated by Igbo desires to dominate the military and the government. The evidence for this conclusion was circumstantial but compelling to northerners, given the already tense ethnoregional political climate and rampant fears of "domination" among ethnic groups. Most damning was the fact that most of the coup plotters were Igbo, whereas none of the twenty-seven key leaders killed was Igbo. Ironsi himself was Igbo. Not only that, but the only regional premiers not killed in the coup were the premiers of the east and the midwest. And, in the four regions where the coup was to be carried out and opposition eliminated, only in Kaduna were they very successful. As final proof of an Igbo plot, Ironsi was now the military head of state.

Ironsi did nothing to allay suspicions of an Igbo conspiracy to control the country. Instead, he reinforced them. For example, of twenty-one officers promoted to the rank of lieutenant colonel under his rule, eighteen were Igbo. Ironsi showed a similar bias, or obtuseness, in his choice of political advisors. The government was now dominated by a small group of Igbo rather than being broadly based. Ironsi also provoked opposition after he announced a new constitution on May 24, 1966, which would abolish the four regions and replace them with groups of provinces. The defunct federal system would become a unitary government, and the federal and regional civil services would be merged. Military rulers would replace civilian leaders. Although Ironsi felt these changes were the only way to eliminate the ethnic and regional strife that threatened to destroy the country, it earned him the enmity of the regional political bosses he was replacing.

Indeed, Ironsi seriously miscalculated the strength of ethnoregional sentiments, especially in the north. Northerners were now convinced of the south's intentions to eradicate northern power. They believed that the new unified civil service would result in southern domination of the civil service because of the southerners' superior educational qualifications. Rumors also circulated that northerners in the army were to be eliminated by Ironsi. In general, Ironsi was unable to resolve ethnoregional rivalries or to implement successful economic or political reforms that might have increased his support among the people.

The north reacted with growing demonstrations and violence. Students and civil servants in the north staged demonstrations against Ironsi's plans to reorganize the government. Politicians incited fears of Igbo domination. Late in May 1966, students at Ahmadu Bello University and the Institute of Administration in Zaria demonstrated against the loss of regional government jobs that would result from the abolishment of the federal system. Gangs invaded Igbo neighborhoods, looting and killing shopkeepers. The violence escalated, and Igbo living in the north found themselves subjected to increasing physical attack in the main cities, where they played a prominent role in commerce and transportation. Riots spread, along with claims of Igbo exploitation of northerners. The evidence suggests that these attacks on the Igbo were orchestrated by senior civil servants, officials of the former Native Authorities who had been given power during the colonial period, and local politicians. Finally, with the violence escalating, between 300,000 and 500,000 Igbo fled the north in fear for their lives.

Ironsi tried to salvage the situation. In a nationwide tour, he sought to justify the May 24 decree to local chiefs and kings, but his efforts were in vain. Earlier, Ironsi had tried to consolidate his position by alliances with local chiefs and the civil service. He gained the support of most of the civil service but at the cost of alienating the chiefs. Government efforts to centralize power and strengthen the civil service allowed the civil service to usurp most of the power and authority of the chiefs. For example, customary courts lost jurisdiction, and chiefs lost seats on government boards and local councils. Ironsi and the other military leaders might have been successful in holding onto power if they had been able to maintain the support of the chiefs and had been perceived as neutral and above regional and ethnic loyalties. Unfortunately for the government, this was not the case.

On July 29, northern military officers staged a second coup and ended the Ironsi government. Initially, northern officers had been reluctant to stage a coup against their own military brothers. However, out of concern that Ironsi was plotting Igbo domination, northern officers planned to use the coup to disarm Igbo officers and troops throughout the country. Instead of simply disarming the Igbo, many Igbo officers and troops were killed in the coup. Among the casualties were the military governor of the west and many officers and troops in the north and the west. Oddly enough, the coup failed in the east, even though the majority of the troops there were from the north.

After the July coup, many northern military officers called for secession of the north, but civilian leaders urged keeping the country united. Lieutenant Colonel Yakubu Gowon, a Middle Belt Christian from a minority ethnic group, became the new head of state. Unfortunately, under Gowon, events in Nigeria would go from bad to worse.

The Civil War

Gowon set about implementing another restructuring of the government. The regional system was restored, and Gowon proposed a constitutional conference to consider the creation of a stronger central government and more states. The latter reform would break up the four regions into numerous states and state governments. This would provide more power and resources for minority ethnic groups. The conference was held in September of 1966. The army, politicians, intelligentsia, and regional representatives were all divided. Most delegates opposed Gowon's plan to create a strong central government, preferring instead to strengthen their regions in a federation with a weak central government. Every region had a list of grievances. The Yoruba in the west were led by Chief Awolowo (of the AG), who demanded more power and a bigger share of national revenue. The Yoruba, he claimed, were victims of discrimination and injustice. Delegates from the midwest were divided; some wanted to remain an autonomous region, while others wanted to join with the east. The north was also split. The emirs and staff of the Native Authorities benefited from being, and wanted to remain, one region. Others liked the idea of more states because it would mean more government jobs and money.

Soldiers from northern minorities, and other northern officers, realized that an autonomous north with a weak central government would be politically and economically weak. They finally convinced the northern delegation at the conference to support the new federal government and the creation of new states for the following reasons:

- The division of the regions into the proposed twelve states would prevent any one region from dominating the others.
- Northern development depended on access to the sea through southern ports at Lagos and Port Harcourt (in the east); therefore, autonomy would be economically suicidal.
- By 1966, Nigeria's potential oil wealth had become known. Most of the oil was in the south, mainly in the southeast. On its own, rather than as part of a unified Nigeria, the north would get no share of the oil wealth. Moreover, a strong central government in control of oil revenues would be needed to ensure that the entire nation, not just the oil-rich regions, would benefit.

The east, by contrast, was in favor of greater regional autonomy and opposed the idea of a strong central government. In fact, as early as 1966, many Igbo were calling for secession. The July 1966 coup had effectively destroyed the military as an agent of national unity. This was especially true in the east where, during the coup, northern troops killed 240 southern army officers and troops, 75 percent of them easterners. Lieutenant Colonel Odumegwu Ojukwu, the Igbo military governor in the eastern region, refused to recognize Gowon as the new head of state. Ojukwu thought Gowon was anti-Igbo. Moreover, he contended, there were more senior and competent officers than

Port Harcourt oil drilling rig (William Campbell/Corbis Sygma)

Gowon who should have been given the job. The Igbo and many others in the south also feared that Gowon and the new military government signaled Hausa-Fulani domination of the country. These fears were only partly dispelled when Gowon released many political prisoners and promised to deal equitably with the problems of regionalism.

Unlike in the north, autonomy or even secession by the east had real advantages. Although the midwest also had oil, most of Nigeria's oil wealth was in the eastern region of the south. With autonomy or independence, easterners would have the oil wealth to themselves and not have to share it with other regions. The other regions had already made it quite clear that they were counting on a share of the oil money to transform their own regional economies. For this reason, they were proposing a new revenue allocation formula that would require the federal government to distribute oil money to the states based on population size and need.

Although the conference debates continued into October, events occurred in the north that virtually doomed efforts to maintain Nigeria's unity. In early October, widespread violent attacks were made on the Igbo and other easterners living in northern cities. This led to retaliatory violence against northerners in the east. Within a few days, as many as 50,000 people were dead, most of them Igbo. Between 1 and 2 million more Igbo fled the north and went back to the east (in addition to those who had done so in May). It is alleged that members of the northern elite provoked the attacks against the Igbo by inciting citizens and soldiers. In one account of what precipitated the violence, people in the north were told that northerners had been massacred in the east. Mounting tensions and the problems of absorbing the huge numbers of Igbo refugees led Ojukwu to order all noneasterners to leave the east for safety reasons.

Talk of secession was now widespread throughout the country, but especially in the east. Such talk was nothing new. In the past, it had been northerners who most often threatened secession. In the 1950s, Ahmadu Bello, sardauna of Sokoto and head of the NPC, had considered secession out of fear of southern domination when independence for Nigeria was proposed. The north also threatened to secede if it did not have 50 percent of the legislative seats in the new federal government. In the northern House of Assembly and House of Chiefs in 1956, a resolution was passed that virtually endorsed secession. Northerners were not the only ones who had threatened or discussed secession, however. In 1954 at the Lagos constitutional conference, the Yoruba-dominated AG party demanded that the new constitution include a clause that allowed secession. In 1964, after the contentious 1963 census, Michael Okpara, premier of the east, threatened secession. He went so far as to establish a committee to work out a detailed plan for such action. This plan was later adopted by Ojukwu when the east did declare its secession from Nigeria. In 1966, in another incident, Isaac Boro declared independence on behalf of the Niger Delta People's Republic. (This occurred after the first coup and during Ironsi's brief rule.) Boro feared Igbo domination of eastern minorities. His new republic lasted twelve days before being put down by the government.

The northern coup in July and the riots of September also had strong separatist undertones. The initial demand of the northern troops had been secession. The western region, which preferred to maintain the federal system, endorsed the right of states to secede. In May 1967, western leaders proclaimed that if the east or any other region seceded, the west would consider the federation to be at an end. In other words, the west, too, would become an independent country. The western proclamation also considered fear of domination by another region to be legitimate grounds for secession.

Whatever the truth was, opinion in the east was that the north and the federal government were bent on their destruction. For instance, the east believed that the massacres of easterners in the north were deliberate and planned by both northern civilian and military leaders. The northerners wanted to eliminate easterners from the North, from the army, and from political equality with other Nigerians, easterners contended. The easterners felt their fundamental constitutional rights had been violated, yet the government was doing little to investigate or punish the offenders. Even worse, many easterners felt that the government in Lagos was in league with the perpetrators of violence against them. Under the circumstances, government preparations to reassert authority over the east were widely viewed in the east as further evidence of a plot to destroy the people of the east. They felt that only an independent state that the east controlled could ensure the protection of the eastern peoples.

In late May 1967, eastern leaders believed that they had legitimate grounds to secede and that there would be little resistance from the rest of the country. By some accounts, western leaders requested in early May that Ojukwu give them twenty-four hours notice before they made any declaration of secession. This would give them time to take the west out of the federation at the same time. Western fears of northern domination appear to have motivated this action, and western leaders professed solidarity with the east.

The military government worked hard throughout this tense period to convince leaders around the country, including Ojukwu, that their problems could be solved best through continuing the federation rather than through secession. It was also made clear that force would be used if necessary to prevent the breakup of the country. In fact, as early as February 1967, minority

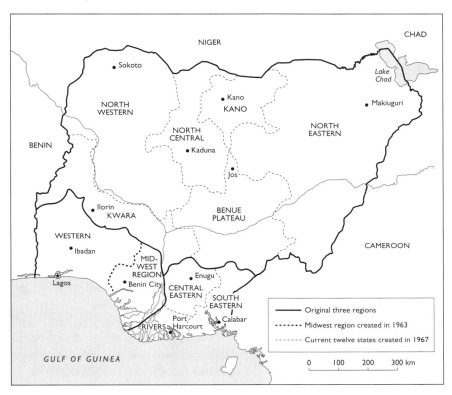

Map 6.1
Nigeria by 1967

group leaders (who had become much more influential in the government and in the military since the July 1966 coup), military leaders, and federal government officials in Lagos had come to agree that it was absolutely necessary to restore federal authority over eastern Nigeria. Gowon had been trying to deal with Ojukwu, but things were at an impasse.

Events came to a head on May 27, 1967. After the failure of a meeting with Ojukwu and the rest of the Supreme Military Council in Aburi to resolve their differences, Gowon declared a state of emergency. Among other actions taken, a naval blockade of the east's two ports, Port Harcourt and Calabar, was imposed. Gowon also issued his plan for reorganizing the government. In this Twelve-State Decree, the former four regions were transformed into twelve states with the possibility of more in the future. The north was to be divided into six states, and the west and the east were to be divided into three states each. The main objective was to address the fears of domination of one group by another. Northern power was reduced, as new states gave more power to minorities.

One of the new eastern states was almost all Igbo, but two states were created for minorities. The hope was that splitting minorities from the Igbo and giving them their own states would divide the east and prevent most of the region from seceding. Not accidentally, the new ethnic minority Rivers State had most of the east's oilfields, which would now be removed from Igbo control. The east's two seaports would also be located in the minority states.

Another change was a strengthening of the central government, which would have primary responsibility for economic development. The states, now larger in number but smaller in size, would have fewer economic resources and less power. Regional leaders were co-opted into the new system by being offered attractive government positions. Co-opting the regional leaders this way would prevent them from backing the east and its calls for secession. The strategy appeared to be working, as such political luminaries as Chief Awolowo (who had promised that the west would secede if the east did), Chief Enahoro of the midwest, and J. S. Tarka of the Middle Belt, among others, became members of Gowon's new Federal Executive Council.

Awolowo's defection to the government's side is considered by many Igbo even now to have been an act of betrayal. However, there were rational reasons for the west not to support the Igbo cause. The main reason to support the Igbo was the fear both the east and the west had of northern domination. The west resented northern domination of the federal government and the government's intervention in western internal politics earlier in the 1960s. However, if the east were to secede, the west would lose the east's presence with them as a counterweight to domination by the numerically superior north. Also, the west realized that an independent east could pose a threat to the west. The east would have control of the oil wealth, which could be used to acquire military power. This could allow the east to expand and dominate its neighbors. For instance, an Igbo-dominated nation might try to take over areas in the midwest with large Igbo populations or extend itself elsewhere in the south and even into the north.

The Middle Belt also supported the government and was unsympathetic to the east. After the July 1966 coup, minorities, especially those from the Middle Belt, comprised a large percentage of people in the military. They were for the first time in a position to gain more power, influence, and access to top civil service jobs in Lagos. They would have little to gain from the breakup of the federation.

Feeling increasingly threatened by the federal government and alienated from the rest of Nigeria, Ojukwu declared secession and the birth of the new

Republic of Biafra on May 30, 1967. He justified this decision by asserting that the Nigerian government was unable to protect the lives of its eastern citizens. Ojukwu's declaration is also carefully worded to include offshore territories in the new republic, which would ensure Biafra's sovereignty over offshore oil resources. Below is part of Ojukwu's independence declaration:

> Fellow countrymen and women, you, the people of Eastern Nigeria: Conscious of the supreme authority of Almighty God over all mankind, of your duty to yourselves and posterity;
>
> Aware that you can no longer be protected in your lives and in your property by any government based outside Eastern Nigeria;
>
> Believing that you are born free and have certain inalienable rights which can best be preserved by yourselves;
>
> Unwilling to be unfree partners in any association of a political or economical nature;
>
> Rejecting the authority of any person or persons other than the Military Government of Eastern Nigeria to make any imposition of whatever kind of nature upon you;
>
> Determined to dissolve all political and other ties between you and the former Federal Republic of Nigeria;
>
> Prepared to enter into such association, treaty or alliance with any sovereign state within the former Federal Republic of Nigeria and elsewhere on such terms and conditions as best to subserve your common good;
>
> Affirming your trust and confidence in me;
>
> Having mandated me to proclaim on your behalf, and in your name, that Eastern Nigeria be a sovereign independent Republic,
>
> Now, therefore, I, Lieutenant-Colonel [later General] Chukwuemeka Odumegwu Ojukwu, Military Governor of Eastern Nigeria, by virtue of the authority, and pursuant to the principles, recited above, do hereby solemnly proclaim that the territory and region known as and called Eastern Nigeria together with her continental shelf and territorial waters shall henceforth be an independent sovereign state of the name and title of "The Republic of Biafra." (http://www.dawodu.com)

The war began shortly after Ojukwu's defiant proclamation. In July, the Nigerian army invaded Biafra. After early advances by Biafran forces against government forces, the government attacked by air, sea, and land. Each side was optimistic about its chances for victory. The government in Lagos expected a quick victory over Biafra's smaller and less well equipped military forces. The Biafrans, too, expected success. They anticipated foreign support, especially from the transnational oil firms that hoped to enrich themselves with Biafran oil. The Biafrans expected these firms to pressure their respective governments and the international community to support the Biafran cause. The Biafrans were also skeptical of the ability of Nigeria's corrupt and incompetent government leaders to wage a successful campaign against them.

It was not long, however, before the government began to quickly retake territory controlled by Biafra. Biafra had little industry and was highly dependent on imported food and materials. Their main source of revenue was oil, but they lost the oilfields to Nigerian forces early in the war.

Despite the odds against Biafra, they did gain some popular foreign support from other nations, in part by waging a potent public relations campaign that presented the war as a genocide and an attempt by Islamic northerners to dominate or exterminate Christian easterners. France, Portugal, Israel, and South Africa were sympathetic to Biafra and provided the Biafrans with arms. Portugal let the Biafrans use Lisbon as a base of operations, and France provided relief supplies as well as weapons. However, Haiti was the only country outside of Africa to give Biafra formal recognition. In Africa, official recognition of Biafra as an independent country was given by only Tanzania, Zambia, Gabon, and Côte d'Ivoire (Ivory Coast). On the other hand, Great Britain, the United States, and Russia backed the Nigerian government. Only the British and the Russians, however, would sell Nigeria the weapons it wanted, including planes, armored cars, and howitzers. These weapons proved essential to the eventual success of the government's military campaign.

Although the civil war is often thought of as a war against Igbo secessionism, it is important to mention that only 64 percent of the east's population was Igbo. Other ethnic groups, the largest being the Efik and Ibibio, comprised more than one-third of the population. As the effort to divide the easterners by creating two minority states suggests, the Biafrans were not all unified in the Igbo-led secessionist cause. Certainly most of the Igbo supported Ojukwu and secession, but many minorities in the east were not comfortable with Igbo domination, nor did they support secession. The Ogoni people, who live in the Niger delta where most of Nigeria's oil is located, were especially ambivalent about secession and suffered greatly during the war.

By the end of 1967, federal troops were in control of the midwest region and the Niger delta area in the east. Despite valiant resistance by the Biafrans, other areas continued to fall to government forces, which vastly outnumbered the Biafrans. It was not long before Biafra was effectively reduced to the Igbo heartland. At this point, Biafra was cut off from supplies from the sea. It would only be a matter of time before Biafran resistance would be unsustainable.

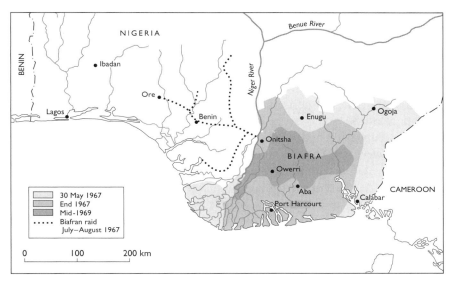

Map 6.2
The Biafra Civil War

Ultimately, Biafra's cause was lost when it could not get support from any other region in Nigeria. Biafra's only real hope of success depended on Nigeria's quickly breaking up into its regional parts. When this did not happen, Biafra was left as the "odd man out." Even most of the eastern minorities eventually declared their support for the federal government. When Ojukwu resorted to coercion against the errant minorities, he further weakened his support among them. Even among the Igbo, support for secession and war were not universal, but as in wars everywhere, such voices of dissent tend to be suppressed or muted once actual war is declared.

The war dragged on for thirty months and inflicted tremendous suffering in the east. Many of the civilian casualties were not direct victims of warfare. Rather, the federal government's military superiority was accompanied by a policy of starvation against the civilian population. The federal government's embargo cut off most of Biafra's supplies of both food and medicine, not just military supplies. As a result, disease as well as starvation and malnutrition were widespread. The Biafran people were in such fear of the federal government, a fear promoted in part by Biafran government claims that the war was genocide against them, that many believed rumors that the Nigerian Air Force was causing kwashiorkor (a protein deficiency disease) by spreading poison over Biafra. Fears of genocide kept the Biafrans fighting but also led them to reject desperately needed emergency food and medical aid. In June

1968, for instance, Great Britain offered to send humanitarian aid to save lives, but the Biafran government turned down the offer. The rumor spread that the food had been refused because the British had convinced the Nigerian government to poison it in order to exterminate the Biafrans. Both anti-Nigerian and anti-British sentiment was behind such behavior.

In the end, Biafra could not withstand the federal government's military onslaught or the effects of the embargo. The war finally ended on January 15, 1970. Between 2 and 3 million people had died, most of them easterners. There were more than 3 million Igbo refugees. The economy of the area was in ruins, along with much of the east's infrastructure and ability to meet even the basic needs of the region's population. Fortunately, and despite the heavy casualty rate, there was no credible evidence of a deliberate campaign of genocide by the federal government.

To his credit, Gowon realized that a successful reintegration of the east back into the Nigerian nation required a policy of reconciliation rather than retribution. Igbo personnel were allowed to reenter the civil service and the military. There were no trials, and only a few individuals were imprisoned. Ojukwu, the Biafran secessionist leader, was treated leniently. After fleeing the country at the war's end and living in exile in Côte d'Ivoire, Ojukwu was allowed to return to Nigeria to live in 1982.

Ukapi Asika, an Igbo who had remained loyal to the government during the war, was suitably rewarded for his stance. He was named the chief administrator of the new East Central State, which encompassed the Igbo heartland. His all-Igbo cabinet included people who had been part of the secessionist government. Asika was considered a traitor by many Igbo, however, and his administration was marred by corruption and incompetence.

Despite the difficulties, the short-lived Biafra was reintegrated into Nigeria. With federal assistance, much of the region's industry, public utilities, and social services were restored, although not to prewar levels. Biafra and the eastern region no longer existed as entities. The east was now part of a new Nigeria, which had twelve states rather than four regions. All of the original ethnoregional states were now divided in the hopes that a new, more balanced system would replace them and prevent the fears of domination that had proved so tragic for Nigeria.

Effects of the Civil War

There was much at stake in the outcome of the civil war in Nigeria. Obviously, the most direct and immediate consequences would be for Nigerians, whose future as a country was in the balance. There were also important international ramifications. To be better understood, Nigeria's civil war must be viewed within the international context of the time. For this reason, this topic will be discussed here. Next, this chapter will assess the consequences of the Biafran crisis for Nigeria as a nation.

Nigeria, like most of the countries of the so-called Third World, was the product of colonialism. After World War II and the creation of the United Nations, the international consensus was that the process of decolonization was to be based on the right of self-determination of all colonial territories. However, the concept of self-determination was not to be applicable once independence was attained. In other words, there would be no general or universal right to secession. Biafra challenged this position and, as noted above, gained little international recognition or support from other nations. The fear was that if Biafra was successful in its efforts to secede from Nigeria, other disgruntled groups within newly independent nations (or more established nation-states, for that matter) might assert a similar right to self-determination through secession. The implications for conflict and chaos in the international order were obvious and not to be tolerated.

This same concern led the Organization of African Unity (OAU) to incorporate into its charter the principle of the territorial integrity of the borders of newly created African countries. Given the multiethnic and fragile nature of most of these countries, African leaders understandably feared that if one country succeeded in changing its boundaries and creating a new country, the whole continent could explode in a series of ethnically based secessionist wars. This reasoning largely dictated the lack of support for Biafra from almost all of the new African states.

As for the effects of the war on Nigeria itself, the war has had contradictory effects on ethnicity and politics. On the one hand, the war taught Nigerians the destructiveness of ethnic conflicts and the need for creating institutions to lessen the possibility of such conflicts in the future. Among the most important institutional changes to prevent future conflict was the reorganization of the country into twelve states. The power of the Big Three ethnic groups was weakened, and more power was given to ethnic minorities. This strategy of "ethnic balancing" has been characteristic of many Nigerian political reforms since the war, although the results are decidedly mixed.

Other efforts to address ethnic conflict include suppressing it by force when deemed necessary. At the extreme, a major justification for the military governments that have overthrown civilian governments has been to save the nation from ethnic conflict that threatens to destroy national unity. National unity has become, in fact, a deeply embedded national value, and the government has acted quickly to stop conflict that it perceives as a serious threat. National security and national unity have become virtually coterminous. To promote identification with the Nigerian nation and not just with regions or ethnic groups, nation-building policies have been implemented. Encouraging greater interaction, tolerance, and understanding among groups is part of this goal. One example of nation-building efforts is the National Youth Service Corps (NYSC). In the NYSC, graduates from universities or other higher education institutions spend one year in community service in a state outside their home state. By 1990, more than 1 million young people had served in the NYSC.

Despite the efforts to lessen ethnic and regional strife in Nigeria, these issues continue to be flash points for tension and conflict. The Igbo play a central role in many of these conflicts, which is an unfortunate legacy of the war. On the positive side, Gowon's "no victor, no vanquished" policy toward the Igbo helped to reintegrate the east and the Igbo back into the nation without harsh government retribution. This is a great tribute to the wisdom and foresight of Nigeria's leaders. It was government policy to protect Igbo property in the north that had been abandoned during the civil war; this property was returned to them at the end of the war. The government was also determined to ensure Igbo access to all major universities in the country and to civil service jobs. This set an example for all groups in the country that the government could be trusted to maintain the rule of law. It also helped to restore a sense of nationhood. Recently, Gowon even apologized to the Igbo for the war and the suffering the Biafrans endured.

Less positive is the widespread popular resentment toward the Igbo since the war. The Igbo have been blamed by many Nigerians for the war and the devastation it caused. This resentment has sometimes resulted in discrimination and prejudice against the Igbo. Indeed, despite the official efforts to reintegrate the Igbo into Nigeria, there has apparently been an unofficial effort to neutralize and marginalize them both in the military and in the civil service. This resentment and discrimination in turn has reinforced the Igbo's sense of alienation from the country, which helped lead to the war in the first place. In fact, the war and its aftermath are considered to be the source of a sense of common Igbo ethnic identity. It emerged for the first time in Nigerian history as a result of the shared civil war experience. Although there are still a great many divisions among the Igbo, the elite have become more cohesive. Igbo author Chinua Achebe has referred to "the Igbo problem" that colors perceptions the Igbo have of themselves and the popular perception of them among other groups. The Igbo elite believe that the Igbo are more cosmopolitan, more open to other cultures and change, more individualistic and competitive, and more willing to live and work in other parts of the country than other Nigerians. In contrast to their evaluation of themselves, the negative stereotype of the Igbo held by others is that they are aggressive, arrogant, and clannish.

Along with a greater sense of ethnic unity, the Igbo continue to distrust the Yoruba, with whom they realize they must forge an alliance to prevent "northern domination," a fear that has intensified rather than lessened over time. Igbo distrust makes alliance with the Yoruba difficult. As one Igbo leader writes, the great Igbo leaders from Nnamdi Azikiwe on shared the nationalist principle that what was good for Nigeria was good for the Igbo. (This perception harkens back to the Igbo-led NCNC party of the 1950s, which was the only party that attempted to be national and transethnic.) The Yoruba and the Hausa-Fulani, on the other hand, under such leaders as Obafemi Awolowo and Ahmadu Bello, operated on the principle that what was good for their ethnic group was good for Nigeria.

The tendency of many Nigerians to associate the war with the Igbo ignores the fact that in many ways the events leading to secession and then war reflect regionalism as much as ethnicity. The attacks on military personnel in 1966 were not just directed against the Igbo but against officers and troops from the east, which included many non-Igbo. The northern massacres and resulting refugee outflows also involved easterners from a variety of ethnic groups, not just Igbo. When troops throughout the country were ordered to return to their regions of origin, this included all the ethnic groups in the east returning to the east. Ojukwu was appointed as the east's military governor, and his actions initially had wide regional popular support. It was only as events came to a climax and the government managed to divide the minority groups from the Igbo in the east that the effort to create an independent Biafra became largely an Igbo cause. The force of regionalism remains strong and is evident in the persistent complaints about northern or southern domination.

Another result of the war on ethnic relations is that the war and subsequent ethnic conflict and violence have reinforced ties of ethnicity as a means of security. The massacres of Igbo in northern cities, for instance, have demonstrated to the Igbo quite clearly the importance of having a safe place to which to return and people on whom to rely in times of hardship. Ties to ethnic kinsmen and the proliferation of ethnic associations reflect this insecurity, also felt by many groups other than the Igbo. The importance of identifying with a hometown, a topic discussed earlier, has the same function.

Of great political significance, the war changed the role of the military and its relationship with civilian government officials. This is most evident in the back-and-forth pattern of movement from civilian rule to military rule and back to civilian rule that has gone on up to the present. Once the sacrosanct rule that the military should not intervene in civilian politics was broken, the tendency to revert to military rule when the military decided it was in the national interest to do so proved to be irresistible. This was especially true once it became apparent how great the economic and political payoff would be. Once in power in top political and civil service positions, military officers were able to use the revenues of the state to enrich themselves. After the war, the first military government and subsequent military rulers became increasingly greedy and corrupt.

Greed, corruption, and hunger for power were not limited to the military, however. The same vices, along with arrogance and a lack of accountability, were pervasive among nonmilitary members of the civil service. These vices were encouraged after the military government came to power in 1966 and during and after the war. The military did not have the skills or experience to run the government. The military needed the civil service and believed that civil servants, unlike civilian politicians, had integrity and competence. However, with the concentration of power occurring at the federal level during and after the war, the civil service became corrupted by too much power. After the war ended in 1970, instead of promoting a return to democracy, the civil service encouraged the military to stay in power in order to protect the civil servants' enhanced positions that military rule had made possible. Instead of integrity and competence, the civil service increasingly became characterized by its abuse of power and its inefficiency. Rather than allocating government resources in an open and rational manner, patron-client relationships have often governed government decisions on the distribution of resources to communities and citizens. Such practices have occurred widely at both the federal and state levels of government, because civil servants had become insulated from any democratic checks and balances. Although reforms to correct these problems have been implemented over the years, they continue to have a negative impact on governance.

Although war resulted in the creation of new states, the autonomy of the states was compromised by the concentration of power at the federal level (the center). Before 1967, the regions had been largely financially self-sufficient. During and after the war, the federal government gained control over the oil revenues beginning to flow into government coffers. The federal government used an allocation formula to distribute a share of oil revenues to each of the various states. The states became solely dependent on these revenues and were not allowed to raise their own revenues internally. This dependence even included reliance on the federal government to pay the states' civil servants. The states also now had less influence in the central government, because power was divided among twelve smaller regional entities rather than four large regions. None of the states had the size or resources to challenge the center.

With military rulers playing the major role in Nigerian governments after 1966, the composition of the military became more significant in ethnoregional terms. As already mentioned, the military had long been a multiethnic entity. Before the war, a disproportionate number of officers had been Igbo and other educated south-easterners. After the war, the military remained multiethnic, but the Igbo were largely excluded from the officer corps. The officer corps was increasingly dominated by northerners, most of them Muslims. Under the circumstances, many in the south doubted the military's commitment to national unity or the national interest as opposed to the interests of the north and the northern ruling elite.

A bloody war had been fought and won in the name of the Nigerian nation and to maintain the unity of the country. Although regional self-interest can explain much of the motivation behind the opposition to secession, there also came into existence a strong allegiance to national unity among most of Nigeria's leaders. This nationalist sentiment is analogous to the Union's determination to prevent the south's secession from the United States in the American Civil War. Like the United States, a united Nigeria is seen as vital to the country's integrity and future development. On the other hand, as economic and political conditions have deteriorated in Nigeria, many Nigerians from all ethnic groups are questioning the sentiment that national unity is sacred and that secession is illegitimate.

In fact, there has been a resurgence of secessionist sentiment among the Igbo. Many of them believe that the original cause for an independent Biafra was just. They feel that the Igbo people continue to face discrimination and mistreatment in Nigeria, including the threat of genocide. Islamization of the country through the imposition of shari'a (Islamic religious law) and the domination of the north are threats that the Igbo and other Christians face. Various Igbo associations have been formed to further the goals of an independent Biafra, to be achieved, it is said, by peaceful means. Advocates for Biafra point out that it was the Nigerian government under Gowon that declared war and used violence in the first place, not the Biafrans. Some even refer to Nigeria as "BiafraNigeria" to indicate Biafra's continuing existence as a distinctive entity in the minds of its adherents.

The most significant secessionist group is the Movement for the Actualization of the Sovereign State of Biafra (MASSOB). MASSOB is an Igbo movement that seeks an independent state of Biafra but also acts as a force to protect the Igbo against violence, especially in northern Nigeria. Such violence is seen as a repeat of the massacres that led to the original declaration of Biafran secession. MASSOB sympathizers continue to feel that the government does too little to protect Igbo communities residing in the north from acts of violence by northerners that continue to the present; therefore, MASSOB feels justified in retaliating against Muslim northerners, especially those living in the south. MASSOB also encourages Igbos in the north to use force to defend themselves against such violence. Harkening back to the pre–civil war period, many Igbo continue to believe that they can't rely on the government to protect them from northern violence. As one might expect, MASSOB is a controversial group in Nigeria. MASSOB's defenders claim that members have been subject to government harassment, murder, and illegal arrest. This sense of persecution by the government further reinforces Igbo separatist sentiments. MASSOB will be discussed in greater detail in chapter 9.

Without a doubt, the civil war of 1967–1970 has been the single most traumatic event in Nigeria's short history. The colonial legacy, the failings of the First Republic civilian governments, divisions within the military, and ethnoregional competition and conflict all played a role in creating the conflict between the eastern region and the federal government that eventuated in secession and civil war. The scars of the war remain, and some Nigerians believe that the country could find itself in another civil war if the country's economic and political problems are not solved and if communal strife worsens.

There has already been a brief discussion of the role of the First Republic in bringing Nigerian politics to such a low point that the military felt it had to stage a coup and establish a military government in order to save the country. The next chapter will examine in more detail the role of party politics and civilian governments during the entire course of the postindependence period. The chapter will focus on the First and Second Republics, the aborted Third Republic, and the tumultuous road to the democratically elected civilian government headed by Obasanjo. The chapter will also show the impact of ethnicity, region, and religion in shaping party politics and government during the relatively brief periods of civilian rule.

Timeline

1960–1966	The First Republic
January 1966	The first military coup occurs; a military government under Ironsi is established
July 29, 1966	A northern-led military coup overthrows Ironsi; Gowon comes to power in a military government
May 27, 1967	Gowon declares a state of emergency over Biafran secession
May 30, 1967	Ojukwu declares Biafra's independence
July 1967	Nigerian forces invade Biafra
December 1967	Nigerian forces take control of the midwest region and the Niger delta area
January 15, 1970	Biafra is defeated; the civil war ends

Significant People, Places, and Events

AHMADU BELLO UNIVERSITY This northern university, located in Zaria, is now the largest university in Nigeria, with about 35,000 students. It was founded in 1962.

BORO, ISAAC Boro was a major in the Nigerian military. He is considered a hero by the Ijaw people of the Niger delta and was killed in the civil war.

GOWON, YAKUBU Gowon was born in the Middle Belt region of Nigeria. After joining the army in 1954, he moved up in rank and became Chief of Staff after the first coup of 1966. He then became Supreme Commander. After the second coup, Gowon became the first military head of state in Nigeria.

IRONSI, JOHNSON AGUIYI Ironsi was not the leader or a coconspirator in the first 1966 coup. He governed for six months before the second coup occurred and he was killed. That coup was led by Major Theophilus Danjuma, who became minister of defense in the Obasanjo government.

OIL The search for oil began in 1937, and in 1956 huge oil deposits were discovered in the Niger delta. The first exports of oil began in 1958, and by 1967 there were 627 oil wells in Nigeria. By 1970, oil became Nigeria's main export.

OJUKWU, C. ODUMEGWU Ojukwu was one of the first Nigerians in the army to have a university degree. After joining the army in 1957, he quickly moved up in rank. He became the military governor of the eastern region in 1967 and the only head of state of the Republic of Biafra. He was a presidential candidate in the 2003 elections.

ORGANIZATION OF AFRICAN UNITY (OAU) The OAU has been the association of all of the states of Africa since independence. Its purpose was to promote peace, security, and economic and social development on the continent. The OAU has reorganized recently and renamed itself the African Union (AU).

Bibliography

Aborisade, Oladimeji, and Robert J. Mundt. 1998. *Politics in Nigeria.* New York: Longman.

Ayoade, John A. A. 1985. "Party and Ideology in Nigeria: A Case Study of the Action Group." *Journal of Black Studies* 16 (December): 169–188.

Diamond, Larry. 1990. "Nigeria: Pluralism, Statism, and the Struggle for Democracy." Pp. 351–409 in *Politics in Developing Countries.* Edited by Larry Diamond. Boulder, CO: Lynne Rienner.

Falola, Toyin. 1999. *The History of Nigeria.* Westport, CT: Greenwood.

Feit, Edward. 1968. "Military Coups and Political Development: Some Lessons from Ghana and Nigeria." *World Politics* 20 (January): 179–193.

Ibrahim, Jibrin. 1999. "Political Transition, Ethnoregionalism, and the 'Power Shift' Debate in Nigeria." *Issue: A Journal of Opinion* 21 (1): 12–16.

Metz, Helen Chapin, ed. 1992. *Nigeria: A Country Study.* Washington, DC: Library of Congress.

Nixon, Charles R. 1972. "Self-Determination: The Nigeria/Biafra Case." *World Politics* 24 (July): 473–497.

Nkpa, Nwokocha K. U. 1977. "Rumors of Mass Poisoning in Biafra." *Public Opinion Quarterly* 41 (autumn): 332–346.

Othman, Shehu, and Gavin Williams. 1999. "Politics, Power, and Democracy in Nigeria." Pp. 15–71 in *African Democracy in the Era of Globalization.* Edited by Jonathan Hyslop. Johannesburg, South Africa: Witwatersrand University.

CHAPTER SEVEN

Party Politics and Civilian Government

I N NIGERIA'S SHORT HISTORY AS AN INDEPENDENT NATION, it has been under military rule for most of that time. A civilian government ruled the
country during the First Republic. The Second Republic lasted an even
shorter period of time, from 1979 to 1983. In both cases, civilian rule was
ended by a military coup. Civilian rule was restored and a Third Republic established in what became a chaotic election held in 1993, but within less than
a year, the military took power once again. Then in 1999, after intense national
and international pressure on the military government and the unexpected
death of the military dictator, a new elected government came to power.

Throughout these tumultuous years and changes in government, Nigerian politicians and political parties have actively competed for office and for
the economic spoils that government office makes possible. Parties have
changed frequently, as have the rules for party participation and elections.
In each case, the changes were efforts to address the failures of previous civilian governments and party politics.

Each time civilian rule was restored, it was with the hope that competent
and honest political leaders could overcome the corruption and misrule of
previous governments, be they civilian or military. As already discussed, the
preference for effective, stable, democratic governance is firmly rooted in
Nigeria's political culture, despite the country's failure to achieve this lofty
goal. A major reason for the failure of civilian governments is that the regional structure of society and resulting patterns of competition for power
based on ethnicity, region, and religion have created a political process that
is not only corrupt and inefficient but also a threat to the unity of the country. Poor governance results in the failure of the state to provide economic
development and a better life for most of Nigeria's people. Poverty, hope-
lessness, and frustration in turn provide fuel for ethnic, regional, and sometimes religious tensions, which the politicians exploit for political purposes.

This chapter will look at party politics and governance in the First and
Second Republics to understand the ethnoregional dynamics at work in the

competition for and use of power. The topics discussed will be party politics in the First and Second Republics, the aborted return to democracy in 1993, and the restoration of civilian government in 1999 under President Olusegun Obasanjo. Perhaps the major lesson to be learned from the following discussion is that party politics in Nigeria cannot be understood as simply a contest among ethnoregional political parties for support among their corresponding ethnoregional voters. The situation is much more complex than this. It is true that parties do tend to be dominated by certain ethnic groups; however, politicians from particular ethnic groups frequently enter into alliances with politicians and parties of other ethnic groups; they also switch alliances. In addition, there is conflict and competition within political parties among members of the same ethnoregional affiliation. Furthermore, identities such as class can complicate ethnoregional political allegiances. Such identities can result in more than one ethnically based party in the same region competing for the same ethnic supporters. These complexities will also be evident in chapter 11's discussion of the April 2003 presidential elections.

The First Republic (1960–1966)

Before Nigeria's independence in 1960, there were three major parties contending for power. These parties were the National Congress of Nigeria and the Cameroons (the NCNC, led by Nnamdi Azikiwe or "Zik"), the Action Group (AG, led by Obafemi Awolowo), and the Northern People's Congress (NPC, led by Ahmadu Bello). The NCNC, the AG, and the NPC came to be associated primarily with the east and the Igbo, the west and the Yoruba, and the north and the Hausa-Fulani, respectively. None of the parties succeeded in being national in appeal, and the politicians running for office under a party label usually were unknown and had little or no support outside their local region. In fact, most of the politicians had little mass appeal at all. The politically active population included mainly the educated middle class, business interests, better-off farmers, and labor union brokers. To gain sufficient mass support to win elections, politicians appealed to the local and regional issues, interests, and identities that were most real to ordinary people.

It is important to remember that, under the colonial system, Nigeria had never been ruled as one integrated unit but as three separate regions. Other than the desire to be free of colonial rule, no other interests or identities had much salience. Even the nationalist quest for independence and a unified country was not shared universally. Northern leaders in the 1950s at first opposed independence, and all three regions had considered becoming independent nations. It was the British who brokered the deal that created a unified Nigeria. Once the federal structure of the new government was agreed upon in the constitution, the country was set for intense party competition along regional lines as control of the new central government in Lagos became crucial. Controlling political office at the center was the main way to acquire public resources and gain from deals with foreign firms. Also, whichever region gained control of the federal government, leaders of that region would be in a position to dominate other regions and rival political parties.

Why was controlling the government so important? The colonial system had kept most of the economic power and wealth in the hands of the British and a few other foreign businesspeople. The African middle class and working class were quite small, and the large majority of the population was poor peasant farmers. Most of the African nationalists came from the middle class of professionals and civil servants. With the modern economy at independence still dominated by Europeans, ambitious Africans found that it was through political power that they could best hope to advance themselves. Moreover, the new African government, not the private sector, was expected to play the leading role in developing the country; therefore, even African entrepreneurs found that access to government was the main way to get loans, licenses, contracts, or other business opportunities.

Party politics was not a simple division along ethnic, regional, or religious lines. Given the way Nigeria's regions were defined, the north would have as many people as the two regions of the south combined. The east was the smallest of the three groups. Each region had somewhat different interests, as defined by the leaders of the dominant ethnic group in each region. As the smallest of the Big Three ethnic groups, the Igbo needed alliances with other ethnic groups to maximize their chances for some political offices at the center. As the second largest ethnic group, the Yoruba were also unable to win control of the center by themselves. It would seem logical for the Yoruba-dominated AG party and the Igbo-dominated NCNC to work together to balance the power of the north. This would seem particularly advantageous in light of the fact that the NPC quite obviously intended to win control of the federal government.

In the late 1940s, most of the Yoruba did support the NCNC. The NCNC also had support from some minority parties in the north. The NCNC lost much of its Yoruba support, however, when it advocated the creation of new regions to give more power to minority ethnic groups and to increase the influence of the east against the larger west and north. Many Yoruba did not want to see the west divided and Yoruba influence diluted, so they left the NCNC and started the AG. Not all of the Yoruba abandoned the NCNC, however. Ibadan, the major Yoruba city outside of Lagos, continued to back the NCNC due to the effective patronage system established by the NCNC's local leader. The loss of most of its Yoruba support left the NCNC as mainly an Igbo party. The southern parties were now competing with each other rather than uniting against the dominant north.

The north was not entirely united either, another piece of a complicated political picture. The NPC represented the interests of the traditional northern elite. Over the years of colonial rule, a small class of younger, Western-educated and reform-minded northerners had developed. They were alarmed by the backwardness of the north and blamed it on the feudal emirate political and economic structure that was perpetuated at independence. In response to such concerns, the Northern Elements Progressive Union (NEPU) was formed to challenge the NPC. NEPU was the most radical of all of Nigeria's political parties. It focused on programs and class interests that appealed to many in the north who were discontented with the emirate system. Among the discontented were many poor and exploited peasants. Also attracted to NEPU were Muslim groups hostile to the NPC and non-Muslims in the Middle Belt, who resented Muslim domination in their region. NEPU advocated eliminating the feudal aristocratic privileges of the emirs and other notables and addressing the problem of widespread poverty in the north. The leader of the party was Aminu Kano, who wanted to see political power in the hands of the common people rather than the wealthy minority. NEPU proved to be so popular in the north that the NPC was forced to begin to modernize itself and its program in order to curtail NEPU's growing influence.

There were other minority parties besides NEPU. Most of these parties represented mainly the Middle Belt but also minority northern interests. These minor parties were UMBC (United Middle Belt Congress); UNIP (United Nigerian Independent Party); BYM (Borno Youth Movement); KPP (Kano People's Party); and MDP (Midwest Democratic Front).

Although none of these parties could hope to win at the regional or national level, they did provide a source of alliance for the three major national parties to enable them to extend their support outside their regions. The NPC, for instance, allied with the MDP to gain support in the midwest. The AG linked up with the UMBC. Although their total support in the elections was less than 15 percent, the alliances small parties made with the major parties gained them some patronage jobs, such as appointments to boards and parastatals (state-owned enterprises).

By the time the federal elections were held in 1959, the political parties were using blatant appeals to ethnic and regional prejudice to win votes at the expense of meaningful discussion of party programs. Violence and harassment against opponents and their supporters were commonplace. The NPC won the most votes in the national elections. It now dominated the center by having the most seats in the national legislature; it also controlled the north. In accordance with a prior agreement made by the south to get the north to join with a united Nigeria, a northerner, Abubakar Tafawa Balewa, was selected to be the new prime minister. This was the beginning of a pattern of almost every head of state in Nigeria being a northerner, which in turn justified southerners' complaints about "northern dominance."

The NCNC, rather than allying itself with the AG, decided to form a coalition government with the NPC instead. One explanation for this decision is that the NCNC wanted to bridge the north-south divide in the interests of promoting national unity. Both the NPC and the NCNC also resented the AG for competing for votes in their regions in order to get minority ethnic group support. Still another explanation for the NCNC-NPC alliance is that the NCNC thought it had a better chance of benefiting from political patronage if it allied itself with the party in power.

In the early years of civilian rule, the pattern was set for politicians and parties to jockey for power and for the spoils of office as their major concern. Parties used every means to keep their rivals from office, and almost every party, north and south, wanted to contain overbearing NPC dominance. The NCNC found it had struck a poor bargain and had gained little from its alliance with the NPC, whereas the NPC had managed to neutralize both the Igbo and the Yoruba parties. These party rivalries required financial resources in order for the parties to engage effectively in patron-client relationships with other politicians, party supporters, and clients for government resources and services. Politicians and parties became increasingly mired in corruption, including bribery by foreign firms hoping to do business in Nigeria. For example, politicians and their business allies became sole distributors, shareholders, and representatives for their foreign business patrons. The state became the arena for intraclass conflict among Nigeria's elite, who used the guise of promoting ethnic and regional interests to advance what were primarily their own personal ambitions. In reality, the interests of the peasants and other ordinary Nigerians in achieving a better life were mostly neglected.

The patron-client system that mainly benefited the elite led ordinary people and communities to identify with and support ethnoregional parties and politicians if they hoped to get a share of public resources for schools, health clinics, and factories. It became a "zero-sum game," in which gains for one community were at the expense of outsiders from other parties or regions. If a community's party or politicians (that is, its patrons) lost power, the community would lose out to communities whose party and politicians won the election; government benefits would dry up for the losers but be lavished on the winners. With the stakes so high, political conflict among and within the parties intensified; it increased among regions, subregions, and communities as well.

In 1962, internal rivalries within the Yoruba party, the AG, led to a split between the faction backing Awolowo and a rival faction backing S. L. Akintola. Akintola was the premier of the western region. He succeeded Awolowo in this position after Awolowo made an unsuccessful attempt to become the elected prime minister of the federal government. Akintola favored the AG being a Yoruba regional party, and he disagreed with Awolowo's democratic socialist politics. When the party split, Akintola entered into an alliance with the north and effectively divided the Yoruba politically. This further strengthened the NPC's grip on power. The NPC also used the AG split to gain political inroads into the western region through an alliance with the minority Nigerian National Democratic Party (NNDP). When Awolowo tried to unseat Akintola, he was arrested and imprisoned for treason.

Akintola renamed his wing of the AG the United People's Party (UPP). To form a majority in the western regional government, the UPP joined the Igbo-dominated NCNC. The NCNC now had control of the east and the midwest. It was also part of the coalition government in the west. This UPP-NCNC alliance worried the NPC. They feared that a unified south would create a north-south split that could undermine the NPC's chances of maintaining control of the federal government in the upcoming 1964 national elections. The NPC managed to break up the coalition. They convinced Akintola to form a new party, the Nigerian National Democratic Party (NNDP), and the UPP-NCNC coalition was dissolved. The NCNC cabinet members were told to join the new party or give up their posts. Some NCNC members caved in and joined the NNDP. This gave Akintola's new party a majority and cut off the NCNC from power in the west.

The power of the NPC was exerted in other ways in addition to the party split. The NPC got Akintola's government in the west to approve the controversial 1963 census that maintained the north's population majority and thus electoral superiority over the south. The midwest also was coerced into approving the census or face losing its federal aid. The NCNC, which had led the effort to block ratification of the census results, was outmaneuvered. After that, opposition to the census dwindled.

By the time the 1964 elections were to take place, the economic and political situation was deteriorating. Worsening economic inequality led to increasing labor unrest. A general strike in June 1964 brought the country to a virtual standstill for thirteen days. Huge disparities in wealth and wages were more galling by being accompanied by massive corruption and conspicuous consumption on the part of the elite. The economic polarization was accompanied by political polarization. The multiple parties of the first election had now been consolidated into two coalitions of parties. One coalition was the UPGA (United Progressive Grand Alliance). The UPGA was composed of the NCNC, AG, NEPU, and UMBC. This made the UPGA a multiregional group with parties from every major region of the country. The other group of parties was the NNA (Nigerian National Alliance), which included the NPC, the NNDP, and some other minor southern parties. The NNA was clearly dominated by the NPC. Ideologically, the UPGA was progressive and nonregional. The NNA was conservative and regional.

In the 1964 national elections, competition was so intense that abuses were rampant. Dirty tricks, intimidation, the use of thugs, violence, and bribery of electoral officers were standard practices on both sides of the political divide. In the west, campaign abuses were so bad that 30 percent of Akintola's NNDP candidates were unopposed, despite the fact that the party was unpopular. In the north, 88 percent of the 174 NPC candidates were unopposed for the same reason. Abuses by the NCNC in the east occurred as well. Instead of ensuring fair and free elections by clamping down on such party excesses, the Federal Election Commission largely ignored them. Without any official means to check abuses and ensure the security of candidates, voters, and others involved in the electoral process, abuses spiraled out of control.

In such a dubious environment for fair elections, the NNA "won" in a huge landslide. Initially, Azikiwe, who was president of Nigeria, refused to validate the results. He called on Prime Minister Balewa to form a new government. Under pressure and with the promise of a political deal, Azikiwe finally agreed to accept the election results. The deal was that the new government would include broad-based representation from both coalitions. Political expediency resulted in unconstitutional practices at all levels of government. The result was to further undermine the credibility of the politicians in the eyes of the people.

Conditions further deteriorated in the west in the 1965 regional elections. Despite its general unpopularity, Akintola's party was the ruling party in the region. To win the 1965 elections, the NNDP resorted to massive fraud and coercion. The popular outrage that followed culminated in mass protests and an explosion of violence. Discontent with the politicians and the government was magnified by the weakness of the economy. Salaries were not paid regularly, and, to raise revenues, the government lowered prices paid to cocoa farmers by nearly half. Violence in the rural areas and cities became widespread, and the government proved unable to respond effectively to the crisis.

It was in this climate of government misrule, a discredited political party system, economic inequality and decline, and public protest and disorder that the military stepped into the picture. In 1966, Nigeria's first military coup took place. As discussed in chapter 6, Akintola, Balewa, and Bello, among others, were killed. Civilian rule had become so disreputable in the eyes of the public that the coup and the end of democracy was widely welcomed. During the following year of political turmoil, the unity of the country was at stake. Secessionist sentiments were growing in all three regions of the country. In the east, secessionism culminated in a declaration of independence in 1967 for a new country, Biafra. Firmly under control of the military, Nigeria would not see a return to multiparty democracy until 1979.

Many scholars have analyzed what went wrong in the First Republic. How could things have turned out so badly after the hard-won battle for freedom and democracy? The major problems can be summarized as follows:

- At independence and beyond, Nigeria lacked national unity and a commitment to nationally shared values that could supercede loyalties to regions and ethnic groups that had been created, for the most part, during the colonial period.
- Ethnic fragmentation and regionalism, much of it created by British colonial policies and the constitutional framework of the country, made it difficult for groups to work together. As a result, Nigeria's economic underdevelopment and heavy reliance on control of the state for economic advancement made politics a "winner takes all" game. The losers were left with nothing unless they could ally themselves with the winners.
- The goal of politics was not to serve the public or the national interest but to gain control of public resources for private gain. In the arena of political competition, ethnic rivalry and grievances were manufactured or exploited by politicians.
- With no fair and impartial institutions to manage competition and settle grievances, conflict and violence resulted.
- Oriented toward controlling power for personal gain and to support ethnoregional patron-client relationships, the government was unable to effectively overhaul the colonial and neocolonial structures of society

that kept Nigeria underdeveloped and poor. Without a developmentalist agenda, Nigeria would continue to be rent by ethnoregional and religious strife.

The Second Republic (1979–1983)

Nigerians did learn valuable lessens from the failure of the First Republic and from the near breakup of the country in the civil war over Biafra. First, it became evident to all that the regional system was a major problem linked with much of the ethnoregional turmoil in the country. Something had to be done to give more power to minority ethnic groups and to divide the Big Three ethnic groups. It was hoped that creating new states would prevent the dominance of any of the Big Three and encourage political alliances among eth-

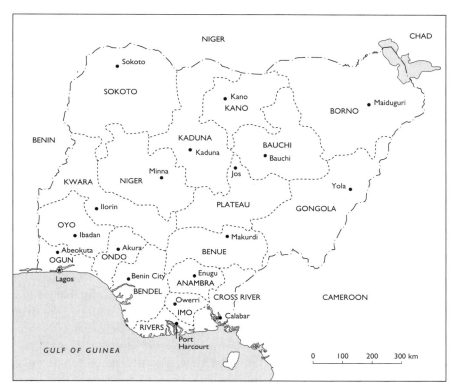

Map 7.1
Nigeria's Nineteen States, 1976–1991

nic groups if they hoped to win in national elections. In 1963, a new state, the midwest region, had been created from the western region, but this had been insufficient to quell ethnoregional discontents. During the civil war, the number of states was increased to twelve, but the clamor for additional states continued.

In 1976, the number of states was increased to nineteen. There were now several new minority states. The major Yoruba state was split into three states, and the major Igbo state was divided into two states. There were now four predominantly Hausa-Fulani states, four Yoruba states, and two Igbo states.

There were numerous other reforms designed to further promote a more balanced ethnoregional political system. Among the reforms, the new 1978 constitution prohibited ethnic political parties. All parties had to demonstrate that they had broad ethnic representation among their supporters and candidates. The structure of government also was changed to an American-style presidential system, replacing the British-style parliamentary system. The president, rather than a prime minister, was head of state, and he appointed his cabinet. The president had to demonstrate that he had broad national support to be elected. He had to have at least 25 percent of the vote in at least two-thirds of the states. Other changes were the creation of a new National Assembly (a bicameral legislature), an independent judiciary, and a Supreme Court. Human rights protections and a Code of Conduct for Public Officers (with a bureau and tribunal to enforce it) were also included in the constitution. The public was encouraged to participate in developing the new constitution, which inspired public optimism and gave the constitution and new political system widespread legitimacy. Finally, a new federal election system, the Federal Election Commission (FEDECO), was set up to certify parties and regulate and monitor campaigns. Other moves to defuse ethnoregionalism and also religion in politics included asking traditional chiefs and religious leaders to remain nonpartisan. Furthermore, ethnic, religious, and cultural groups (such as ethnic associations) were not allowed to contribute money to political parties.

There were some inherent problems with the new reforms that would prove to undermine them, despite the good intentions behind them. For one, the new constitution sought to reflect Nigeria's "federal character" by ensuring that the composition of government at every level (local, state, national) reflected the ethnic makeup of the locale it controlled. At the national level, at least one minister in the cabinet had to come from each of the states. There could be no centralization of personnel from any one ethnic group or region. One problem with this quota system was that in many local governments, candidates had to be "indigenes" (that is, regarded as locals). This could often exclude minorities ("strangers")—Nigerian citizens that had moved to an area other than the area of their birth—regardless of how long they had lived in the area. This resulted in many Nigerians being treated as alien elements rather than as equal and welcome members of their adopted communities. Such treatment also lessened migrants' sense of identity with the community and people where they resided. Instead, ties with the migrants' ethnic hometown and regional ties were reinforced, because it was only "back home" that they were fully accepted. However, there were exceptions to this pattern of ethnic discrimination. Since the 1950s, seats in the Ibadan city council were open to any resident. Hausas, Ijebus, Edo, and Igbo, among others, had all been elected regardless of their place of origin.

The emphasis placed on federal character and the delicate ethnic balancing in access to government offices and resources often had the opposite effect than what was intended. It heightened the salience of ethnicity and region and led to new tensions based on perceptions of fairness or discrimination. The importance of ethnicity was also strengthened because identification with an ethnic group and geographic area became essential for political participation and rights to resources.

Another problem emerged during the first elections for the presidency. Recall that the president had to have 25 percent of the vote in two-thirds of the states. Here was the problem: two-thirds of nineteen is not an even number. What if the presidential candidate with the most votes got the required percentage of votes in only twelve states? Would there have to be new elections until an additional state was won by 25 percent of the vote? Or should some other formula be used to ascertain a winner? This dilemma was, in fact, what happened. The resolution of the problem had a lasting and negative impact.

Before discussing the results of the presidential elections, this chapter will look at what happened overall in the first elections. When the decision was made by the military to return the country to a civilian government, the political parties from the First Republic were either defunct or unprepared to compete in new elections. Parties were not given enough time to organize or to expand their constituencies outside of their old ethnic and regional bases. Several new, innovative parties were in the process of organizing, but few of them were able to organize sufficiently to meet the deadline in 1978 for filing or to get certified by FEDECO. Of fifty emerging parties, only five became eligible to run for the elections. Four of these parties were mostly copies of the parties in the First Republic with the same old politicians in charge: UPN (Unity Party of Nigeria), led by Awolowo; NPN (National Party of Nigeria), led by Shehu Shagari, a leader in the old NPC; NPP (Nigerian People's Party), headed by Azikiwe, leader of the old NCNC; and PRP (People's Redemption Party), under Aminu Kano, the founder of NEPU. The only really new party was the GNPP (Great Nigerian People's Party) under the leadership of Azeri Ibrahim; the GNPP had split from the NPP.

The new parties were broader-based than parties had been before. The NPN, the largest party, was in fact Nigeria's first genuinely national party. Although its base was the aristocratic and technocratic northern Muslim elites, there were significant numbers of Yoruba, Igbo, and minority political and economic elites in the NPN. The party even had good support from the Christian areas of the Middle Belt. The NPN had managed to garner this impressive interethnic membership by agreeing to rotate political offices by region. Most of the GNPP support came from the Muslim north and minority areas of the southeast. It campaigned on a platform of promoting national unity and integration of the country as a secular state. The UPN and PRP were the least parochial in their ideology, but their actual support was more regional. Awolowo had tried to recruit more politicians from the north but failed, leaving his party with mainly western support. The PRP remained largely a party of more radical northern reformists.

All in all, there were few new parties or politicians with new ideas. The political field was mainly open to affluent, self-employed career politicians. New elements, such as students, academics, labor union members, or civil servants, were largely excluded. The parties were, for the most part, dominated by politicians from the First Republic. In the end, with little time to develop new messages and approaches to campaigning, they resorted to the old familiar appeals to ethnoregionalism and religion.

Although the elections were considered relatively honest, all of the parties complained of fraud and victimization in the areas they lost. The biggest controversy was over the presidential elections. Shagari, of the NPN, won a majority of the votes; Awolowo, of the UPN, was second. The UPN challenged Shagari's victory because he had won 25 percent of the votes in only twelve states rather than in two-thirds of the states as the constitution required. The electoral commission eventually ratified Shagari's victory under what many of Awolowo's backers considered to be dirty, behind-the-scenes politicking by the NPN. The commission's logic in favor of Shagari was that, in addition to the twelve states he could claim, he had won two-thirds of 25 percent of the vote in a thirteenth state. Shagari's tainted victory created much antagonism between the UPN and NPN, and, even now, many Yoruba are convinced that the northern politicians had over successive elections worked to rob Awolowo of his rightful place as Nigeria's head of state.

So disgruntled were the opposition parties over the election results that the nine elected governors from the UPN, GNPP, and PRP began meeting in 1979 to plan their opposition to the NPN. They called themselves the "nine progressive governors." The NPN was able to undercut this opposition by using patronage to get the unofficial support of some NPP, GNPP, and PRP federal legislators. The PNP also began making political inroads in both Yoruba and Igbo states; even Azikiwe allied himself with the northern politicians in hopes of gaining rewards for his Igbo compatriots.

In the north as well, cleavages were developing that indicated that competing class interests, not just communal ties, were influencing political loyalties. For example, the conservative NPN found itself sharing power with Aminu Kano's reformist PRP. The PRP had managed to carry both Kano and Kaduna in the 1979 elections. PRP election victories indicated growing class conflict in the cities of the north. In 1980 to 1981, however, factionalism caused a split in the PRP. The more radical wing was supported by many young people, intellectuals, and some legislative representatives. The PRP radicals came into conflict with the dominant NPN in Kaduna State when PRP governor Altai Abdulkadir Musa and his young, idealistic backers sought to mobilize the peasants to overthrow the traditional system of class privilege in the north. Despite opposition from the NPN-dominated legislature, Musa managed to institute new socialist policies, abolish exploitative taxes, investigate questionable land transactions that had cost peasants their holdings, and establish a mass literacy program. In the end, Musa was impeached and removed from office in June 1981. In July 1981, violence erupted in Kano State; many government buildings were burned down, and the governor was killed. The riot apparently was organized by NPN supporters, who were determined to undermine the radical PRP agenda for change.

Adding to the new political complexities, ethnic minority states had gained influence as swing states in federal elections, and parties had to compete hard for their votes by appealing to their economic interests rather than to their parochial ties. Oil in particular became a new focal point for political divisions and alliances among the states. The southern states, where most of the oil was located, found themselves joining together over the distribution of oil revenues in opposition to the nonoil states that depended on a share of oil revenues for their state budgets.

In general, the northern-dominated NPN government did little to address the nation's problems, such as poverty, the decline in oil revenues, increased dependence on food imports, and overall economic instability. Corruption had become a massive problem due to the fact that oil had provided the government with a huge source of revenue to exploit for patronage purposes. In order to gain or keep power at both the federal and state level, all of the parties resorted to human rights violations, harassment of political opponents by thugs, electoral abuse by politicians in concert with corrupt judges and police, and violence as standard weapons in their political arsenals. Corruption was not only rampant, but it usually went unpunished. Political cronies were given government licenses and contracts, and real entrepreneurs got little support. The cronies then sold their licenses to importers, who added the cost to the price of goods to consumers. Commodities and foodstuffs, such as milk and rice, were hoarded by speculators in order to drive up the price. Party men were given construction contracts at inflated costs. They then produced shoddy, substandard work or sometimes failed to do the job at all. Politicians demanded or took kickbacks and bribes, a percent of which was deposited in party coffers.

There were numerous outrageous cases of corruption that came to light over the years. In 1983, in one such case, the minister of finance had "mishandled" $2.5 billion in import licenses. In another case, legislators had accepted bribes from a Swiss firm. A state governor tried to smuggle millions of naira (the Nigerian currency) into Great Britain, and another official cost the country almost $1 billion in a payroll fraud case. The list of improprieties was virtually endless and robbed the politicians of any legitimacy they might have had in the eyes of the public. Added to this, politicians also tried to maintain or gain support by providing resources, such as development projects and money, to their home areas. It is important in Nigeria's patron-client system to cultivate the support of people back home, who are a core part of politicians political support, by showering them with contracts, jobs, and university positions. This was one area in which ethnicity and religion remained potent sources of identity. The results are similar to what Americans would call "pork barrel" spending, that is, wasteful spending on projects or activities that benefit a politician's constituents.

With so much at stake in elections, losing became an intolerable tragedy. It meant economic failure, not just political defeat from which one could recover or move on from into other endeavors. For one thing, if one backed a losing candidate, one could face retaliation from the victor and his party. For example, a farmer might be denied access to fertilizer, or a businessman could be turned down for a loan or a license. Consequently, to maintain its hold on power, electoral fraud on the part of the party in power, the NPN, was especially widespread and flagrant. NPN electoral abuses were so effective, however, that they enabled the party to win elections even in areas controlled by rival parties. Unfortunately, NPN tactics led to violence in some areas, such as Ondo State, which was a stronghold of Awolowo's UPN, and most of the electorate came to view the entire political process as a sham and a farce.

The impact of fraud, corruption, and mismanagement of the nation's financial resources were compounded by the country's declining economic fortunes. Oil prices had fallen in the 1980s, which led to a decline in government revenues, which were based mainly on the sale of oil. Nigeria's earnings from oil declined from $24 billion to only $10 billion between 1980 and 1983. The country faced a skyrocketing national debt and a depression simultaneously. The public was faced with growing shortages, rising prices, growing unemployment, unpaid teachers and civil servants, and labor unrest. At every level of government, evidence of government failure to fulfill its obligations was palpable. School and hospital construction was left unfinished, roads were unmaintained and full of potholes, public equipment was abandoned and forgotten, and badly needed wells for safe drinking water remained undrilled.

The 1983 elections were the last straw. Rather than uniting against the NPN, the major opposition parties, Azikiwe's NPP and Awolowo's UPN, opted to compete with each other for the presidency, which would virtually ensure Shagari's return to power. Both parties, however, did campaign against NPN corruption and got widespread support from disgusted voters around the country, even in the northern states. Given the NPN's sorry record, most people expected serious election losses for NPN politicians. Imagine their astonishment when the NPN won by a landslide! The NPN stole the election through massive and systematic fraud, including acquiring ballots and marking them in advance, bribing electoral officials, and using chicanery to disenfranchise entire communities. Not only did Shagari win easily against Azikiwe and Awolowo, the NPN also managed to increase its control over state governorships from seven to thirteen (of nineteen) states. Even governors known for being the most corrupt were reelected. The NPN also increased its numbers in the National Assembly from a slight majority to more than two-thirds. Incredibly, the courts upheld almost all of the challenged elections, despite obvious "irregularities."

Much of the population was outraged at the NPN's theft of the elections. Demonstrations broke out in several areas of the country as citizens voiced their frustration. In the Yoruba states, where electoral fraud was the worst, some protests became violent. More than 100 people were killed, and more than $100 million in property was destroyed. Feeling pushed to the limit, the military stepped in and staged a coup on December 31, 1983. A bogus "democratic government" once again had fallen, a victim of the excesses and abuses of its leaders. And once again, a disillusioned Nigerian public welcomed its demise.

In comparing the First and Second Republics, one can see some important similarities as well as differences. Ethnoregionalism continued to characterize much of the dynamics of the political process, but class cleavages and ideology appear to have played a greater role in the Second Republic. Also, by changing the structure of states and the rules (via the constitution), parties were forced to become less parochial and to seek crosscutting ethnic and regional alliances. However, ethnic and regional appeals and mobilization remained a major force, if no longer the only force at work. Some skeptics note that parties crossed ethnic and regional lines not to promote national unity but to build alliances for the strategic purpose of gaining political office and stealing public resources. These alliances were, in other words, a truce among thieves to share the loot, although not in equal shares. The strongest still took the most, and the competition remained intense among the rest to get their share.

Intraclass rivalry among the elite is certainly crucial to understanding the political dynamics that led to the failure of the Second Republic, but ethnoregional identities and competition among the nonelite classes played a role as well. In the 1980s, common location, shared language and customs, and religion remained the primary bonds for most people. Support for ethnic associations and political parties identified with one's ethnoregional group were a logical extension of such identities. In a situation of economic scarcity, for example, when there were too few government jobs (the main source of employment), ethnic rivalries intensified, especially when access to many jobs had to reflect the "federal character" of the states. Ethnic quotas were a response to the competition for jobs and resources and ensured that in their own states, the dominant ethnic group would have preferential access and less competition from members of other ethnic groups. This arrangement had the unfortunate consequence, however, of leading to a proliferating demand for the creation of new ethnically based states. By concentrating ethnic groups within more ethnically homogeneous states, isolation from other ethnic groups resulted. This, in turn, necessitated policies that compelled political parties to build interethnic party coalitions.

The reliance on kin and ethnic group membership was only partially lessened by class-based identities. Workers in trade unions, for example, would work for class interests in times of economic duress and when wage issues were at stake. On most issues, though, family and ethnic group remained primary. Even within unions, ethnicity sometimes could be divisive, and social life at work often remained noticeably influenced by common ethnic group ties. Where residential segregation in wards and quarters existed, ethnic stereotyping, ignorance of other groups, and lack of interaction reinforced ethnic boundaries that could be exploited and inflamed by political demagogues.

The Aborted Third Republic (1993)

The period between 1983 and 1993 was marked by a string of corrupt and increasingly despotic military regimes. The government that directly preceded the 1993 return to democracy was headed by Major General Ibrahim Babangida. Babangida came to power in a military coup in 1985. The population's discontent with Babangida and military rule in general intensified as a deteriorating economy, mounting corruption and political scandal, crime, and religious and ethnoregional conflict discredited the regime.

Bending reluctantly to pressures to reestablish civilian rule, Babangida began a lengthy period of transition to democracy. In an effort to postpone losing power as long as possible, he repeatedly announced and then cancelled dates for elections. Finally, however, Babangida did implement a transition program for elections that took place in 1993. As part of the transition program, in 1987, Babangida created a committee to revise the 1979 constitution. The revised constitution, which was ratified in 1989, mandated a major overhaul of the structure of the political system. The presidential system of government from the 1979 constitution was extended to state and local governments. A major change in the constitution was a limit in the number of political parties to only two. The rationale was that a two-party system would minimize ethnoregional politics by compelling transethnic political coalitions in national elections. To avoid a north-south polarization in presidential elections, the provision of the 1979 constitution was retained that the winner had to have 25 percent of the vote in two-thirds of the states. This idea was extended to the states as well: governors now had to have 25 percent of the vote in two-thirds of the local government areas of their states. In 1991, the number of states was once again expanded from nineteen to thirty; a presidential winner now would have to win at least twenty states.

Modeled closely on the two-party system in the United States, Babangida's two-party system has provoked considerable commentary and controversy. To its critics, the whole thing was bizarre. Babangida personally created the two parties, named them, funded them, and wrote their party platforms. In summarizing their ideological positions, critiques have remarked that one

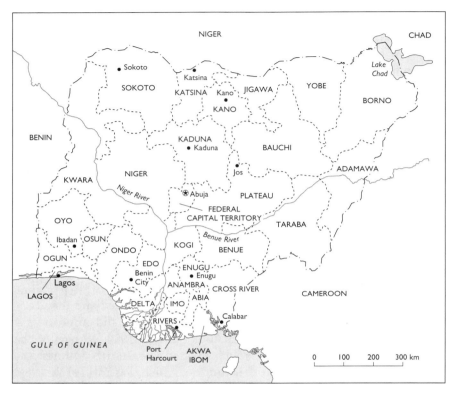

Map 7.2
Nigeria's Thirty States, 1991–1997

party was "a little to the left"; the other party was "a little to the right." The left of center party was the Social Democratic Party (SDP); the right of center party was the National Republican Convention (NRC). Completing his efforts to control the parties, Babangida retained the right to ban any politician from participating. To its architects and defenders, the two-party system, however artificial in its origins, was a beneficial reform. It made real progress in reducing the influence of ethnicity, region, and religion in politics and forced parties and politicians to broaden their appeals and constituencies. Defenders claim that another positive result was to shift some power from the north to the south.

It was hoped that the new party system would encourage not only new ethnoregional alignments but also new leaders who were untainted by the sordid history of the discredited, old-line politicians. This proved to be somewhat true, as new contenders for power had emerged. Some had gained fortunes in business in the 1970s and 1980s and now hoped to gain access to the economic spoils of government office. Retired generals, many of whom were now in business, were another group seeking access to even greater wealth through political careers in a new civilian government.

The established politicians were not to be sidelined easily. Many of these politicians had amassed a great deal of money and influence as well as extensive patronage networks. They managed to dominate the two parties. When the presidential nominees of each party were announced, it was familiar party stalwarts who were chosen. Moshood Abiola, a leading figure in the former dominant NPN party, was the SDP candidate. The NRC candidate was Bashir Tofa, also a former NPN man. The backgrounds of the two candidates reveal a great deal about power politics in Nigeria. For one, a north-south split in the elections was introduced. Abiola was a Yoruba from the south; Tofa was a Kanuri from the north. Tofa, however, was little known in the country, whereas Abiola was a prominent businessman highly regarded for his philanthropy in both the north and the south. As a result, Abiola had considerably more national appeal than Tofa. Both men were Muslims with close ties to the northern military elite. Abiola had the advantage of having close personal and business ties to Babangida.

It is tempting to draw the conclusion that Babangida and other powerful figures in Nigeria were orchestrating things to ensure that both presidential candidates would be acceptable to the military and would be no threat to their intentions to retain much of their power by working through the civilian government. It also seems that the cards were being stacked in favor of Abiola. Babangida may have wanted to consolidate his personal influence, if not control, over any new president. Abiola's candidacy and election would have the further advantage of muting the constant carping from the south, especially from the Yoruba, that the north was determined to control the presidency by preventing a southerner from being elected.

Many analysts believe that Babangida really wanted no candidate to win. He hoped that the election would produce a north-south split in the vote and disaffection of the south because both candidates were Muslims. Babangida, in fact, did work behind the scenes to stop the elections from taking place. These efforts failed, however, and the elections were held on June 12, 1993. Abiola won 58 percent of the vote in what is considered to be Nigeria's freest and fairest elections in its short history. Abiola even outpolled Tofa in his home state of Kano.

Before Nigeria's electoral commission could announce Abiola's victory, Babangida shocked the country when, by fiat, he annulled the elections on June 23. Apparently, the northern, military-dominated oligarchy had decided

Youths in Lagos hold newspapers headlining the June 1998 death of military leader Sani Abacha. (AP/World Wide Press)

that Abiola might be too independent once in office and a threat to their power and control over the country's oil revenues. Protests broke out across the country, especially in the southwest, and prodemocracy organizations were out in force to save Abiola's presidency. Southerners were convinced once again that the forces of "northern domination" had asserted themselves. Secessionist sentiments among the Yoruba began to spread along with demands for the creation of an "Oduduwa Republic."

Babangida helped to fan the flames of north-south and ethnic division to prevent the country from unifying against him. He charged, for example, that Abiola was a stooge for Yoruba interests. While working to discredit Abiola, Babangida also worked to divide the parties against each other and to weaken the SDP's loyalty to Abiola. He promised that new elections would take place, an obvious ploy to gain NRC support for a chance to reverse the original outcome of the elections. Another tactic of his was to use intimidation. For instance, Babangida threatened to abolish the two parties and other democratic institutions. Then, with the country in turmoil and fears of another military coup (this time against him) in his mind, Babangida pulled another surprise. In an about face, Babangida announced his resignation from the presidency on August 23, 1993. This did not result in Abiola gaining the position, however. Instead, Babangida installed an Interim National Government with innocuous Ernest Shonekan as its caretaker president. Shonekan was a southerner and a Yoruba from Abeokuta, as was Abiola. Babangida's substitute for Abiola failed to quell continuing public unrest, and the new government had little popular legitimacy.

Nigeria's High Court stepped in and declared the interim government illegal, but neither this decision nor ongoing prodemocracy activism was able to reverse the situation. What brought the Shonekan government down only a few months after its creation was a military coup by General Sani Abacha on November 23, 1993. Abacha abolished all of the elected national and state assemblies and sacked all of the states' elected executives.

Local councils and political parties were also abolished. Meanwhile, Abiola had gone into exile to seek international support for his presidency. By remaining out of the country, he was unable to help prodemocracy forces to maintain the momentum necessary for a restoration of democracy and his presidency. Abiola returned to Nigeria, and, in June 1994, declared himself Nigeria's president. Undaunted, Abacha had him arrested for treason on June 23. Abiola remained imprisoned until his death on July 7, 1998. With Abiola out of the way, Nigeria's latest military dictatorship under Abacha was firmly entrenched.

The Restoration of Democracy (1998–)

Between 1993 and 1998, Nigeria was ruled by the most corrupt and despotic regime in its history. Under Abacha's rule, the country's economy was a disaster, in part due to the enormity of corruption and mismanagement by military rulers in government office and by their cronies. Widespread ethnic, regional, and religious strife were worsening. Brutal government repression only exacerbated the growing contempt for the government and the violence that threatened to engulf the country. But even Abacha was eventually compelled by popular and international pressure to initiate a transition to democracy and a restoration of civilian government. From the beginning of his regime, Abacha had promised that his rule would be temporary and that his intentions were to restore democracy. He vowed to gather representatives from all of the country's major ethnic groups together to revise the constitution and discuss how to build a peaceful, unified nation. In 1994, a constitutional conference did meet and make minor changes to the constitution. In 1996, the ban on political parties was lifted. This led to the creation of five new political parties: the United Nigeria Congress Party, the Committee for National Consensus, the National Center Party of Nigeria, the Democratic Party of Nigeria, and the Grassroots Democratic Movement.

Showing his true contempt for democracy, Abacha denied registration to any parties with links to the imprisoned Abiola and excluded any other groups from participation that might be opposed to Abacha. Elections were scheduled to take place in 1996 and 1998, but the military declared itself to have the prerogative to disqualify any candidate it found to be unacceptable. With the political field so limited, the political parties that were allowed were assumed to be either pawns of Abacha or thoroughly cowed. Few people had any confidence in the political process or in the parties.

Any credibility the parties might have had evaporated when Abacha managed to get all five parties to nominate him as their presidential candidate. Although some intimidation may have been involved, bribery and the promise of lucrative opportunities in office apparently were sufficient to gain the cooperation of the parties.

In what some Nigerians regard as an act of providence, Abacha's grab for power came to naught. He died under "mysterious circumstances" on June 8, 1998, and his body was quickly cremated by senior military officers. Officially, he was the victim of a heart attack. Those who thought Abacha's death would result in freedom for Abiola and his assumption of the presidency had their hopes dashed. In an astonishing turn of events, Abiola died in prison (as noted above) on July 7, 1998; he suffered a heart attack while meeting with a U.S. delegation.

Abacha's successor, General Abdulsalami Abubakar, quickly moved to assure a shaken nation that he would oversee a genuine transition to democracy. The five parties established under Abacha were dissolved in July 1998, and new parties were allowed to form. A new electoral commission was established to register parties and manage the electoral process. Twenty-six parties applied for registration, and nine were approved.

Power sharing was a big concern, as many politicians hoped to avoid the pitfall of destructive ethnoregional and religious conflict that had doomed party politics and civilian governments before. Their call was for "true federalism" in which everyone would receive fair treatment and secure rights. Unfortunately, most of the politicians and candidates for office were mostly corrupt, and wealthy, politicians from previous governments or men who had acquired their wealth due to patronage from past governments. None of these people were likely to seriously attempt to clean up the system.

Three major parties emerged to compete for power: the People's Democratic Party (PDP), the Alliance for Democracy (AD), and the All People's Party (APP). The PDP had the broadest support. It developed from "G 34," a group of thirty-four eminent Nigerians from all over the country. Many of them were wealthy retired generals with large patronage networks. The northern elite in the PDP realized the need for a political "power shift" to the south in the presidential elections, but they wanted to make sure that a southern presidential nominee would be acceptable to the northern elite and not a threat to their dominance. The AD was mainly a southwestern, Yoruba party. It was most vocal in support of "true federalism," which would give more power to state and local governments. The AD also favored the allocation of government revenues (mostly from oil) on the basis of "derivation" (origin of the oil) and a power shift away from northern dominance. The AD was an offshoot of Afenifere, a pan-Yoruba group. The last major party, the APP, got most of its support from the north and some from the east. In December 1998, local government elections were held; the PDP was the overall winner. Then, in preparation for the presidential elections of 1999, the APP and AD formed an alliance to offer a single candidate to run against the PDP. They chose Olu Falae, a Yoruba and a southerner from the AD, as their presidential candidate and Alhaji Umaru Shinkafi, a northerner from the APP, as the vice-presidential candidate. The selection of Falae and Shinkafi split the APP. Many Igbo and others from the southeast left the APP and joined the PDP.

The PDP nomination was contested by two candidates: former military head of state, General Olusegun Obasanjo, a Yoruba, and Dr. Alex Ekwueme, an Igbo. Ekwueme had the support of the old NPN party of Shehu Shagari and had donated 2 million naira to the PDP. Obasanjo outdid Ekwueme with the help of allies among the retired northern generals after he gave the party 130 million naira. It has been alleged that money won the nomination for Obasanjo, but there may well have been other factors at work besides money in the selection of Obasanjo by the PDP. The northern elite had decided to back a southern candidate, but it had to be the "right" candidate. Although both presidential candidates would be Yoruba if Obasanjo were selected to run on the PDP ticket, Obasanjo's candidacy would not constitute a genuine power shift to the south. Obasanjo actually had little support among the Yoruba; he was more closely allied with the northern power elite. Obasanjo's candidacy was allegedly engineered in part by his ally Babangida, the former military dictator, because Babangida and many of the other northern elite saw Obasanjo as a southerner who would not challenge northern interests. Alex Ekwueme, on the other hand, was unacceptable, because he was seen as too close to the Igbo and their interests. Falae, the APP-AD candidate, was also unacceptable to the north. He was perceived as a Yoruba candidate the north could not count on to preserve their interests. Falae and Ekwueme were supported by Afenifere and Ohanaeze Ndigbo, the major pan-ethnic associations of the Yoruba and Igbo, respectively. Both groups represented their ethnic group's interests and supported greater regional autonomy, goals contrary to northerners' interests in maintaining control from the center. The North also figured that it could count on Igbo support without backing an Igbo presidential candidate, because many Igbo politicians were part of the northern military's patronage networks. Moreover, many of the Igbo resented the APP-AD for choosing the Falae-Shinkafi ticket while rejecting an Igbo candidate.

A question readers might have is why the northern elite were willing to support a southern president in 1999 but not in 1993, when Abiola was running. After all, Abiola was a southerner but also a Muslim with close ties with the northern elite. Apparently, Abiola was kept from office due to northern fears that he would be too independent as president. This was based in part on the fact that Abiola had widespread support in both the north and the south; therefore, he would not be dependent enough on northern support to defend mainly northern interests. To buttress this fear, there were unsubstantiated documents circulating in the north that suggested that Abiola's intentions as president were to reverse northern dominance. The southern candidates for the 1999 elections, especially Obasanjo, were not seen to be such a threat to the north.

The PDP won a landslide victory. Obasanjo got almost 63 percent of the vote and at least 25 percent of the vote in thirty-two of the thirty-six states. It is noteworthy that he got only 20 percent of the Yoruba vote. The four states Obasanjo failed to carry were Lagos, Ondo, Osun, and Oyo, all in his home region. The PDP had won strong majorities in both houses of the National Assembly as well as the presidency. As the northern elite anticipated, the Igbo turned out strongly for Obasanjo and the PDP. Despite Ohanaeze Ndigbo urging the Igbo to vote for the APP as a protest for the PDP's rejection of Ekwueme, Obasanjo won 76 percent of the vote in Ekwueme's home state, Anambra. All of the governors and National Assembly members selected in Igbo areas were PDP candidates.

In the return to democracy, the public had been hopeful that a genuine end to "ethnomilitary rule" by the northern traditional and military elite would occur. As Darren Kew observes, most people were "cautiously optimistic" to see "what sort of new arrangements the military would allow the civilian politicians to struggle over, and what in turn the civilians would offer the public." People saw the elections as "the military choosing to submit to a relatively open contest for power in which the [PDP] party of their civilian friends and former military officers could bring to bear the incredible resources they had amassed under years of military rule." One voter commented, "I think the powers-that-be have already chosen our leader for us" (Kew 1999, 29).

Despite international monitoring of the elections, observers concluded that there was massive fraud on the part of all parties. This included bribery of election officials, ballot stuffing, and gross manipulation of the voter rolls and reported voter turnout. Paid thugs assaulted and intimidated opposition candidates, ballot boxes were stolen, and votes were rigged. PDP abuses were worse than those of the APP or AD, because the PDP had more resources provided by their military backers. According to election monitors, in both the National Assembly and presidential elections, "massive corruption" oc-

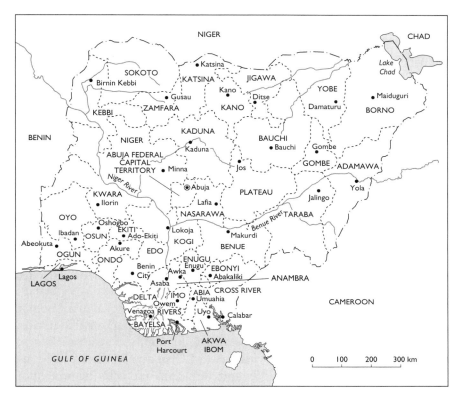

Map 7.3
Nigeria's Administrative States, 1996–Present

curred in one-third of the states; one-third were "comfortably corrupt"; and one-third were generally honest, mostly in the southwest and parts of the north where a dominant partly was largely unchallenged by rivals. Despite these abysmal statistics, most election monitors accepted the election results for fear that the military would use a repudiation of the elections as an excuse to stay in power. One of the election monitors was former U.S. president Jimmy Carter, and he was so disgusted by abuses during the election that he refused to endorse the results.

Obasanjo's election was seen by many as a victory for the northern-dominated military elite. The military bought Obasanjo's nomination by the PDP and, according to some observers, paid off APP delegates to determine the APP-AD candidate as well. They helped Obasanjo outspend Falae by four to one during the campaign. The National Assembly was dominated by PDP members. The military elite had a huge amount of money to oil their large patronage networks and to protect their interests. The 1999 constitution passed by the military still continues at present to give most of the power to the northern-dominated federal government.

Under the circumstances, there was widespread doubt that Obasanjo would have enough power to implement necessary political and economic reforms in the country, most of which were opposed by the north. Obasanjo came to power in a country suffering economic stagnation, dependence on oil revenues, infrastructure decay, a brain drain of many of its best educated citizens, corruption, fraud and mismanagement by the government, crime and gang violence, disaffection in the east and southwest, conflicts over oil revenues, ethnic and religious extremism and conflict, issues of power distribution between the federal government and state and local governments, and threats of secession or civil war. A crucial issue is how to consolidate democracy and curb military interference in politics to prevent another coup. It is hard to imagine how any president, even under the most favorable circumstances, could make a serious positive impact given the enormity of the problems at hand.

Obasanjo has tried to reassure the skeptics that he is his own man and not a pawn of the PDP and the north. Some of his actions indicate that he sees the parties, including the PDP, as obstacles to his ability to act as he sees fit. Nigerian professor Omo Omuruyi argues that Obasanjo has always had contempt for Nigerian political parties and politicians and is in the process of trying to divide and weaken them. Obasanjo was not a founding member of the PDP but was drafted by them to run for president. As early as May 1999, Obasanjo declared at a party convention at Jos that his intentions were to be independent of the party. After his election, Obasanjo proceeded to ally himself with certain powerful political loyalists in key government ministries. One objective has been to increase his weak support among the Yoruba. The late Minister of Justice and Attorney General Bola Ige and Minister of Internal Affairs Sunday Afolabi worked to put together a new pro-PDP, pan-Yoruba organization, the Yoruba Council of Elders, to support Obasanjo's re-election in 2003. Obasanjo has used patronage in the form of government offices to divide the PDP and lure party members from the APP and AD, thereby fragmenting and weakening the opposition. One example of these efforts is Bola Ige, mentioned above. Ige was a major leader of Afenifere, the pan-Yoruba group that had opposed Obasanjo in the elections, but then he became a major Obasanjo backer.

Obasanjo has been independent enough by spreading appointments and resources around the country that he has alienated some of his northern backers, including Abubakar Rimi, one of Kano State's most powerful political leaders. Rimi supported Obasanjo in 1998, but after being rejected for the vice-presidency and the foreign minister's position, Rimi is now a vocal critic. His sentiments are echoed by others in the North. "Obasanjo came to power," claims Rimi, "with a hidden agenda to exact vengeance on the North. He forgot that it is the North that chose him, invited him to run, supported him, campaigned and voted for him. But when he came to office he was against the North. It was unbelievable, unexplainable, and you can even call it treacherous" (Onishe 2001).

Conclusion

The record of democracy and party politics in Nigeria has not been impressive. The election process has been plagued repeatedly by fraud and violence, which results in little confidence on the part of the people that the winners are in any true sense the representatives of the people. Instead, history shows that parties and politicians are representing mostly themselves and powerful political patrons. The government under civilian leadership has become subordinate to a northern ethnomilitary elite that, by working through politicians and parties, maintains its control over the political system and government oil-based revenues. Their dominance allows the elite to enrich themselves and their cronies at the public's expense. The results are massive corruption, mismanagement, and economic underdevelopment and widespread poverty. Festering economic and political problems fuel ethnoregional and religious conflict, which is in turn exploited by the political class to win elections. When conditions deteriorate to such a point that the survival of the country is in question, the military takes over control of the government.

Currently, Nigeria is in its most recent phase of democratic civilian government after a long period of control of the government by the military. Democracy has survived elections in 1998 and 1999, and new elections were held in April and May 2003, in which Obasanjo and the PDP were victorious in the hotly contested elections. Although it is too early to tell the fate of the Obasanjo government in a second term, opposition claims of electoral fraud could undermine the government's ability to rule effectively. If political chaos threatens, another military coup is not out of the question, which could once again bring an end to democracy. These and other topics associated with the Obasanjo government and current politics will be discussed in chapter 11. The next chapter will turn attention to Nigeria's noncivilian rulers, the military, and will examine who its most powerful members are and how they are linked to the ethnoregional and religious dynamics of

Nigeria. Readers will see the impact of military rule on Nigeria and assess whether or not it has been an improvement on the civilian governments it has in the past chosen to replace.

Timeline

1960–1966	The First Republic, including the following parties: NCNC (National Congress of Nigeria and the Cameroons), AG (Action Group), NPC (Northern People's Congress), NEPU (Northern Elements Progressive Union), plus minor parties
1962	The AG splits between Akintola and Awolowo; Akintola forms the UPP (United People's Party)
1964	National elections are held, including the following two coalitions: UMBC (United Middle Belt Congress); UPGA (United Progressive Grand Alliance: NCNC, AG, NEPU); and NNA (Nigerian National Alliance: NPC, NNDP, etc.)
1966	A military coup ends civilian government
1967–1970	The Biafra civil war takes place
1979–1983	The Second Republic, including the following parties: UPN (United Party of Nigeria), NPN (National Party of Nigeria), NPP (Nigerian People's Party), PRP (People's Redemption Party), GNPP (Great Nigerian People's Party)
1983	National elections held; a military coup ends civilian government
1993	National elections are held and annulled by Babangida; an interim government is installed and overthrown in a military coup; active parties are SDP (Social Democratic Party) and NRC (National Republican Congress)
1994	General Sani Abacha declares himself president
1998	Abacha and Abiola die; General Abdulsalami Abubakar becomes the temporary head of state
1999	National elections are held; Olusegun Obasanjo is elected president; active parties are PDP (People's Democratic Party); AD (Alliance for Democracy); and APP (All People's Party)

Significant People, Places, and Events

ABUBAKAR, ABDULSALAMI General Abubakar began his career in the Air Force and then transferred to the army. After rising through the ranks, he became head of state for several months in 1998 until elections were held that returned Nigeria to civilian rule.

AFOLABI, SUNDAY Afolabi, a Yoruba, has had a long political career. During the Second Republic, he was a member of Awolowo's UPN. He served as deputy governor of Oyo State when Bola Ige was governor there. He later switched to the northern-dominated NPN party and served as the minister of education in the Shagari government. Afolabi was one of the few Yoruba politicians to back Obasanjo's bid for the presidency.

AKINTOLA, S. L. Akintola was a journalist and lawyer and an early member of the AG (Action Group). His disagreements with Awolowo led to a split in the party. He was premier of the western region when he was killed in the 1966 coup.

BABANGIDA, IBRAHIM Major General Babangida, a northerner from Niger State, joined the army after high school and rose quickly through the ranks. Since leaving the presidency in 1993, he has remained a powerful behind-the-scenes force in Nigerian politics.

BALEWA, ABUBAKAR TAFAWA Balewa was a teacher before becoming involved in politics. He was Nigeria's first prime minister and was killed in the 1966 military coup.

EKWUEME, ALEX Ekwueme was defeated for the PDP party presidential nomination by Obasanjo in the 1999 elections. Ekwueme informed party delegates of an alleged plot by Obasanjo to bribe the delegates with as much as 250,000 naira to vote for him. Ekwueme's supporters told the delegates to take the money as a "return of the loot from the moneybag politicians" but then to vote for Ekwueme as a vote for "freedom and democracy."

FALAE, OLU An economist, farmer, and former general, Falae has had a long political career. Notably, in the 1980s, his work on economic reform for the Babangida regime earned him the unflattering nickname "Mr. SAP," referring to the unpopular structural adjustment program imposed on Nigeria by the IMF.

IGE, BOLA A former governor of Oyo State, Ige was a key government minister in Obasanjo's government. In 2002, Ige was assassinated. His death may have been the result of political conflict among the Yoruba, most of whom opposed Obasanjo.

INTERNATIONAL MONITORING In the 1999 national elections, the United States Agency for International Development (USAID) spent $600,000 to train Nigerian government election officials and local monitors. Additional money was spent to provide international monitors from such organizations as the Carter Center, an organization founded by former

U.S. president Jimmy Carter to promote democracy and peace in the world, to observe the elections and vouch for their fairness. Most monitors accepted the results despite numerous reports of fraud and other irregularities.

KANO, AMINU Kano was a teacher before he established two northern political parties, NEPU (Northern Elements Progressive Union) and later the PRP (People's Redemption Party). Kano was a strong advocate for the poor and opposed the dominance of the north by conservative elites.

SHAGARI, SHEHU Shagari was a teacher before dedicating his career to politics. An early member of the NPC party, he held several prominent political offices before being elected president of Nigeria from 1979 to 1983 on the NPN ticket. Shagari remains a prominent member of the northern political class.

SHINKAFI, ALHAJI UMARU Shinkafi was the vice-presidential candidate of the APP-AD coalition in the 1999 presidential elections. He is a son-in-law of the late sardauna of Sokoto and politically is ultraconservative.

SHONEKAN, ERNEST Shonekan was a former chair of the United Africa Company, the former British trading company in the colonial period, before becoming head of the interim government created by Babangida to deny Moshood Abiola's election to the presidency in 1993.

TWO-PARTY SYSTEM In 1989, under Babangida, a two-party system was imposed. The new system was set up with the help of the Center for the Study of Democratic Institutions, renamed the Center for Democratic Studies (CDS). The party manifestos were drawn up by the Nigerian Political Science Association. The manifestos were never used by the parties, as these entities did not survive Babangida's time in office.

Bibliography

Aborisade, Oladimeji, and Robert J. Mundt. 1998. *Politics in Nigeria.* New York: Longman.

Diamond, Larry. 1990. "Nigeria: Pluralism, Statism, and the Struggle for Democracy." Pp. 351–409 in *Politics in Developing Countries: Comparing Experiences with Democracy.* Boulder, CO: Lynne Rienner.

Enemuo, Francis C. 1999. "Elite Solidarity, Communal Support, and the 1999 Presidential Election in Nigeria." *Issue: A Journal of Opinion* 27 (1): 3–11.

Falola, Toyin. 1999. *The History of Nigeria.* Westport, CT: Greenwood.

———. 2001. *Culture and Customs of Nigeria.* Westport, CT: Greenwood.

Kew, Darren. 1999. "Democracy-Dem Go Crazy-O: Monitoring the 1999 Nigerian Elections." *Issue: A Journal of Opinion* 27 (1): 29–33.

Lincoln, Joshua. 1999. "The 'Persistent' Federation: Nigeria and Its Federal Future." *Issue: A Journal of Opinion* 27 (1): 17–25.

Ojo-Ade, Femi. 2001. *Death of a Myth: Critical Essays on Nigeria.* Trenton, NJ: Africa World Press.

Olufemi, Kofa. 1999. "The Limits of Electoralism." *Issue: A Journal of Opinion* 27 (1): 8–11.

Omuruyi, Omo. 2001. "Parties and Politics in Nigeria." Presented at the November 2001 meeting of the African Studies Association in Boston, MA.

Onishe, Norimitsu. 2001. "Winds of Militant Islam Disrupt Fragile Frontiers." *New York Times,* 2 February. Available at http://query.nytimes.com/gst/abstract.html?res=F00E11F63F5A0C718CDDAB0894D9404482 (accessed June 20, 2002).

----------------------- CHAPTER EIGHT -----------------------

Ethnomilitary Rule

T

O UNDERSTAND THE FRAGILE STATE of ethnoregional and religious relationships in Nigeria requires an awareness of what happened in
Nigeria during the years of autocratic rule by the Nigerian military.
Indeed, the military has governed Nigeria during most of the postindependence period. Since the 1960s, the military changed from a professional organization with a mandate to defend the new nation, to an organization
whose main function has been to promote and protect the political and economic interests of a powerful group of officers. After the Igbo-led civil war,
most of these officers have been from the north, one factor in creating ethnoregional cleavages. Each time democratically elected governments have
been in power, they have been replaced by "ethnomilitary rule," that is, rule
by a largely northern, Hausa-Fulani military elite and their allies. Once in
power, military governments became corrupt, incompetent, and repressive.
Promoting their own interests foremost, they have exploited and worsened
ethnoregional and religious tensions and brought the country to the brink
of possible national disintegration. During the years of military rule, there
have been growing fears of ethnoregional and religious domination among
Nigeria's diverse communities, ethnic and religious strife, demands in the
south for "true federalism" (that is, more regional autonomy) and a "sovereign national conference" of ethnic communities to discuss the country's future, and even renewed appeals for secession and the creation of more ethnically and religiously homogeneous nations. Even after the return to civilian
rule in 1999, there remains a justifiable concern that another military coup
could occur and end Nigeria's latest effort at creating a viable democratic
government, with devastating consequences for national unity.

   This chapter will examine the role of the military in sowing the seeds of
ethnoregional and religious discord in the two periods of military rule. For
purposes of discussion in this chapter, the first period was from 1966 to 1979
and, after a period of civilian government, from 1983 to 1985. The second
period lasted from 1985 to 1998. Most of this discussion will center on the

Babangida and Abacha regimes, which ruled Nigeria from 1985 to 1998. This was not only the longest sustained period of military rule, but also the period when the most damage was done to Nigeria's economy, political system, and ethnoregional and religious group relationships. Notable in the first period of military rule was the northernization of the military and the rise of the ethnomilitary elite. The second period included the growing economic and political failures and corruption of the government and the associated deepening of ethnoregional and religious divisions, including intraclass and intrareligious conflict.

Period One of Military Rule (1966–1979 and 1983–1985)

The prelude to Nigeria's first military coup in 1966 is discussed in detail in chapter 5, but this discussion will summarize the key events. At that time, an Igbo-dominated military under General Ironsi staged a coup, which resulted in the deaths of high-ranking government and military leaders, many of whom were northerners. When Ironsi created a new government and reshuffled the military, many Igbo rose into newly created positions of power. Ironsi also announced a new constitution abolishing the federal system and creating a unitary government. Northerners particularly felt threatened by Ironsi's moves and saw them as a blatant attempt by the Igbo to take over the country. In a coup led by northern officers, Ironsi was overthrown and killed, along with many Igbo officers and troops.

A new head of state, Yakubu Gowon, was installed by the military. Gowon was a Christian from the Middle Belt of the northern region. Gowon restored the federal system and proposed a constitutional conference to consider reforms such as the creation of a stronger central government and more states. The Igbo in the east, under the rule of Ojukwu, refused to recognize the Gowon government and began to threaten secession. This threat came to fruition in 1967, when the independence of Biafra was declared. A civil war broke out in 1967, which ended in 1970. During the war, Gowon announced the creation of twelve states to replace the earlier system of four regions. The goal was to lessen the dominance of the Big Three ethnic groups and give more power to ethnic minorities.

In October 1970, Gowon announced a six-year transition back to democracy, after which time elections would be held and power returned to a civilian government. In this early period after Nigeria's independence, the military saw its governing role as temporary. The military had stepped in and ended civilian rule only to save the country from disintegration. Military officers were not yet motivated by the desire to stay in power in order to accumulate personal wealth. As good, professional soldiers, they were eager to return to the barracks once the country was stable enough for a new civilian government to retake control and to avoid the failures of the First Republic. In 1974, however, Gowon changed his mind and cancelled the date for new elections indefinitely. What had happened was that, once in control of the government, members of the new military-political elite discovered the access to riches that accompanied political office. The country's booming oil industry and the enormous revenues it generated made the temptation to stay in power irresistible to Gowon and his cronies. At this time, the military as a whole was still professional enough to reject Gowon's grab for power, and Gowon was overthrown in a bloodless coup in 1975.

Changes were in place, however, that would alter how the military saw its role. For one thing, the size of the military and military spending increased greatly after the civil war and the 1975 coup. During the civil war, defense spending was 43 percent of federal spending and remained 20 percent until 1971 through 1974. Oil revenues paid for much of the 1970s buildup, but it was still a big drain on the economy. Salaries, pensions, and arms spending went up sharply and, until the late 1970s, the size of the army had grown to between 200,000 and 300,000 troops. This laid the basis for the military to be a more formidable force within Nigerian society. Another change was the increase in cronyism and corruption that had grown during the Gowon years. In 1975, many retired military officers had no great wealth accumulated from their positions in government, which indicated a strong level of honesty and probity. On the other hand, by 1970, a network of military officers, civil servants, and multinational firms was emerging. This network was the beginning of the ethnomilitary, northern oligarchy. This oligarchy, dependent on and in collusion with foreign capital, has since come to politically dominate Nigeria and siphon off its wealth for its own enrichment.

The military government that replaced Gowon was headed by General Murtala Muhammed. Muhammed's rise is worth mentioning because it was indicative of early ethnoregional tensions in the military and in Nigerian society. Muhammed was from Kano and began his military career working closely with officers such as Aguiyi Ironsi, the Igbo leader of the first 1966 coup, and Ojukwu, the eventual military ruler of Biafra. However, in the tense period of the coup and the Ironsi government, Muhammed became a leader of the northern officers who overthrew and killed Ironsi in the second 1966 coup. The northern officers believed that the Igbo were biased against them and were preventing their advancement in the military. The northerners also came to believe that there was an Igbo conspiracy to launch

Abuja was constructed in central Nigeria during the 1980s and replaced Lagos as the capital of Nigeria in 1991. (Liz Gilbert/Corbis Sygma)

a second coup to completely eliminate northern officers from the military. Some even thought that the Igbo were planning to kill all northern males, both civilian and military. These fears led to the second coup. They were also a factor in the massacres against Igbo civilians living in the north at the time.

Initially, after the second coup, Muhammed urged the north to secede from Nigeria. This was opposed by Gowon and other Middle Belt officers, who feared Hausa-Fulani dominance in an independent northern nation. In the end, northern soldiers chose Gowon to become Nigeria's new head of state. After the civil war, Muhammed became a minister in Gowon's government but later led the coup that ousted Gowon. Among the leading participants in the coup were other northern officers including Shehu Yar'Adua, Ibrahim Babangida, and Muhammed Buhari, who were destined to become major figures in Nigeria's ethnomilitary elite. Their names recur in this and other chapters.

Muhammed was probably the only military ruler held in high esteem by most Nigerians. Personally incorruptible and at heart a professional soldier, he tried to implement policies that would restore a viable democracy and reform the military. He initiated a major purge of both the government and the armed forces. Commissions were set up to investigate scandals involving public officials and to make recommendations on the creation of additional new states. Five months later, seven new states were created, increasing the number from twelve to nineteen. The controversial movement of the capital from Lagos to a new city, Abuja, also was initiated by Muhammed. He planned to return the government to civilian rule on October 1, 1979. Unfortunately, his reform efforts were cut short on February 13, 1976. A failed military coup by disgruntled middle-ranking officers, who felt excluded from political power, resulted in his death.

The military officer who replaced Murtala Muhammed was Olusegun Obasanjo, Murtala Muhammed's deputy. Remarkably, Obasanjo initiated a transition to democracy and willingly handed over power in 1979 to his civilian successor, Shehu Shagari. Obasanjo is the only military head of state to leave office rather than be overthrown in a coup or die in office.

After 1983, a new generation of mostly northern military officers emerged to dominate the military and the political system. The process of "northernification" of the military began in the 1960s when the northern political elite began to push for a greater number of northern officers in the then southern-dominated officer corps. The purge of Igbo officers by northern officers in the second 1966 coup and the aftermath of the civil war furthered the process. Since Gowon came to power in 1966, every military head of state but Obasanjo has been a northerner. The connection between military misrule and northern rule has been close in the minds of many Nigerians, especially those in the south, and has been a major source of ethnoregional tension.

The army is not entirely a northern monopoly, though, to be sure. Other groups also are represented. In fact, many minority ethnic groups have found joining the military to be a major avenue for social mobility. One-half to two-thirds of all military personnel come from the Middle Belt and the south due to their higher levels of education and skills. Minorities have found that they have a better chance of holding important political offices by becoming army officers than by competing for office through election. Nonetheless, the presence of many different ethnic groups in the military, and in the officer corps especially, has not altered the fundamental dominance by northern officers in the higher ranks. By 1985, about 70 percent of senior officers were from the north or the Middle Belt, although most administrative, technical, and logistical jobs were held by southerners. Moreover, ambitious minority officers have had little incentive to challenge the system of northern dominance, because they depend on the northern elite who control the government to appoint them to government positions. At

Former president of Nigeria Shehu Shagari (William Campbell/Corbis Sygma)

the local and state levels, the reliance on "federal character" in appointments to offices (that is, appointments that reflect the ethnic makeup of an area) guaranteed Yoruba officers power in Yoruba areas, Tiv officers power in Tiv-dominated areas, etc. In this ethnically based spoils system, nonnorthern groups have been bought off as a means to maintain northern dominance at the key federal level of government.

After the 1983 coup that ousted Shagari, General Muhammed Buhari became head of state. Buhari did try to make some reforms to lessen the most egregious excesses of previous governments and to address the growing ethnic, regional, and religious divisions in the country. Under the aegis of a "war against indiscipline," Buhari sought to instill a sense of patriotism, nationhood, and discipline down to the level of the ordinary citizen. For example, people were made to wait their turn in lines, show up on time at work, and clean up their neighborhoods. After Buhari pledged to punish corruption and eliminate waste, more than 300 top civil service, police, and customs officials were fired. Hundreds of politicians were arrested and detained, and huge amounts of illegally obtained funds were seized from the homes of leading politicians. The Buhari government created many political enemies, especially among southerners who felt they were being singled out while northerners went free. Eventually, Buhari lost the support of most Nigerian citizens, who began to resent his hectoring and intrusions in their lives. His efforts to replace ethnoregional divisions with nationalistic fervor failed and were considered ludicrous when all around them people were confronted with poor leadership, greed, and a failing economy that imposed increased hardships. Moreover, in a backlash against a growing chorus of its critics throughout society, the Buhari government began to crack down and become more repressive and authoritarian.

Buhari's reform effort was also alienating the northern politico-military class, whose support was critical to his hold on power. They had sanctioned Buhari's efforts to restore order and discipline in politics, the economy, and society; but they did not want their power and wealth undermined by such efforts. As economic and political conditions continued to deteriorate, the military decided, once again, that a regime change was needed. On August 27, 1985, Major General Ibrahim Babangida carried out a coup that removed Buhari from power. Babangida, like his military predecessors, promised to restore democracy and good government and bring the country's economy back on track.

Period Two of Military Rule (1985–1998)

Babangida initially reversed the antidemocratic, authoritarian measures implemented by the Buhari government and vowed to hold elections and return the country to civilian rule in 1990. Babangida, however, made it clear that the military still regarded itself as the ultimate political arbiter and would not hesitate to intervene to preserve national unity and stability. At first, Babangida tried to address the persistent problems of patronage, corruption, and elite dependence on government as the means to acquiring wealth. His plans to attack the economic basis of cronyism and corruption were part of a broader program to return the country to civilian rule in 1993. To lessen ethnoregionalism in politics, he initiated a restructuring of political parties. His goal was to force parties to organize around issues and be inclusive of a variety of ethnic and regional groups. Toward this end, Babangida created a new two-party system: one, the SDP (Social Democratic Party), would be the left-of-center party; the other, the NRC (National Republican Congress), would be right of center. To prevent the corrupt, ineffectual politicians of past civilian governments from undermining the new party system, Babangida banned the politicians from the Second Republic.

Another major issue Babangida tried to address was the overcentraliza-
tion of power at the federal level. This was especially contentious among the
various regions of the country because the central government controlled the
distribution of oil revenues to the states. The demand for the creation of additional and more ethnically based states in 1991—the number grew from
nineteen to thirty—was a way for various ethnic groups to get a bigger share
of economic resources and jobs. Under Babangida, the idea of decentralization was extended to local government, and forty-seven new local governments were created. The sentiment was that local governments should be
given a greater share of revenues to provide social services and economic development at the local level. There was also a feeling that local governments
should be allowed to raise their own revenue via taxation. It was hoped that
decentralizing power and resources would give citizens more control over
government and lessen the premium ethnic groups placed on control over
power at the national level.

Unfortunately, what appeared on the surface to be a worthy reform was
tainted by politics. Creating all of these new governments meant creating
new capitals, new administrations, and new jobs all of which required new
money and other resources from the central government. There would also
be a huge number of new contracts to various businesses to equip the new
governments. In other words, vast new opportunities for patronage were
created. For one thing, patronage politics played a major role in the location of states and capitals. As an example, Asaba, the hometown of Babangida's wife, Maryam, became the capital of the new Delta State. Similarly, Babangida used the expansion of state and local governments as an
opportunity to reward his close supporters in the military. Because so
much was at stake economically and politically, the decisions made often
provoked demonstrations and ethnic violence between communities in several northern and southern states.

Babangida's other efforts at reform were also in trouble almost from the
beginning. As criticism mounted, Babangida backed away from serious reform efforts and became more authoritarian. This tendency became more
pronounced after a December 1985 coup attempt against him. Babangida
was understandably worried that he was alienating the powerful northern
political networks that were the most threatened by serious reforms. One
way Babangida tried to appease the northerners was to appeal to northern
religious interests. In one of the most contentious moves in Nigeria's history, Babangida surprised the country by making a unilateral decision to
have Nigeria become a member of the Organization of the Islamic Conference (OIC). One justification for membership was the promise of financial

assistance from OIC countries for Nigeria's troubled economy. In another controversial move, Babangida began to appoint powerful northern military strongmen to his ruling body, the Armed Forces Ruling Council (AFRC). Both of these moves, but especially the OIC membership, alarmed and outraged many Christians and southern ethnic groups throughout the country. Babangida's OIC decision was seen as evidence of the north's attempts to use the government to "Islamize" the country in total disregard of constitutional guarantees that Nigeria would be a secular state. Communal violence broke out in many areas where Christians and Muslims lived in proximity to each other.

On another equally explosive religious issue, Babangida backed off somewhat from his seemingly pro-Islam policies. When the 1979 constitution was being revised in 1988, some Muslim leaders began to demand that shari'a (Islamic law) be given greater legal standing and jurisdiction. Babangida appointed a Committee of Elders, made up of eighteen leaders from various religions to study the issue and make recommendations. The committee recommended that shari'a remain in the constitution, but its application was to be limited to Muslims. The government accepted this recommendation and reaffirmed that Nigeria was a secular state.

On the economic and political fronts, Babangida's reforms stalled and then failed altogether. Corruption continued unabated, and banned politicians retained their dominance in the political parties and most government institutions. One result was the continuing stagnation of the economy. Babangida was eventually forced to accept an unpopular structural adjustment program (SAP) imposed by the International Monetary Fund that was a condition for new loans. Among other measures, the SAP required the government to cut spending and devalue Nigeria's currency. As a result, spending on social services was cut, many government workers were laid off, and the cost of imported goods greatly increased. The public and local industry suffered greatly as a result of the structural adjustment measures that were imposed. Unemployment and inflation mounted while incomes and living standards plummeted. As will be discussed in chapter 11, many of Nigeria's best educated, mostly southern, professional people (including its educators) fled the country, leading to a skills shortage in many areas. Health, education, and other public services declined as government budgets were slashed. While ordinary people suffered, flagrant corruption and misuse by officials of public funds was becoming more outrageous and scandalous.

The current discussion of northern political dominance needs to be refined at this point to include the reality of intraclass competition, conflict, and cooperation among the Nigerian elite within and across ethnoregional lines. To get a clearer understanding of this, one can look at a powerful segment of the northern elite called the Kaduna Mafia. The Kaduna Mafia was started by northern elites who began their careers in the northern government bureaucracy under Ahmadu Bello, the northern premier in the First Republic. They were for the most part better educated than the traditional emirate elites that dominated northern politics. Mafia members had close ties to the military and were able to establish themselves in the federal government, industry, and gentleman farming. The city of Kaduna was the center of their business, social, and political activities. They also controlled many state agencies and financial institutions. Members of the Kaduna Mafia opposed General Ironsi, who had tried to eliminate the federal system and create a unitary state after the first 1966 military coup. They gained positions of political and social influence during the decade of military rule after the 1967–1970 civil war.

When Shehu Shagari and his cronies came to power in 1979 during the Second Republic, the Kaduna Mafia lost the competition for control of the main northern party, the NPN, and was excluded from party and state patronage. Frustrated by this, the Mafia members allied themselves with Yoruba leader Awolowo and his party against Shagari and the NPN. Shagari won but was overthrown by the military shortly after the 1983 elections. The coup was apparently engineered before the elections by the Kaduna Mafia and their allies within the senior ranks of the military. The leading figures in the Buhari government, which replaced Shagari, were mostly northerners with close ties to leaders of the Kaduna Mafia.

It was also the Kaduna Mafia that pushed for shari'a courts of appeal in the north during the Babangida regime as a way to mobilize popular political support among Muslims. When Babangida's military government refused to support this initiative, the Kaduna Mafia was weakened. Unfortunately, the shari'a issue still persists and continues to provoke animosity between Muslims and Christians.

Members of the Kaduna Mafia were also central players in the 1993 presidential elections. One of the major contenders for the SDP (Social Democratic Party) nominations for president was Major-General Shehu Yar'Adua, a member of the Katsina aristocracy with close ties to the Kaduna Mafia. As mentioned above, Yar'Adua (along with Babangida) was one of the masterminds of the 1975 coup that removed Yakubu Gowon from power. He became Vice-Chairman of the Supreme Military Council when General Obasanjo became head of state from 1976 to 1979. Apparently, Yar'Adua's appointment was an effort to appease the Hausa-Fulani for the death of Murtala Muhammed in the coup that brought Buhari to power. Yar'Adua retired from the military a very wealthy man and, at the age of thirty-six, became a major-general. The Kaduna Mafia remains an active, often unacknowledged, force in Nigerian politics, especially in the factional fighting within the northern oligarchy.

Eventually, the pressures on Babangida's failing regime to complete its promised transition to democracy became overwhelming. Babangida created his two parties and went through other steps in the process of moving the country toward elections. At the same time, Babangida tried to cling to power by subverting the democratic process and resorting to divide and rule strategies. He played off parties against each other, Christians against Muslims, and north against south. He used his power to ban or unban people and groups involved in politics. He aborted the 1992 party primaries and, five days before the scheduled 1993 elections, provided funding for a pro-Babangida group seeking an injunction from the courts to halt the elections. This ploy failed, and the elections took place anyway. After annulling the election—which was won by Moshood Abiola, a close Babangida associate—Babangida and other northerners tried to incite ethnic and regional fears by claiming that Abiola would promote Yoruba interests at the expense of other groups if he were allowed to take office. Facing demonstrations and strikes at home and international condemnation, Babangida's hold on power became untenable. He resigned the presidency on August 26, 1993. After Babangida's annulment of the 1993 elections, an interim government was established under Ernest Shonekan.

After a few months in existence, the Shonekan government was overthrown on November 27, 1993, by another northern general, Sani Abacha, who appointed himself Nigeria's new president. Abacha had been an ally of Babangida, and they shared much in common. The rule of both men can be characterized as despotic, with democratic rights and human rights routinely abused. Corruption and cronyism reached new extremes, while public trust in government fell to an all-time low. Ethnic, regional, and religious strife increased during Abacha's rule. The plundered and mismanaged economic system produced mass destitution for average people, and extravagant wealth was acquired by illicit means and flaunted by the rich and powerful. The destructive forces in society grew stronger and threatened to plunge the country into communal unrest unknown since the 1967 civil war. With both Babangida and Abacha obstructing the presidency of Moshood Abiola, many southerners became convinced that the north would never cede power to a southerner. The only escape from northern domination would be through a radical reconstitution of the federal system or the breakup of the country.

Personally, both Babangida and Abacha likely hold the record for malfeasance in office, each becoming multibillionaires as a result of the political power they held. Both men were able to hold onto power in part because of their use of patronage and their support from the northern military elite. Although efforts were made to pass patronage around to a variety of leaders from different ethnic groups and states, most appointments went to northern military officers, the key king breakers and king makers in Nigerian politics. Having effectively destroyed democracy, the military was now almost totally discredited in the eyes of the people. Any credibility it once had as the guardian of national unity and as the country's savior from bad governance had evaporated. The military had descended to naked "predatory rule" over the country.

Realizing his lack of legitimacy even among segments of the northern political and military elites, Abacha's rule was characterized by the worst repression in Nigeria's history. Such powerful ex-military figures as former president Obasanjo and Shehu Yar'Adua of the Kaduna Mafia were arrested after being critical of Abacha's overthrow of democracy. Abacha created a Presidential Strike Force to destroy his critics and opponents. The media, political parties, and the judiciary were all suppressed. Abacha would tolerate no criticism or opposition. The army, police, and civil service were packed with his northerners who would be loyal servants of Abacha's regime. Alleged coup attempts were used as an excuse to purge Abacha's rivals in the military. Those purged included officers that Abacha feared might be too powerful or disloyal to him. He replaced the top ranks of the military almost entirely with northerners he felt he could trust or co-opt through patronage.

Among those Abacha felt he could not trust were the Yoruba. In 1997, the government claimed to have uncovered a coup plot against Abacha. Of the more than 100 alleged conspirators arrested, most were Yoruba. After this incident, almost all Yoruba in the armed forces, including the officer ranks, were purged. Abacha's fears were not unfounded paranoia. Factional rivalries within the military led to bombing attacks against the homes and offices of prominent military officers. One victim of such a bombing was Abacha's son, who was killed by a bomb.

Abacha was a master at using ethnic groups against each other to control his rivals. He artfully created alliances with the leaders of some groups, who were able to get wealthy through the patronage process, while denying access to others or repressing them. Conflicts intensified among the states and among ethnic groups within states over the allocation of government resources. Disgruntled groups clamored for the creation of more states and argued over the distribution of jobs on the basis of "federal character." Interethnic violence was encouraged in part by the fact that the government did so little to stop it or to prevent conflict from becoming violent. With little or no protection from violence coming from the government, ethnically and religiously based vigilante groups, militias, and pan-ethnic solidarity associations were formed to provide security to their members. With ethnic and religious groups lashing out at each other, they were unable to unify against Abacha and his corrupt, autocratic regime. More analysis and examples of this interethnic and religious conflict are discussed in chapter 9.

Abacha did more than fail to respond to growing violence; he actually provoked it. He could then point to "tribal violence" and religious strife as a justification for the military to stay in power. He would counter calls for democracy with the claim that the country was not ready for democracy and that democracy would end in "tribal warfare." The country would break apart, claimed Abacha, without the strong arm of the military holding things together. Another argument was that a "strong state" was needed to manage economic development.

By repressing his opposition and pitting ethnic groups and states against each other, Abacha managed to maintain his control over Nigeria's oil revenues. He maintained that he was implementing structural adjustment reforms to help the economy, reduce poverty, and protect the environment. In reality, however, most of Abacha's economic reforms were a sham. Greater privatization and support for the private sector mostly provided opportunities for Abacha and members of his patronage network to accumulate fantastic wealth at the risk of a collapse of the country's financial and commercial sectors. Economic reforms also provided an important avenue for Abacha to attack his political opponents and rivals. Among those Abacha attacked were prominent members of the northern elite who opposed him, which included his former associate, Babangida, and his political network. One member of Babangida's network that Abacha attacked was powerful northern politician Ibrahim Dasuki, the Sultan of Sokoto and, as such, a Muslim spiritual as well as political leader. Abacha also went after Alhaji Ado Bayero, the emir of Kano and a prominent member of the Kaduna Mafia. The Kaduna Mafia had opposed Abacha's seizure of power and was alleged to be supporting the prodemocracy National Democratic Coalition (NADECO).

Under Abacha, the Nigerian economy was decimated by corruption, cronyism, and theft on an unprecedented scale. From 1993 to 1998, Abacha personally amassed about $6 billion. His finance minister embezzled $2 billion that was supposed to have gone to servicing Nigeria's $30 billion foreign debt. In some years, government leaders stole as much as 25 percent of export earnings. Nigeria's precipitous economic decline was disastrous in its impact on the country's standard of living and quality of life. The professional middle class, decimated by years of inflation, poor working conditions, and low wages, continued to flee the country.

Both official and civilian lawlessness and criminality, including massive drug trafficking, reached their peak under Abacha. The police were unwilling or unable to protect the public or apprehend perpetrators. In fact, sometimes the police were in league with the criminals. Without adequate police protection, ethnically based militias and vigilante groups developed in many communities to protect them from the out-of-control crime wave. Such groups have become the instigators of some of Nigeria's worst communal violence.

By 1998, it became obvious to even the most naïve Abacha supporters that he would not give up power willingly. The promised transition to democracy would be subverted so that Abacha, as a civilian candidate for president for all five political parties, could continue to run the country. What the exact fate of the country would have been is unclear, but it would have been disastrous. The issue is now moot, however, as Abacha died on June 8, 1998, before the elections could take place. Abacha's successor, General Abdulsalami Abubakar, wasted little time in trying to reverse some of the abuses of the Abacha years. Many political prisoners were released, including Obasanjo, who became president in 1999.

With Abacha gone, there was a chorus of calls for a reordering of the country or for breaking it up into more ethnically and religiously homogeneous countries. One of the most contentious issues was the question of shari'a, which by now had become a key element in the Christian-Muslim and north-south divide. Despite these unresolved issues, there remained hope in many quarters that, with a return to democracy, a unified Nigeria might yet survive the dark years of military rule.

Conclusion

It would be nice to be able to end this chapter with a reassuring nod to the victory of democracy over tyranny in Nigeria with the end of military rule. Unfortunately, dysfunctional economic and political structures and communal tensions have become entrenched over the years of military misrule that will be difficult to manage by even the most honest, efficient, and patriotic of governments. The first and perhaps biggest problem is the power of the northern-dominated military itself. Currently, the civilian government rules with the consent of the military. Nigeria's latest experiment with democracy may fail if the military perceives that the civilian government is instituting reforms that pose a threat to the ability of the military elite and their civilian allies to maintain their monopoly over public offices and resources for their personal enrichment.

Another problem is that after years of misrule, ethnoregional and religious distrust and hostility is at an all-time high and could plunge the country into chaos and a return to military rule. If the country becomes so fragmented by unmanageable ethnoregional or religious strife that the unity of Nigeria is at stake, the military will put itself back in control. It will not matter that years of misrule by the military caused most of the strife to begin with or that the nation's leaders failed to manage it in a just and effective way.

Over the years, one way communal interests and antagonisms have been expressed is through ethnic and religious associations and movements. Too often, the focus on these groups, which have the potential to fragment the country, lead one to overlook the variety of organizations and associations that transcend ethnicity and religious differences and promote national interests and identities based on human rights, democracy, and religious tolerance in a unified Nigerian nation. The next chapter will look more closely at civil society in Nigeria to get a better understanding of both types of groups and their impact on their country.

Timeline

1966	The first military coups occur; the First Republic is overthrown
1966–1979	The first period of military rule is established
1975	Yakubu Gowon's regime is overthrown by the military
1975–1976	Murtala Muhammed rules in a military government
1976–1979	Olusegun Obasanjo is head of state
1979–1983	Civilian rule returns in the Second Republic
1983–1985	After a coup, military rule returns under Buhari
1985–1993	After a coup, Babangida becomes head of state
1993	Presidential elections are held, but the election is annulled; an interim government is installed and overthrown; military rule is reestablished
1993–1998	Abacha rules in a military government
1998	Abiola and Abacha die; an interim government takes power under Abubakar
1999	Civilian government returns under Obasanjo

Significant People, Places, and Events

Abuja Abuja is a new capital city located in the center of Nigeria. It has been controversial because of the huge cost involved in its construction, the fact that much of its architecture favors Islamic styles and buildings (such as mosques), and because it is virtually empty except for the government institutions that are located there. Lagos, the former capital, remains Nigeria's leading city.

Dasuki, Ibrahim Dasuki, the former Sultan of Sokoto, traces his lineage back to the original Fulani jihad leader of the nineteenth century, Uthman dan Fodio. In 1996, Abacha removed Dasuki from his position and banned him from Sokoto.

Muhammed, Murtala Muhammed became the head of state after the coup against Gowon. He, in turn, became the victim of a coup. In honor of his service to his country, Nigeria's main airport is named after him: Murtala Muhammed International Airport.

1985 Coup The coup plot against Babangida involved one of his former schoolmates, Major-General Mamman Vatsa. Vatsa and the other coup plotters resented their exclusion from key political appointments and saw Babangida as unfit to rule. After a secret trial, Vatsa and nine other officers were executed.

Yar'Adua, Shehu Yar'Adua was one of the most powerful political figures in Nigeria until he opposed military dictator Sani Abacha. Abacha had him imprisoned in 1995; he died in prison in 1997.

Bibliography

Aborisade, Oladimeji, and Robert J. Mundt. 1998. *Politics in Nigeria*. New York: Longman.

Diamond, Larry. 1990: "Nigeria: Pluralism, Statism, and the Struggle for Democracy." Pp. 351–409 in *Politics in Developing Countries: Comparing Experiences with Democracy*. Edited by Larry Diamond, Juan J. Linz, and Seymour Martin Lipsit. Boulder, CO: Lynne Rienner.

Enemuo, Francis C. 1999. "Elite Solidarity, Communal Support, and the 1999 Presidential Election in Nigeria." *Issue: A Journal of Opinion* 27 (1): 3–11.

Falola, Toyin. 1998. *Violence in Nigeria: The Crisis of Religious Politics and Secular Ideologies*. Rochester, NY: Rochester University.

———. 1999. *The History of Nigeria*. Westport, CT: Greenwood.

Lincoln, Joshua. 1999. "The 'Persistent' Federation: Nigeria and Its Federal Future." *Issue: A Journal of Opinion* 27 (1): 17–25.

Metz, Helen Chapin, ed. 1992. *Nigeria: A Country Study.* Washington, DC: Library of Congress.

Othman, Shehu, and Gavin Williams. 1999. "Politics, Power, and Democracy in Nigeria." Pp. 15–71 in *African Democracy in the Era of Globalization.* Edited by Jonathon Hyslop. Johannesburg, South Africa: Witwatersrand University.

Reno, William. 1998. *Warlord Politics and African States.* Boulder, CO: Lynne Rienner.

CHAPTER NINE

Civil Society and Ethnoregional and Religious Issues

MUCH OF THIS BOOK'S ATTENTION thus far has been focused on the role played by civilian and military elites in postindependence Nigeria. The ruling class is divided along ethnic, regional, and religious lines, although crosscutting alliances are made to promote the class interests of the elites, which are to monopolize power and wealth. Even the military elite is not unified, and coalitions are created and break down, with new alliances forming. Previous chapters have also observed that common ethnic, regional, and religious identities do not foster monolithic group solidarities among ordinary Nigerians, either. In other words, there is a great deal of factional competition and conflict within ethnic, regional, and religious groups as well as between groups.

Among the elites, the object of all of this jockeying for position is to maximize the accumulation of wealth and resources for self-aggrandizement and for patronage networks through control of the government, especially at the federal level. The rest of the population has been largely impoverished and oppressed by a succession of military regimes. Whenever popular discontent with government corruption and authoritarianism threaten elite interests, the tendency is for Nigerian leaders to use ethnic, regional, and religious divisions to turn communities against each other. Communal tensions are also manipulated in the intraclass competition among politicians and military leaders as they seek to gain support for themselves or undermine their rivals. As economic and political conditions have deteriorated, communal conflict has been easier to exploit and has increased in intensity and frequency.

Nigeria's people are not passive victims of social forces and efforts to manipulate them. As individuals and collectively, ordinary people have tried to promote their own interests, cope with adversity, and build a more secure space for themselves within the social system, even though the system is fraught with sources of insecurity over which people have limited control.

To cope with the conditions they face, many groups and associations have been formed. Many of these groups are a response to the failure of government to function in ways that meet people's needs for security, social services, or economic development. Some groups seek to make the government more accountable to the people and force the authorities to respect people's rights and the rule of law. Other groups seek to promote and protect their economic, political, or religious interests in opposition to other groups or to the government. All of these types of groups and associations are part of what is known as "civil society." Among other things, civil society provides individuals with a collective means to oppose the state, gain support from the state, or supplant the state (for example, by performing functions or providing resources that government fails to provide).

The vitality and size of a country's civil society is often used to gauge the strength of its democracy. Authoritarian political systems want to minimize civil society because they do not want any popular competition or opposition to be mobilized against them that would lessen their control. Therefore, independent groups, such as political parties, labor unions, or human rights organizations, are banned or put under state sponsorship and control. By contrast, more democratic societies are known for the large number of associational groups that represent a variety of "special interests" in society. These include groups organized to promote the interests of women, religion, professionals and businesspeople, the environment, and so forth.

The focus in this chapter will be on how civil society associations reflect, promote, or attempt to lessen ethnoregional and religious differences. The chapter will look first at groups associated with specific ethnoregional or religious groups. Then, it will examine prodemocracy, human rights, women's, and labor groups as examples of organizations that transcend ethnoregional or religious differences and appeal to other Nigerian identities and interests.

Nigeria is noted for the large number and variety of its associational groups, despite decades of authoritarian rule. It was such groups as labor unions and prodemocracy groups, for example, that brought pressure on military governments to return to democracy. However, there are some caveats about civil society that should also be kept in mind. One caveat is that civil society development is not uniform in Nigeria. The south, for instance, with its history of less centralized, authoritarian rule and greater exposure to western liberal values, has far more associational groups than the north. Notably, the north has few human rights or civil liberties organizations. Most northern groups are more traditional, community-based, and less formal in organization. The south and the Middle Belt have most of the prodemocracy groups and have groups with a more formal structure, a more highly educated staff, and more links with the international donor community.

Another caveat is that many civil society groups are not necessarily democratic or forces for extending democracy and tolerance. Some are narrowly sectarian or oriented toward rights or resources for their group at the expense of others. Or, in an effort to promote traditional values, they would deny democratic rights to others, for example, fundamentalist Islamic groups that oppose women's rights. The use of violence by some groups is also antithetical to democratic values and practice. Finally, even groups that profess to be progressive and prodemocracy may be undemocratic in their own structures. They are in many ways a microcosm of the authoritarian structure of Nigerian society. For instance, many groups are dominated by a single individual or a small group of individuals, not infrequently family relatives. Decisions are made by a few officers, and meetings of the entire membership are few. Changing officers is sometimes difficult, allowing the leadership to become entrenched and less responsive to its members. Corruption is also sometimes a problem, especially in the north, where some organizations are known to have presidents who are in office for life.

With this introduction to civil society, the discussion can now turn to some of the types of groups most relevant to our understanding of ethnicity, region, and religion: first, ethnic associations designed to promote specific ethnic group interests; next, Islam and Christianity and religious groups associated with them; last, more broad-based groups that are a force for nation building and transcending communal and sectarian interests. These include some religious groups, human rights and prodemocracy groups, women's groups, and labor unions.

Ethnic Associations

Three types of groups will be discussed in this section. The first is the hometown association. This will be followed by a look at ethnic unions and then ethnic gangs and militias.

Hometown associations are the least controversial type of ethnic association. Hometown associations and related community development associations have become widespread and important in Nigeria as a result of the worsening economic and political situation in the country over the years. As government funding for development and social services shrank and community competition for resources intensified, many towns formed hometown associations to get community members living outside as well as within the town to provide financial and other forms of support. Hometown associations are not political but are self-help groups that seek to improve the hometown and the everyday lives of people there. There is, however, a political dimension to the spread of hometown associations, in that growing ethnic and religious violence and political repression have led many Nigerians to seek a safe haven they can always go to and count on for help in times of turmoil. This search for security often means identification with a local, ethnically based community. Another political ramification of hometown associations is that connections with a hometown often provide the launching point for political careers and a nucleus of political support that translates into patron-client relationships between politicians and their ethnic and regional constituencies.

Hometown associations are found mainly in the south and much of the Middle Belt. They are largely absent in the north, both in the Hausa-Fulani emirate states and in the largely Kanuri regions. Those that do exist in the north are created by southerners to deal with issues both in the communities where they are living and in their home areas. The absence of hometown associations in the north reflects the precolonial and colonial differences between the north and the south that influenced patterns of economic and political openness, levels of education, and popular participation in public life.

The earliest hometown associations were formed before 1925, during the colonial period, to improve local services and development. Hometown associations, then and now, seek to promote the interests of their hometowns in competition for scarce resources with neighboring towns. This competition might be for the location of a new road, school, factory, or health clinic. Associations also provide services to migrant sons and daughters "abroad." Living abroad means living in Lagos, Ibadan, or elsewhere outside the town. As late as the 1960s, it was almost obligatory to belong to a hometown association, because a person who did not associate with his or her hometown was ostracized. Also, even those who acquired money and lived away from their hometowns during most of their lives planned to return there to retire; therefore, it was important to maintain hometown ties.

Hometown associations and their provision of migrant services through urban welfare chapters in large cities have been instrumental in maintaining identification with local ethnically based communities. This reinforcement of ethnicity is seen by some as a negative aspect of hometown associations that works against nation building. Many observers had predicted that greater geographical mobility, urbanization, and ethnic mixing would create a more homogeneous national culture and new identities that would transcend ethnoregional loyalties. Instead, however, ethnic associations allow people to limit interaction with others outside of their ethnic group or local area. People are also less likely to identify with or feel a responsibility toward the community where they reside if they feel their primary loyalty is to their hometown and its people.

Nigerian concepts of "indigenes" (locals) versus "strangers" (migrants) also contribute to the attachment to hometowns and hometown associations. The proliferation of states and local governments in Nigeria is designed to guarantee indigenes preferential access to jobs, public office, and public resources. This keeps strangers in a permanent position as outsiders and second-class citizens when they are anywhere in the country outside of their ethnoregional "home." Such discrimination perpetuates ethnoregional identification and hinders any sense of national identity; it can also promote conflict in the competition for scarce jobs and resources.

Lillian Trager's study of the Ijesa Yoruba illustrates important aspects of the hometown association phenomenon and its connection to the persistence of ethnoregional identities. She points out that internal and international migration are a basic fact of life for many Nigerians. As most economic opportunities are in the bigger cities, most people leave their home places and reside elsewhere for much of their lives. They may rarely go back home. Many people born in the city may never have been to their hometown (see below); often their parents and relatives were migrants. Yet hometown identities remain an important component of the multiple identities people have (for example, class, religion, occupation, etc.). This identification with a place where one has rarely or never been may seem puzzling until one understands the socially constructed concept of hometown. A person's hometown is not necessarily where they were born, grew up, or ever lived. To some extent, people choose their hometown and may even have more than one. For instance, one's hometown is where one has kin and usually where one's father or husband's lineage is from. The hometown is essentially a web of social connections that provides security in people's lives. In a telling comment, Trager observes that if people could move anywhere and be "at home," the need for a hometown would not exist. But in Nigeria, the hometown is the only place many people feel they will be protected. Trager adds that most people have little identification with their state or local government area.

Not surprisingly, hometown associations' most prized members are politically and economically successful people. This includes well-educated professionals, members of the national elite, and Nigerians living out of the country. These individuals are expected to help raise money for development, help solve local problems, and to participate in local rituals and celebrations. They also help the community by providing remittances, that is, money sent back home for family members or community development projects. Those living outside the hometown are in turn provided with security and a place for recreation and discussions with other hometown people. Ties to the hometown remain so strong for most individuals that even now most people return home in their old age.

Community Day celebrations are a major means used to bring members back home and to reinforce ties between locals and those living abroad. Among the Ijesa of Trager's study, elites and professionals who live in big cities like Lagos do most of the planning and management of these events. Local obas (traditional Yoruba rulers) and chiefs are invited as well as the townspeople, who are organized into various clubs and associations. Trager describes these events as exercises in "invented traditions," that is, consciously created rituals that incorporate ideas of past practices into contemporary enactments for the purpose of creating community solidarity. For example, speeches are given that commemorate mythic town founders, and largely honorific chieftaincy titles are given to town benefactors by the oba. There are some common themes relevant to contemporary concerns in the speeches that are given. One is the emphasis on self-help, because the government cannot be counted on for help. Another theme is the need for unity of all the community's ethnic group members, although appeals for loyalty to the state and the nation are also made. Indicating concerns that such loyalties are weakening, speakers often lament the lack of solidarity and the idea that people are becoming too individualistic. Another theme is a call to those abroad to come home and physically be a part of the community and help with its development.

As benign as ethnic associations may seem, there are concerns that they may promote, and be a reflection of, growing "tribalism." Critics argue that they separate one ethnic group or subethnic group from others rather than helping to unify people as Nigerians. They may also encourage the formation of ethnic unions, which are viewed as more threatening. Some leaders are aware of the dangers. For example, in the early 1990s, E. A. Ifaturoti, the chairman of the Ijesa Solidarity Group, discussed the federal government's neglect of Ijesaland and the need for self-help initiatives to develop the region. But in helping the Ijesa, he argued against the trend toward "stateism," in which groups clamor to create new states to benefit their own ethnic group and region and in which they discriminate against nonindigenes. Coming together should not involve being against other ethnic groups, he cautioned. It should mean coming together to accomplish things hard to achieve as individuals or in small groups. This includes such goals as economic growth and modernization. Promotion of the integration of all Ijesa should be accompanied by recognition of the need to integrate all of Nigeria's diverse people. The problem with such ethnic solidarity appeals as those made by Ifaturoti is that there is little indication of how ethnic solidarity can be transcended to encompass national unity. There seems to be an assumption that if every group looks out for its own group's interests in a positive way, the national interest will be served. This overlooks the Nigerian reality that, too often, looking out for one's own group leads to a zero-sum game in which one group's gain comes at the expense of others.

The next type of ethnic association is the ethnic union. Whereas hometown associations work to improve the town, ethnic unions work to promote the interests of the ethnic group. In the constructed claims of ethnic unions, their ethnic groups are primordial entities of ancient origin and duration. National identities are viewed as recent, arbitrary, and artificial products of colonialism and imperialism. If they have any legitimacy at all, they are secondary to that of ethnicity. The Ijesa Solidarity Group, mentioned previously, would be an example of an ethnic union, although it actually encompasses only one subgroup of the Yoruba.

Ethnic unions began forming in the late 1920s and are more directly linked to political activism than are ethnic associations. Ethnic unions are concerned largely with the status of their ethnic group relative to others. They are less interested in local political affairs and more politically involved at the regional and national levels. As such, they are closely linked with the formation of ethnically based political loyalties and parties in Nigeria. For example, the Egbe Omo Oduduwa (also known as Afenifere) is a Yoruba ethnic association started in 1948. Its founder was Obafemi Awolowo, the Yoruba's most prominent politician and a founder of the Action Group (AG) political party. Another ethnic union is the Igbo Union, whose former president was Nnamdi Azikiwe, a founder of the National Council of Nigeria and the Cameroons (NCNC) political party.

The close association between ethnic unions and political parties encourages the widespread perception that parties are instruments for the advancement of ethnic group interests. For one, ethnic unions are largely responsible for the creation of pan-ethnic identities and for using ethnic appeals to mobilize political support for specific political parties and politicians. By promoting parochial interests and identities, ethnic unions are viewed to be working against larger public interests and national identities. On the other hand, some supporters maintain that ethnic unions represent Nigeria's real nations (the ethnic groups), unlike the artificial "nation" British colonialists cobbled together in 1960 from Britain's colonial holdings. There is some truth to both of these perceptions. Ethnic unions and parties have contributed to problems of national integration. The constant monitoring of one's ethnic group's status relative to others tends to perpetuate a sense of victimization and unfair treatment. Although the proliferation of states based on ethnicity has been a response to this problem, it has by no means solved it. Instead, it leads to a situation in which the only place in Nigeria where a person is a first-class citizen is in their home area. There is no equality of citizenship based on the identity "Nigerian." As long as this is the case, there is little basis for people to identify with this label.

The Nigerian government has contributed to the problem by not creating and enforcing institutions and policies that ensure equality of treatment and social justice for all throughout the country. The proliferation and importance of ethnic unions is a response to the perceived unfairness of the system. The widespread perception in the south of northern domination, along with the fears of minorities in the south and the Middle Belt of domination by the Big Three ethnic groups, are factors that explain why hometown associations and ethnic unions are largely southern and Middle Belt phenomena.

Since the 1980s, as the Nigerian government became increasingly northernized and repressive under successive military regimes, southern ethnic associations became more politicized and militant. An increase in ethnic and religious violence in the country led in 1962 to Babangida's banning all associations deemed to be political, other than the two government-approved political parties. The main targets of the ban were such groups as the Northern Elders' Committee (based in Kano) and the Middle Belt Forum (in Jos). Pan-Yoruba and pan-Igbo groups were other suspect organizations. Sani Abacha had repeated violent clashes with the Oodua People's Congress (OPC), a pan-Yoruba organization. Ethnic organizations in the Niger delta, where most of Nigeria's oil is located, also formed and resorted to violent tactics in response to the exploitation, neglect, and environmental abuses suffered by minority ethnic groups at the hand of the government and its foreign oil company partners. Indeed, almost every ethnic group now has formed an ethnic union, partly as a defense against other organized ethnic groups. Unfortunately, militant ethnic associations are fighting each other with growing frequency. The flash points involve competition and conflict over scarce resources in a declining and inequitable political and economic environment. As conditions worsen, ethnic tensions mount, sometimes leading to violence. Because the police are unwilling or unable to control communal violence, ethnic unions become more militant and arm themselves to protect their members. With all of these groups now possessing armed militias, when conflict occurs, it is more likely to become lethal. Violence leads to retaliation and more violence. Hatreds intensify, making violence more likely to occur over seemingly minor provocations.

Let us look in more depth at one of Nigeria's most notorious ethnic unions, the Oodua People's Congress, as a case study of the causes and consequences of the militarization of ethnic associations. The OPC began in 1994 as a grassroots resistance movement in response to the Yoruba's perception of their marginalization by the northern oligarchy after the annulment of Mashood Abiola's election to the presidency in 1993. Outraged Yoruba were convinced that the north was determined to maintain its dominance of the federal government and would never allow a "power shift" to the south. The OPC's president, Dr. Frederick Fasehun, explained the organization's mission as "defending the rights of every Yoruba person on earth."

In 1999, the OPC broke into two factions. Fasehun's faction insisted that it used dialogue, not violence, to achieve its goals. The more radical, militant group, under Ganiyu Adams, began to engage in violent clashes with the police. In 1999 alone, OPC-police violence was reported in Ilesa, in Osun State, and in Lagos, where twenty-three people were killed. Conflicts with other ethnic groups, especially the Hausa, also occurred. In July 1999, for example, fighting between OPC members and Hausa settlers in Shagamu in Ogun State resulted in fifty deaths. In a retaliatory strike, Hausa militants attacked the Yoruba in Kano; more than 100 people were killed. OPC youth also clashed with Ijaw youth in Lagos in 2000, leaving twelve people dead. In February 2002, another violent episode involving the OPC and the Hausa left fifty-five people dead and many injured.

The OPC defends its actions by claiming it fights to protect Yoruba interests, sometimes against armed robbers and other criminals who threaten Yoruba neighborhoods in Nigeria's crowded and crime-infested cities. Ganiya Adams accused the police of taking bribes and colluding with criminals, who are often released shortly after they are arrested, if they are arrested at all.

The OPC is not the only ethnic association to become more militant and violent. Allegedly in response to OPC attacks, the Hausa established their own ethnic association and militia, the Arewa Peoples' Congress (APC), in 1999. The APC is led by retired army captain Sagir Mohammed. Mohammed states that the purpose of the APC is to safeguard and protect northern interests and to respond to attacks on northerners anywhere in the country, but especially in Lagos where the OPC is attacking them. The APC plans to provide self-defense training to northerners so that they can protect themselves against OPC attacks. Yoruba-Hausa violence has increased in both the

Ganiyu Adams, the leader of a violent faction of the militant wing of the Oodua People's Congress (OPC), talks to his supporters November 6, 2001, after his release from detention in the Mushin district of Lagos. Ganiyu Adams was tried for murder and other crimes. (AFP/Corbis)

southwest and the north, and the spread of armed militias has played a key role. As an APC member in the northern city of Minna put it, "We fight all the time They kill us. We kill them Because there is OPC, there must be APC. If there is only OPC, who will defend us?" (Singer, 2001: 6.)

The Igbo have two ethnic associations of note, the Ohanaeze Ndigbo and the Movement for the Actualization of the Sovereign State of Biafra (MASSOB), that are active in Nigerian party politics. Ohanaeze is a pan-Igbo organization that seeks reparations for the 1967–1970 civil war and an end to discrimination against the Igbo in Nigerian society. MASSOB is more radical but complementary to Ohanaeze. It describes itself as a nonviolent Igbo civil rights movement. Like Ohanaeze, MASSOB believes that Igbo rights have been consistently abused by the Nigerian state and that the civil war was an act of genocide against the Igbo people. MASSOB has clashed with the government over its renewed campaign for Biafran secession from Nigeria. On May 27, 2000, MASSOB's leader, Ralph Uwazurike, unsuccessfully declared an independent state of Biafra. MASSOB also has an armed militia and has had several violent confrontations with the police, and its members have been subject to arrest and detention.

Most of the ethnic militias are made up of young males, many of them unemployed and facing bleak prospects in Nigeria's stumbling economy. Although many are motivated by ethnic loyalty, others appear to be little more than young thugs who find militia activities to be an opportunity to destroy or loot property and engage in other criminal activities and violence under the guise of defending their ethnic group or preventing crime. Some also receive the outright approval of community members and government officials. For example, in June 2001, the governor of Lagos State publicly invited the OPC to help the government fight crime, which was apparently beyond the capacity of the police.

One of the most controversial youth militias is the Bakassi Boys, an Igbo vigilante group founded in 1998 to combat armed robbery. As with other militia groups, the origins of the Bakassi Boys reflect the weak legitimacy of the Nigerian state and the lack of confidence in the government to protect citizens from crime or ethnic violence. The Bakassi Boys began in Aba in southeast Nigeria in response to armed robbers who were a constant threat to local traders. The traders originally funded the Boys with some help from the state government. The number of Bakassi Boys was 500 at first, but that has increased over time. The group has gained such widespread popular approval that the governor of Anambra State included them in the state's security system. Until a recent ban by Obasanjo made employing such groups illegal, the Bakassi Boys worked under an official name as the Anambra Vigilante Services. The Bakassi Boys aroused growing alarm due to the tactics and dubious political purposes for which the group was used. Its members are responsible for a large number of executions, arbitrary detentions, and torture of suspects who are given no right to trial or legal protections. These excesses occurred while state officials provided the Boys with uniforms, vehicles, offices, and salaries. Along with its brutal tactics, the Bakassi Boys militia has been accused of intimidating and murdering political opponents of state government officials or anyone who criticized their tactics. Although the group was disbanded by the police in September 2002, the governor is reported to be creating a new group, the ASMATA Boys (Anambra State Markets Amalgamated Traders Association).

Another region that has spawned youth-dominated ethnic militias is the oil-producing Niger delta. The most well known activist group is MOSOP (Movement for the Survival of the Ogoni People). MOSOP got international attention due to the arrest and execution of well-known writer and activist Ken Saro-Wiwa and several of his comrades by military dictator Sani Abacha.

Ken Saro-Wiwa, a leader of the Movement for the Survival of the Ogoni People (MOSOP), was executed by dictator Sani Abacha. Saro-Wiwa was a famous writer as well as a political activist opposed to the environmental damage caused by the oil industry in southern Nigeria. (Greenpeace/Corbis Sygma)

MOSOP had been trying for years to get the government and the oil companies to address the problems of poverty, underdevelopment, and environmental degradation in the Ogoni region. MOSOP is alleged to have a youth militia wing. But the best known ethnic militia in the area is the Egbesi Boys, the militia of the Ijaw Youth Movement that has been resisting the government and the oil companies. The militia has sabotaged oil installations, kidnapped oil workers, and attacked the police in order to stop the ecological damage caused by the oil industry. In retaliation for these actions, the government has sent in the army, which has destroyed whole villages. Sometimes the various ethnic youth groups clash with each other as well as with officialdom. In May 1999, for instance, a fight between Ijaw and Itsekiri youth near Warri caused nearly 200 deaths.

In December 1999, as the rising tide of communal and religious violence was spiraling out of control, President Obasanjo finally cracked down on the militant ethnic associations. He announced that "law enforcement agencies are hereby ordered to arrest and prosecute any person who claims or presents himself as a member of the OPC and similar organizations, all of which are hereby declared illegal, unacceptable and a serious threat to the peace and security of Nigeria" (McGreal 2000). The immediate cause of the ban was an outbreak of violence in Lagos, which resulted in the deaths of more than 100 people and forced 20,000 people from their homes. OPC militants claim they were pursuing thieves into a mainly Hausa area of the city. The violence then spread to other areas. When OPC leader Fasehun refused to join Hausa leaders in demanding a stop to the violence, Obasanjo declared the ban. He went so far as to order that all known OPC members be shot on sight. However, the ban and "shoot on sight" order were not well enforced, nor did they stop militia activities. Ganiyu Adams, leader of the radical wing of the OPC, was declared a wanted man by the police; nonetheless, he traveled around the southwest, publicly addressing rallies and holding press interviews. He was finally arrested in August 2001 in Lagos State, but the OPC remains a potent force, as do other militias. If anything, the ban has driven them more underground.

Repression of ethnic unions is not the only response of the government to ethnic strife. The Obasanjo government is making some efforts to promote ethnic group reconciliation and build greater understanding and cooperation. One initiative is the National Reconciliation Committee, a group of elders from different ethnic groups who travel the country calling for unity, peace, dialogue, and understanding. Another initiative is the Truth and Reconciliation Commission, a human rights panel also known as the Oputa panel. Modeled on South Africa's Truth and Reconciliation Commission, Nigeria's version is an effort to gather evidence on human rights violations by the authorities and other political actors going back to 1966. The commission has been more successful in probing long-past human rights cases than ones involving still living ex-presidents such as Babangida, who not only refused to testify but is also currently suing the commission. Another government program is the National Youth Service. The NYS requires university graduates to perform community service for a year outside their home region. It was hoped that the NYS would promote greater interethnic understanding and development, but there are reports that results have been disappointing. On a more symbolic level, billboards have sprouted up around the country admonishing Nigerians to "Stop, Think. United We Stand. Divided We Fall."

Religion and Civil Society

Religion has become one of the most divisive elements in Nigerian society. Some observers feel that it has become a greater factor in communal conflict and violence than ethnicity. Of course, one must always keep in mind that ethnicity, region, and religion tend to overlap, making it hard to separate them or rank their relative importance. The religious divide is mainly between Muslims and Christians, although both of these religions have internal divisions as well. Religious divisions are not simply doctrinal disputes, however. They reflect the larger economic, political, and social problems of the country. Both Christians and Muslims have become more reliant on religion and religious organizations as secular institutions and leaders have failed to meet people's needs. Religious organizations offer alternative avenues to deal with hardships and to build a better society. They also provide valuable social and welfare functions at a time when structural adjustment programs (SAPs) have forced the government to cut back on public spending. As societal conditions have worsened, religion has become more politicized, and extremism grows more powerful. Political leaders and religious leaders exploit and exaggerate religious differences and demonize their religious rivals in order to mobilize their co-religionists. The process of demonization promotes hatred and mistrust that make violent conflict more likely and tolerance and reconciliation more difficult. When one religious group appears to be favored economically or politically by the government, further antagonisms are created that weaken peaceful coexistence among religious communities. Moreover, they undermine the legitimacy of the state and the nation.

Although Christianity and Islam have been rivals in Nigeria since the nineteenth century, tensions were managed by the colonial state, which made the emirate north off-limits to Christian missionaries. Except for parts of Yorubaland and the Middle Belt, the south became largely Christian. Islam was confined mainly to the north. However, modernization and urbanization have resulted in many Christian southerners moving to northern cities, such as Kaduna and Kano, and Muslim northerners moving to southern cities, such as Lagos and Ibadan. This puts religious communities in greater contact with each other and creates the potential for increased competition and conflict as well. Since independence, the Nigerian state has managed religious diversity through the constitutional stipulation that Nigeria is a secular state that guarantees freedom of religion and equality of all citizens. In a concession to Muslims, the government also allows shari'a (Islamic) law and courts to operate in the north alongside secular common law and courts. Shari'a was to be applicable only to Muslims and to personal life, while common law was to apply to non-Muslims and to criminal cases.

Current religious conflicts date to the 1970s, but their roots can be traced to these earlier foundations. The Muslim north has been poorer, more authoritarian, and less influenced by Western cultural values than the south. In part because they are a minority, southern Christians want to ensure that Nigeria remains secular. They feel threatened by any signs of Islamization of society or the state. Islamic institutions in Nigeria are controlled by a conservative, privileged ruling class, which resists fundamental modernization of Islam or northern society. They are rightfully concerned that the spread of liberal Western values and institutions would threaten their power, wealth, and privilege. From the conservative Muslim's perspective, the northern Muslim social order and way of life must be preserved against alien influences.

Early in Nigeria's postindependence history, Muslims and Christians created organizations to promote their interests. These groups have become a more widespread and active means of expressing popular discontents, in part because religious leaders and groups were less subject to government harassment and repression than other, more overtly political, civil society organizations.

The first, and still powerful today, major Muslim group was the Jama'atu Nasril Islamiyya (JNI). The JNI was the creation of Ahmadu Bello (the sardauna of Sokoto and the first premier of the north) and a group of northern Muslim leaders and intellectuals. The original goals of the JNI were to spread Islam and to educate Muslims about their faith. Founded in 1962, the JNI gained a large membership among politicians and other prominent Muslims all over Nigeria. The group established links with other Muslim countries, including Saudi Arabia, and received funding from Kuwait. The JNI had a political orientation as well as an evangelical-educational mission. It was closely liked with the northern NPC political party and northern members of the civil service during the First Republic. All of the northern emirs were JNI members. It was not long before the JNI became involved in the north-south political struggle. After the 1966 coup, which the JNI perceived to be a Christian Igbo plot against Islam and the north, the JNI became more determined to promote the interests of a unified north and of Islam. The JNI saw itself as being in an adversarial role to the dominant southern Christian organization, the Christian Association of Nigeria (CAN), on major political issues involving religion.

In 1973, the JNI merged with the West Joint Muslim Organization to form the Nigerian Supreme Council for Islamic Affairs (NSCIA), which was recognized by the government as the main representative body of Nigerian Muslims. As such, the Supreme Council would be the only channel of contact between the government and civil society bodies on matters concerning Islam. The Supreme Council's position on the relationship between church and state was the ideological basis for the conflict between Islam and Christianity in Nigeria. Leading NSCIA spokesmen declared secularism to be an attack on Islam and a threat to the country, saying that Nigeria should not be a secular state but a state "under God (Allah)." The JNI has been especially hostile toward branches of the CAN in northern cities, such as Kaduna. The JNI believes that CAN members hate Muslims and are in a conspiracy with southern Christians to promote southern dominance of the north. Many JNI members are convinced that they are victims of discrimination by the state and Christians both, which have worked, in effect, to institutionalize Christian values and institutions. For example, the secular state and Christian Sabbath are given official recognition, and Christians are economically and politically privileged, according to the JNI.

The antithesis of JNI is CAN, the largest and best known Christian association in Nigeria. It was founded in 1976 and includes most of Nigeria's Protestant and Catholic denominations. Catholics are the most influential group in CAN. Other groups in CAN are the umbrella groups, the Christian Council of Nigeria, the Organization of African Instituted Churches, the TEKAN/ECWA, and the Pentecostal Fellowship of Nigeria. CAN is regarded as mainly a Christian political organization rather than a religious one. Given the wide diversity of Christian churches in CAN, many of which are doctrinal and ritual rivals, the organization would long ago have disintegrated into factionalism if it had tried to operate as a religious body. Indeed, even on politico-religious issues, there are differences of opinion, and some groups and leaders are more influential than others. For instance, the northern branch of CAN tends to dominate CAN opinions, and Catholics tend to prevail over other denominations. Since 1980, CAN has become more vocal and militant in response to growing Muslim-Christian violence and the perception that Nigeria is steadily becoming an Islamic state. This fear has led to growing militarization. For example, former soldiers are training Christians to protect themselves, and there is a proposal to create a Christian army to defend Christians and their property and churches against Muslim attacks. CAN has even been accused of organizing an attempted coup by southerners against Babangida in April 1990.

CAN's main political objectives are to mobilize Nigerian Christians to protect the secular status of the country, to prevent Islamization, and to gain more political power and resources for Christians. To spread its views and alert Christians to political issues affecting them, it mixes religious events with political messages, and the Christian and secular media are used to publicize them. CAN also has links with Christian politicians and members of the military. It is quick to complain of discrimination by the government against Christians. In 1990, for instance, CAN protested that the federal government was dominated by Muslims. Indeed, 80 percent of the cabinet members were Muslims, as were twenty-seven federal ministers (versus five Christians). When Babangida changed his cabinet so that all the members were

Muslims, CAN was so outraged that it held large protest demonstrations in several northern cities.

The issues that have created the most ongoing hostility among Muslim and Christian groups are Nigeria's membership in the Organization of the Islamic Conference (OIC) and the expansion of shari'a in the north. In 1985, probably to placate northern Muslim leaders, Babangida secretly made Nigeria a member of the OIC. CAN members protested this move as a major betrayal of Nigeria's secular foundations and as evidence of the Islamization of the country. Even more threatening has been the movement to get greater recognition for shari'a in the constitution and to expand shari'a to criminal cases. To Christians this represents a direct conflict with equal protection under the law, which necessitates a secular legal system. With so many Christians living in the north now, even if shari'a is supposed to apply only to Muslims, it can have an impact on Christians and be imposed on them as well as Muslims. For example, bans on alcohol and attacks on stores that sell alcohol have affected Christians, as has segregation of the sexes in schools and on public transport.

Shari'a was first admitted to the penal code in Zamfara State in 1999 and was subsequently added by eight other northern states. CAN organized large-scale protests in every state, and Cross River State in the southeast threatened to introduce "Christian law" if shari'a law was allowed to stand. In northern Kibbi State, CAN members have promised to do everything, even die, to defend their freedom of religion. The controversy over shari'a has sparked organized as well as spontaneous violence in several northern cities, including Kaduna. Kaduna is now roughly split between Christians and Muslims. In February 2000, Christians in Kaduna organized a large protest against efforts to impose shari'a that led to violence. In May, the Muslims retaliated; 200 people died and hundreds of buildings, including mosques and churches, were burned down. In all, 500 people died in riots in February and May. Similar violence has occurred in Jos, Kano, and Katsina, among other cities.

Religious violence and ethnic violence are sometimes overlapping phenomena and are linked to some of the ethnic associations discussed earlier in this chapter. For example, in 2002, three days of fighting in Lagos between Yoruba and Hausa gang members left at least fifty-five people dead. The conflict started when a young Christian Yoruba boy was caught defecating near a mosque. Local Hausa who worshipped at the mosque were outraged, and fighting soon broke out between the Hausa and the members of the OPC, a Yoruba militant group. Militancy by MASSOB, an Igbo group, is also in some cases a response to violence against the Igbo in northern Nigeria and the introduction of shari'a there. MASSOB's leader, Ralph Uwazurike,

warned that MASSOB members would retaliate against northern Hausa violence by similar violence against Hausa living in the south. He also urged
Igbo in the north to use "every amount of force available" and "any ammu-
nition in their possession" to defend themselves.

Although there are prominent Muslim and Christian leaders calling for
peace and an end to violence, often both JNI and CAN leaders provide legitimacy for violence, which makes it more likely to occur. Some Muslims
give violence a moral justification by calling it "jihad" (holy war). By contrast, many Christians see Islam as being akin to demon worship and feel that
Muslims give them no choice but to defend themselves. Both see the other
as morally inferior and believe that they themselves are never the cause of
violence. They regard themselves as victims and excuse violence as justifiable
for self-defense, revenge, or a means to rid the world of evil. As each group
feels increasingly threatened, more militant groups are coming to the fore-
front. Clashes are provoked, as demonization of the faith and character of
the opposition is answered with violence.

Although this response is more understandable in the north, where religion overlaps with regional and ethnic differences, it is beginning to have a
damaging effect on the long-standing religious tolerance that has characterized Muslim-Christian relations in Yorubaland, where religious differences
occur among the Yoruba ethnic group living in the same region. A newspaper report from December 2001 by Isyaku Dikko, followed by reader comments, tells a revealing story. According to these accounts, some Islamic and
Christian preachers are becoming more extreme and militant and inclined
to stir up conflict. In November 2001, for example, Muslims in Ibadan organized a demonstration in support of the Taliban in Afghanistan, which led
to a clash with Christians. Two weeks after a reconciliation meeting was organized by the Ondo State governor and shown on TV, another clash occurred in Osun State.

The foundation for these clashes is that religious identities were being
politicized by religious leaders and striking a responsive cord among members who felt they were marginalized and victimized by their religious rivals
and by sympathetic government henchmen. Yoruba Muslims fear political
marginalization by Yoruba Christians and feel threatened by the growing
militancy of Pentecostal churches and their efforts to convert Muslims. The
Muslims mobilize in response to these threats through such organizations
as the National Council of Muslim Youth Organization, the Movement for
Islamic Culture and Awareness, and Academic Islamic Propagation. Muslim
groups, such as Isarul-Haq, hold crusades that blame Christians for recent
Muslim-Christian clashes. In an affront to Christians, radical Muslims are re-

ported to have hung banners at the central mosque in Akure and Osobo claiming that Jesus was a Muslim. Muslims also claim that Christians have attacked Muslims who were preaching. In Ondo State, Muslims claim that the state government favors Christians by failing to protect Muslims from attacks by Christian hoodlums. Muslims also point to the small number of Muslims in government positions as evidence of discrimination against them. On the Christian side, they find that Muslim "comparative religion" crusades, which purport to compare Christianity and Islam, make ridiculous claims and distort Christianity and the Bible.

There are different views on what has provoked recent Muslim-Christian tensions. The governors of Osun State and Ondo State believe that it is Muslims outside of Yorubaland who are trying to stir up religious conflicts in order to destabilize President Obasanjo's government. (Obasanjo is a Yoruba and a Christian.) Most Yoruba believe that recent clashes are isolated and so far nonviolent. They think serious religious tensions are a northern problem unlikely to overtake Yorubaland. And, so far, there is very little sentiment in favor of shari'a among southern Muslims, which has been such a problem with Christians in the north. On the other hand, some preachers at mosques and churches are urging their congregations to vote only for candidates of their own faith. And some young, more militant Muslims claim that they would vote for a political party that supported shari'a. Although currently not a major threat to politics in Yorubaland, these are troubling signs that the region may not be immune to the politicization of religion affecting the north.

Religious organizations and movements in Nigeria are not just a response to interreligious differences. Religious movements can also be an expression of opposition to the dominant social, political, and religious order. This has been especially characteristic of the north, which historically has been more rigid and autocratic than the south. Religion becomes one of the few outlets for political expression. Also, traditional Islam makes little distinction between religion and other affairs of society; therefore, the causes and remedies of societal problems are readily couched in religious terms. For example, with poverty and economic and political inequality greater in the north than the south, class conflict is sometimes expressed as religious appeals for reform and justice and a return to God's laws. A good example of this is the Maitatsine movement of the early 1980s, led by Mohammadu Marwa. Marwa and his mostly poor, jobless followers were reacting to the poverty and misrule in northern Nigeria. Marwa was also opposed to most aspects of modernization and Westernization, which he saw as the cause of materialism and moral decadence and a threat to

Islam. Marwa also challenged the northern Islamic religious establishment, especially the Tijaniyya and Qadiriyya brotherhoods. Marwa's radical, anti-establishment message was seen as both heretical and a threat to the social order, especially as Marwa's followers became more antagonistic toward its perceived enemies and the government. Eventually, the group resorted to widespread rioting and violence, which broke out in several northern cities, and thousands of people died. The authorities crushed the movement, and many of Marwa's followers, and Marwa himself, were killed.

In the early 1990s, another large Muslim group emerged, this time in Katsina, under the leadership of Yakubu Yahaya. This movement was associated with the Shi'a branch of Islam. Yahaya's hero was the Ayatollah Khomeini, the religious leader who headed the Islamic Revolution in Iran. Yahaya believed God had sent him to end injustice, exploitation, and oppression in Nigeria. To that end, Yahaya advocated the overthrow of the Nigerian government and an end to the secular constitution and state. They were to be replaced by an Islamic state modeled on Iran. Yahaya accused the Christian governor of Katsina of collaborating with CAN to spread Christianity and secular policies. He also believed the federal government was allowing the mistreatment of Muslims. Yahaya was working under another radical Muslim revolutionary, Ibrahim al-Zakzaky of Zaria, and his followers. Although Yahaya was eventually arrested for rioting, al-Zakzaky and his radical Shi'a sect remained active. During the early to mid-1990s, there was at least one violent incident in places like Kaduna, Kano, and Zaria attributed to the Shi'a. In 1996, al-Zakzaky was finally arrested under the allegation that he was illegally importing weapons and publishing subversive material.

Internal divisions within Nigerian Islam prevent a unified Muslim civil society from emerging to challenge the state or the Christians. For instance, the major Sufi brotherhoods, the Tijaniyya and Qadiriyya, disagree on what a good Muslim is and find themselves competing for followers. There are also anti-Sufi groups, of which the Izala movement is the best known. The Izala appeal to the poor and the middle class with their message that true Muslims should not engage in extravagant expenditures and conspicuous consumption. The anti-Sufis accuse Sufi religious leaders of being partial to the rich, whom they implicitly criticize for the ways they have acquired and used their wealth. The anti-Sufis condemn political corruption and believe that wealth should be acquired through legitimate, productive activities. They also condemn the emirs and religious leaders for exploiting the poor. Although Izala has many ingredients for a more progressive, outward-looking version of Islam, there are some elements in their beliefs that some find problematic as well. For instance, the Izala remain committed primarily to northern Muslim advancement and retain a conservative commitment to very limited roles for women, such as the view that women should remain in seclusion in the home (purdah).

Violent conflicts between the Sufi brotherhoods and anti-Sufi groups began to occur in the late 1970s, and confrontations continue to occur throughout the north. In general, the inability to control the antagonisms among Muslims has weakened the authority of the sultan of Sokoto and JNI as unifying forces and have been a source of embarrassment and concern as well.

Although Nigeria's political leaders have helped to provoke the religious conflicts and violence in Nigeria, the forces of religious intolerance and hatred, once unleashed, can quickly go out of control and threaten the government and the nation. In many respects, radical Islam poses the greatest threat because so many of the Islamic associations refuse to acknowledge the legitimacy of the secular state. Recognizing the threat posed by religious divisiveness, the government has devised several strategies to manage religious conflict. One strategy is the creation of new states that reflect religious as well as ethnic differences. This has not been especially helpful. In 1991, when the number of states was increased to thirty, there were ten mainly Muslim states, ten mainly Christian ones, and ten that were mixed. So far, religious conflict has increased only in recent years, and the one region that is peaceful is the east, which is almost entirely Christian. In the core regions of the north, however, reformist, anti-Christian, and anti-Christian immigrant violence is common. In the mixed states of central Nigeria, often overlapping ethnic and religious violence occurs as largely Hausa-Fulani Muslim dominance is resisted by largely pagan or Christian ethnic minorities.

A second strategy is to promote religious tolerance. Almost every serious outbreak of religious violence in Nigeria is followed by appeals from the government, moderate religious leaders, and intellectuals for tolerance, dialogue, and the search for common ground. The problem is that extreme positions are becoming pervasive and hardened to the point at which no one is really willing to listen to their adversaries' point of view. Neither Christians nor Muslims are showing much tolerance or willingness to compromise for the good of the country. Religious tolerance and compromise are also complicated by overlapping political, ethnic, and class divisions.

A third strategy is to use the schools to promote secular loyalties and values such as nationalism and civics. Unfortunately, the state, which controls the schools, has little credibility on the issue of ethics or civic virtues. A fourth strategy is to ban or curtail the activities of all religious groups. As implausible as this may sound, in 1987, a Nigerian atheist association called both Islam and Christianity alien religions that should be banned in Nigeria.

A fifth proposal is to make everyone of the same religion through either coercion or conversion. This position is already advocated by some of the Islamist groups, and the prospect of its implementation is the greatest fear among Nigeria's Christians, who fear that creeping Islamization is already taking place. Muslims, too, resent and resist Christian efforts to proselytize their members and compete zealously with Christians for "pagan" converts, if not Christian ones. Yet another strategy is to use the military and police powers of the state to stop violence and suppress extremist religious groups and their activities. This approach to conflict management is already widely used. Unfortunately, the efficacy of this approach is compromised by the fact that the government has failed to follow through by addressing the root causes of much of the violence, which are poverty, unemployment, and an unjust and inequitable economic and political system. Moreover, when the government does intervene, it is not trusted or perceived to be an impartial mediator.

Civil Society and Nation Building

As a major source of Nigeria's intergroup conflict and violence, it is not surprising that the government is not the most credible manager of Nigeria's ethnoregional and religious diversity. Nor has it offered people much hope for a more just and democratic society. This has opened space for a multitude of civil society groups and initiatives designed to resolve conflict and promote broad-based, nonsectarian issues such as human rights, democracy, and women's rights. There are also class-based groups, for example, labor unions and professional groups, that are multiethnic and transreligious. Such groups are evidence that Nigerian identities are not limited to parochial loyalties and that there are interests that can bind people together for collective action, not just divide them.

For example, concerned Yoruba are responding to intraethnic and religious conflict as well as conflict with other ethnic groups. To allow the Yoruba to peacefully resolve their differences and prevent intra-Yoruba violence that recently occurred in Ife, Owo, and Modakeke, the Oodua Development Council set up a Boundary Dispute/Communal Clashes Committee. Yoruba leaders are also trying to prevent political opportunism by some politicians and religious leaders from dividing the Yoruba along religious lines. For instance, both Muslim and Christian leaders criticized the call to implement shari'a and the appeal not to vote for someone of a different religion. There is also an increasing effort to promote pan-Yoruba solidarity as an antidote to divisiveness and as a means to promote development of the entire region. Although calls for pan-ethnic solidarity can lead to conflicts with other groups, this does not necessarily have to happen. Being for one's own group doesn't have to mean being against other groups, some pan-Yorubists contend.

A lack of tolerance and respect for people of other faiths has provoked considerable dehumanization and violence by both Christians and Muslims toward each other. That violence can be a catalyst for new groups who oppose violence. In the northern city of Kaduna, James Wuye is the joint leader of a Christian-Muslim conflict resolution association. Wuye is critical of both Muslim and Christian leaders for failing to halt violence, which he has experienced directly. Wuye was the leader of a militant Christian youth gang in Kaduna that was responsible for some vicious fighting in the area. After he lost an arm, he turned his back on violence. His coleader is a former Muslim militant who lost most of his family to religious violence. As yet, there are few such groups, but Wuye hopes that his group can reach other young people who think violence is the way to deal with differences.

Years of violence and human rights abuses by Nigeria's military dictators has spawned a host of human rights groups, some national in scope and membership. One such group is the Civil Liberties Organization (CLO), which was founded in 1987. Its mission has been to expose human rights abuses by the government. The CLO has established branches throughout Nigeria. Among its activities, the CLO has called for an independent investigation of the 1999 large-scale killing of citizens in the village of Odi in Bayelsa State (in the Niger delta). The killings by government troops were in retaliation for the murder of twelve police officers by militant Ijaw youth. Another group is the Lagos-based Social and Economic Rights Actions Centre (SERAC), which filed a case against Sani Abacha in 1996 with the African Commission on Human and People's Rights, a body of the Organization of African Unity (OAU). The case was launched in response to the plight of the Ogoni people in the Niger delta. In 2002, the commission ruled that the Nigerian government should compensate the Ogoni for the abuses they have suffered to their land, environment, housing, and health at the hands of the oil industry and government security forces.

Overlapping with human rights concerns is the effort to promote democracy. Most prodemocracy and human rights groups are southern-based. Only one, the Movement for Democracy and Justice, is a northern organization. In the early 1990s, many prodemocracy groups emerged to contest rule by the military. Among these groups was the Movement for National

Reformation, founded by Anthony Enahoro, a well-known politician for many years. Another group, the Association for Democracy, Good Governance in Nigeria, was established by Olusegun Obasanjo when Sani Abacha was in power. This group was made up of several former heads of state and other prominent citizens. Despite its elitist composition, Obasanjo's group was able to put tremendous pressure on the Abacha regime to restore democracy after his 1993 coup.

The most influential broad-based prodemocracy groups in the 1990s have been the National Democratic Coalition (NADECO) and the Campaign for Democracy (CD). Both of these groups challenged Sani Abacha and his takeover of the government in 1993 by organizing mass demonstrations against him. Both groups include civil and human rights activists and politicians. Both organized protests and other activities to demand a return to democracy and the installation of Moshood Abiola as Nigeria's rightful president. Although most of NADECO's members were Yoruba, some prominent northerners were also members, such as retired general T. Y. Danjuma. The CD is a coalition of forty-two organizations. These groups include the Committee for the Defense of Human Rights, the National Association of Democratic Lawyers, the National Association of Nigerian Students, Women in Nigeria, and the Nigerian Union of Journalists. Like NADECO, the CD has been identified with the Yoruba and is centered in Lagos. The CD predates NADECO, however. It was founded in 1991 to oppose military rule under Babangida. Among the CD's founders were civil rights lawyer Gani Fawehinmi and Beko Ransome-Kuti, a former leader of the Nigerian Medical Association. Ransome-Kuti was arrested in 1992 after Babangida's ban on all political, ethnic, and religious associations except for his approved two parties. After his release, he was arrested again by Abacha, who wrongfully accused him of participation in a coup attempt against him in 1994.

Since Obasanjo's election in 1998, prodemocracy groups are playing a more low-key role as monitors and protectors of the democratic gains that they helped to create. Some are also determined to see that former military rulers who abused their power are held accountable. CD leader Fawehinmi and former police commissioner Abubakar Tsav gave President Obasanjo an ultimatum to arrest Babangida and force him to account for the missing $12 billion in oil revenues Nigeria earned during the Gulf War. They have also demanded that the Oputa panel require Babangida and former military rulers Buhari and Abubakar to testify before the panel about human rights abuses while they were in power. Fawehinmi and Tsav are irate that former military rulers are not being held accountable by the government for the massive corruption and human rights abuses that they are alleged to have committed.

In the struggle to promote human rights and democracy for all Nigerians, including women, effective women's groups play an important role. Nigerian women, especially northern Muslim women, have far less power, wealth, education, and status than men. One of the first women's groups was the Market Women's Association (MWA), formed in the 1920s in the south. The MWA represented market women as economic actors but also played a major role in Nigeria's nationalist struggle. Since independence, there have been numerous women's groups working to empower women and promote their interests, although most are rather conservative and nonfeminist. Women's groups have been constrained by the traditionalism of Nigeria's patriarchal culture and by efforts of past governments generally to suppress or control progressive civil society groups that might pose a threat to the status quo. As a consequence, since independence there have been relatively few women's groups that were independent of the government or that were a threat to Nigeria's patriarchal society and culture. Most women's groups are part of the 1959 government-founded umbrella organization, the National Council of Women's Societies (NCWS). Made up of 400 women's groups, the NCWS has been criticized for the fact that its leadership consists of mainly the wives of powerful men or Western-oriented professionals. It is unrepresentative of Nigeria's women, most of whom are poor peasants.

As one would expect, women's groups in the north tend to be fewer in number and less radical than those in the south. Constrained by the overall Islamic religious conservatism and fundamentalism in the north, women's organizations such as the Muslim Sisters' Organization and the Federation of Muslim Women's Associations of Nigeria encourage women to define their roles within an Islamic context. Unfortunately, with the highest rates of illiteracy and the lowest levels of education in Nigeria, most northern Islamic women have little ability to know what their rights are or to struggle for those rights' enforcement or expansion. However, there is one women's group, Baobab, headed by a Muslim woman, Ayesha Imam, that has fought for northern women's rights, including a recent case that attracted international attention. With the expansion of shari'a law to criminal cases in many northern states, human rights concerns have been raised over what many consider to be draconian and gender-biased laws and punishments in the Nigerian interpretation of Islamic law. The case that drew Baobab's involvement concerned Bariya-Ibrahim Mazazi, a barely literate, unmarried teenage mother who lived in a remote village in the north. According to Baobab, the girl was convicted in an Islamic court in Zamfara State of the crime of "zina," that is, engaging in premarital sex, and "qadhi," that is, false accusation against anyone, especially men in a sexual case. She was sentenced to a beating of 180 strokes with a cane. Baobab is appealing the case using Islamic law. For instance, the girl may have been only thirteen or fourteen when she had sex, and Baobab has discovered that she may have been coerced into having sex with several men by her own father. If these claims are true, Islamic law would exonerate her, and the men involved would be considered to be at fault.

With more than 3.5 million members in the early 1990s, the biggest and most powerful interest groups in the country are labor unions. Trade unions were active in Nigeria as early as the colonial period, and they were participants in the struggle for independence. Since oil came to dominate Nigeria's economy in the 1970s, unionized workers have been involved in many labor actions against the oil companies. In 1975, Nigeria's four trade union federations joined forces to become the Nigerian Labour Congress (NLC). In 1977, as a result of strikes, the government dissolved all labor unions. In 1978, the government replaced the independent NLC with a government-controlled NLC, which all labor unions were made to join.

Anti-SAP (structural adjustment program) activities got the NLC dissolved once again in 1987, although it was recreated in 1988. In 1994, after the presidential elections were annulled, a general strike was called that led to Abacha's replacing the union leaders involved. Participation in the strike by the oil workers' unions lasted for months and seriously cut oil production for the domestic market. A cycle of government restrictions and repression and union strikes and demonstrations continued up to the election of Obasanjo in 1999. Obasanjo won union support by promising to improve wages for Nigeria's workers after years of economic decline. In general, labor unions have been one of the most consistent opponents of military rule and participants in the struggle for democracy.

The labor unions remain a force for democratization and nation building, in part because they provide a national identity for Nigerians that transcends ethnoregionalism and religion. By emphasizing class interests and issues of economic inequality and exploitation, labor unions help to unify their members to attack the real economic and political sources of their problems— that is, government and elite corruption and failure to develop Nigeria for the benefit of all. In a May Day speech in 2002, the NLC's current president addressed thousands of workers and politicians. He cautioned the politicians that labor expects free and fair elections and will carefully consider candidates only on the basis of who will best lead the country, not on the basis of their region, ethnicity, or religion. The following is a Nigerian journalist's reproduction of part of the speech:

If you are a Yoruba candidate, NLC will not support you. If you are an Igbo candidate, NLC will not support you. If you are a Hausa candidate, we will not support you. If you are an Afenifere, Arewa Consultative Forum or Ohanaeze candidate, NLC will not support you because NLC believes that politics should go beyond ethnicity. Politicians hide under ethnic cleavages when they have nothing good to say, to incite and weaken the unity of our people. If they don't have what it takes to build bridges, we as working people of Nigeria, North, South, East, West, we have chosen to constitute ourselves into the Nigerian forum. As Christians, Muslims, and Non-believers, we all have the right to be proud citizens of our country. If you have an Igbo President, and he takes all the money to America and impoverishes our people, will the average Igboman be any more comfortable? If you have a Yoruba President, and he takes all the money to America, will the Yorubaman be more comfortable? If you have a Hausa President, and he takes all the money to America, will the Hausaman be more comfortable? The crowd shouted in response, "No! No!" (Oshiomhole 2002)

Conclusion

Strong civil society groups are essential to a stable and strong democratic society. They compel the government to be accountable for its actions and responsive to the interests of citizens. They also play a vital role in meeting popular needs through private rather than public resources. There are many such groups in Nigeria, and they often have had to operate under adverse conditions of government repression or efforts to control associational life in the country. With the return to democracy, it will be important that such groups remain active to ensure that democracy survives and that the country does not return to a new phase of military dictatorship or regress into greater sectarian violence.

Despite the importance of civil society to democracy, civil society can also pose a danger to democracy and national unity. The return to democracy has encouraged a flowering of associational life, but this has included groups committed to parochial loyalties and interests. Some of these groups condone or engage in violence to serve their goals. Some groups are also undemocratic in their own activities and organization and determined to maintain traditional, undemocratic practices. These include efforts to deny democratic and human rights to women or to promote the dominance of one ethnic group or religion over others. It is unclear whether more democratic, inclusive, and tolerant groups will prevail. The answer depends substantially on whether Nigeria's government leaders can implement needed economic and political changes that will move the country toward a deepening of democratic values and institutions.

On a positive note, there are indications that among some Nigerians, mainly the more Westernized, educated elites and young people, identities based on the extended family, kinship, ethnicity, and religion, while still strong, are declining in importance or being redefined. These changes involve people who have experienced some of the fruits of development that have so far been denied to most of Nigeria's population. Some are people who have migrated to different regions or cities of Nigeria or abroad and who have done well for themselves. They have experienced living among and getting to know people who are different from them. They have lived under conditions that reward individualism, merit, and the nuclear family structure. Able to achieve economic and political security through means other than reliance on kinship connections, patronage, or ethnic/religious ties, they become less dependent on these identities.

However, moving away from the village or home region doesn't necessarily weaken communal ties. As long as such ties are necessary and functional or people have no viable alternatives, ethnicity, region, and religion will continue to play primary roles in most Nigerians' lives. But it is economic and political arrangements that largely determine how important such ties are, what forms they take, and what purposes they serve. This is why achieving genuine, broad-based economic and political development is so important.

Currently, a nascent Nigerian culture is slowly emerging as a unifying force to counter the forces of parochialism and division. The greater the development, the greater the numbers will be of those willing and able to participate in this common Nigerian culture. Education, the media, and globalization are all components in the spread of this common culture. One element of this culture is the use of a common language: English or "pidgin." Much of the culture is derived from the Western world—for example, clothes, music, movies, food, sports, and Western values such as freedom, individualism, and materialism. But it is being adapted by local people and becoming Nigerianized. Living in the major cities, access to education, and higher income are the major determinants of access to this Nigerian culture, and more and more Nigerians want access. This culture represents development, modernity, and the "good life" for growing numbers of people. It is inclusive and tolerant of differences. For instance, one can choose to speak English or a local language depending on the situation, attend a Christian service and then celebrate with Muslim friends, or enjoy a local indigenous religious festival. Although this emerging Nigerian culture is highly Westernized, it is important to add that Nigerians want to preserve their distinctive African cultures as well. This includes local food, dress, music, language, and a regard for communal values. They do not want to be copycat Americans or Europeans.

Chapter 10 will examine a group of Nigerians who are among those most likely to experience the weakening of ethnoregional and religious identities and the incorporation of new social and cultural identities. These are Nigeria's international migrants, who are typically Nigeria's most educated, skilled, and Westernized citizens. They are a creation of globalization forces that have helped to launch a new "diaspora" out of Africa. This new diaspora reflects both desperation and hope. The desperation is due to the lack of economic opportunity and the political despotism that have been Nigeria's curse. The hope is for freedom and opportunity abroad. Nigerians abroad are not only changing themselves but Nigeria as well.

Timeline

1920s	The Market Women's Association is founded
ca. 1925	Hometown associations are started for the first time
ca. late 1920s–1930s	The first ethnic unions are established
1959	The government organizes the National Council of Women's Societies (NCWS)
1960s	The Jama'atu Nasril Islamiyya (JNI) Islamic association is founded
1970s	Serious religious conflicts begin to occur
1973	The Nigerian Supreme Council for Islamic Affairs (NSCIA) is established
1975	The Nigerian Labour Congress (NLC) is founded
1976	The Christian Association of Nigeria (CAN) is established
1980s	The Maitatsine riots break out in the north
1985	Nigeria joins the Organization of the Islamic Conference (OIC)
1990s	Outbreaks of Shi'a militancy occur in the north; the National Democratic Coalition (NADECO) and the Campaign for Democracy (CD) begin activities
1994	The Oodua People's Congress (OPC) is founded

| 1998 | The Bakassi Boys vigilante group begins operations in the east |
| 1999 | Zamfara State expands shari'a law in the north; the Arewa People's Congress (APC) is founded; Obasanjo bans militant ethnic associations |

Significant People, Places, and Events

ADAMS, GANIYU Adams is a cofounder of the Oodua People's Congress.

AFENIFERE This is a Yoruba sociopolitical organization. It created the Action Group, which became the first Yoruba political party in 1950. The Alliance for Democracy (AD) is the latest Afenifere political party.

BAKASSI BOYS Young, male vigilante groups are sprouting up in so many cities and regions that they are given a general name "area boys" by the public and the media.

DANJUMA, GENERAL T. Y. Danjuma's military career includes the arrest of Nigeria's first coup leader and military ruler, Aguiyi Ironsi, during the second 1966 coup. Ironsi was killed during the coup.

DIASPORA The name *diaspora* is given to the involuntary transfer of millions of Africans to the Americas during the Transatlantic slave trade. The new diaspora out of Africa involves voluntary international migration.

ENAHORO, ANTHONY Enahoro has the distinction of having proposed the motion in 1953 in the House of Representatives that Nigeria should become independent in 1956. The motion was defeated due to northern opposition.

FASEHUN, FREDERICK Fasehun is a medical doctor and a cofounder of the Oodua People's Congress. He was tried and acquitted of violence committed by the OPC in Lagos in 2000.

MARKET WOMEN In most West African countries, women dominate trade in local markets. Women sell their produce, handicrafts, or other goods and services (such as sewing or hair styling) to earn money for their families. Market women's groups help to manage affairs among market traders and represent traders in dealings with the government.

MOHAMMED, SAGIR Mohammed is a former operative of the Directorate of Military Intelligence and a retired army captain. He lives in Kano.

OIL COMPANIES Among the major oil companies operating in Nigeria are U.S. firms ChevronTexaco and ExxonMobil. In 1999, Rep. Dennis Kucinich (D-Ohio) urged a congressional investigation into allegations of numerous killings of civilians, human rights abuses, and harassment of environmental activists by the government in collusion with the oil companies. Although some reforms have been implemented, outbursts of violence continue.

Pidgin Pidgin is a creole language of English and various African dialects that develops in urban settings. It provides a common language for Africans of different linguistic backgrounds.

Ransome-Kuti, Beko Ransome-Kuti comes from a distinguished Nigerian family. His younger brother is Nigeria's most famous musician, Fela Kuti. His older brother was a cabinet minister in Babangida's government. His mother, Olufunmilayo, was a noted women's rights activist and politician with the NCNC party.

Sardauna of Sokoto The sardauna is one of the most important traditional rulers of the northern emirate states dating from the establishment of the Sokoto Caliphate in the nineteenth century.

Shi'a Islam There are two major branches of Islam: the Sunni and the Shi'a. The majority of Muslims, both in Africa and the rest of the world, are Sunni.

Social and Economic Rights Actions Centre (SERAC) SERAC is a good example of a Nigerian nongovernmental organization (NGO) with links to international NGOs. The legal case against Abacha and the oil companies was made possible with the help of the New York–based Center for Economic, Social, and Cultural Rights (CESR), which cosponsored the case.

South Africa's Truth and Reconciliation Commission After decades of racial oppression, the apartheid system controlled by whites was replaced by a black majority-rule democratic system in South Africa, which became the model for Nigeria. Rather than engage in retribution against the whites for a long history of human rights abuses, some of which were committed by blacks struggling against the white government, the new government showed its commitment to racial reconciliation by encouraging all perpetrators of human rights abuses and war crimes to admit their crimes and apologize to their victims and their families.

Warri This Niger delta town is the base of operations for leading multinational oil companies, including ChevronTexaco.

Bibliography

Abbott, Charles. 2002. "Hometown Associations and Ethnic Unions in Nigeria: What Are They, Where Are They, and Why Does It Matter?" Paper presented at the

Nigeria in the Twentieth Century Conference, University of Texas–Austin, March 29–31.

Babawale, Tunde. 2001. "The Rise of Ethnic Militias, Delegitimisation of the State, and the Threat to Nigerian Federalism." *West Africa Review,* http://www.west-africareview.com (accessed March 13, 2002).

Dikko, Isyaku. "Religious Crisis in Yorubaland: Genesis and Implications." *Weekly Trust* (Nigeria). http://www.nigeria.com (accessed December 7, 2001).

Falola, Toyin. 1998. *Violence in Nigeria: The Crisis of Religious Politics and Secular Ideologies.* Rochester, NY: University of Rochester Press.

———. 1999. *The History of Nigeria.* Westport, CT: Greenwood.

McGreal, Chris. "Nigerian Government Outlaws Radical Group." *Mail & Guardian* (South Africa). http://www.mg.co.za (accessed October 23, 2000).

Oshiomhole. "Labour Won't Be Neutral." *Vanguard* (Nigeria). http://www.vanguardngr.com (accessed May 9, 2002).

Singer, Rena. 2001. "Militias Fracture Nigerian Society." *Christian Science Monitor* (March 14): 6.

Trager, Lillian. 2001. *Yoruba Hometowns: Community, Identity, and Development in Nigeria.* Boulder, CO: Lynne Rienner.

Walker, Judith-Ann. 1999. "Civil Society, the Challenge to the Authoritarian State, and the Consolidation of Democracy in Nigeria." *Issue: A Journal of Opinion* 27 (1): 54–58.

CHAPTER TEN

Nigerians Abroad

Within Nigeria, ethnoregional and religious identities have become so strong that they are a flash point for conflict and violence. By focusing on incidents of extremism, however, one can overlook the fact that most Nigerians desire to peacefully coexist with their fellow citizens and work together to develop their country. Among Nigeria's better educated, more affluent, and urban population, global influences and development are contributing to a shared culture that allows people of diverse cultural backgrounds to bridge their differences and find common ground. Part of the reason this is occurring is that many Nigerians leave their homogeneous communities and migrate to cities to seek economic opportunities unavailable at home. Although ethnic associations and wards allow many people to maintain ties with their hometowns and ethnic kin, new relationships and identities also form that transcend communal ties. These identities can be based on such things as occupation, class, gender, or nationality.

There is a group of Nigerian migrants living much farther away from home than in Nigeria's large cities. These are Nigeria's international migrants. The emphasis in this chapter will be on who these people are, why they are leaving their country, and where they are going. The chapter will also focus on what happens to immigrants in their host countries and how their identity changes. Of special concern is the process by which new identities or modifications of prior ethnoregional identities occur as migrants adjust to their host country and interact with members of other groups. Also important is the extent of contacts Nigerians abroad maintain with their family and community back home. For instance, do they send money home and become involved in the critical economic and political issues affecting Nigeria? Do they plan to go back to Nigeria and to their hometown some day? The answers to such questions indicate the strength of ethnoregional identities and loyalties.

There is not enough scholarly data to resolve these questions conclusively, but there is enough information to provide a useful, if not definitive, view of Nigerians abroad and the issues of identity that immigration raises. Due to the greater availability of sources of information in this country, this discussion will, for the most part, be on Nigerians in the United States. Specifically, this discussion will first get a demographic perspective on who migrates, that is, what their number and characteristics are and why they leave. Then the discussion will focus on how migrants' identities are influenced by years of living abroad. This will include the nature of the relationships they develop within the host country, including with other Nigerians, and the connections they maintain with people back home. Lastly, the chapter will examine efforts by the current democratic Nigerian government to appeal to migrants' national identity in order to encourage them to increase their involvement with their homeland.

The Demographic Picture

As already discussed in previous chapters, Nigerians have migrated from place to place since prehistoric times. The main reasons for migrations were changes in environmental conditions, the need for grazing lands and farmlands, the pursuit of trade, and war. During the period of the slave trade, millions of Nigerians became involuntary migrants in the first diaspora. With the introduction of the colonial system, most migrants were male, rural dwellers moving to cities to look for wage jobs. In the first decade of independence, rural-urban migration usually involved the movement of thousands of job seekers to other African countries such as Sierra Leone, Cameroon, Ghana, Benin, and Guinea. Since the 1980s, migration abroad has been directed more toward industrialized, richer countries of Europe and the United States.

Both internal and external forces are behind these more recent migratory movements. Before the mid-1960s, U.S. and European immigration laws were highly restrictive and unfavorable to immigrants from developing countries. But a growing need for low-cost labor in the industrial countries resulted in new policies more favorable to immigration from countries like Nigeria. In the early 1970s, in response to the civil war from 1967 to 1970, emigration from Nigeria began to increase somewhat. However, relatively few emigrants at that time left for Europe or the United States; most went to other African countries. The booming Nigerian oil industry after the war created a temporary period of rapid economic growth and development, which lessened the need for most Nigerians to look abroad for work. Then, in the late 1970s and 1980s, everything began to go downhill. Oil prices collapsed, as did the economy in general. A long period of political instability and military rule replaced democratically elected governments. Political repression, corruption, crime, and a vast inequality in wealth between the rich and everyone else led to a corrosion of social cohesion. In such an environment of societal decline, communal strife found fertile ground. Compounding these problems were painful structural adjustment programs (SAPs) forced on Nigeria by the World Bank and IMF since the 1980s. These efforts to reform the economy led to sharp cutbacks in jobs, wages, and social services, such as health care and education. Although the poor suffered the most from the imposed "austerity programs," the educated middle class was decimated by a combination of low wages, job losses, and high inflation. As almost every African country at this time was in the same boat as Nigeria, they offered little attractive alternative for Nigerians struggling with such adverse conditions. In fact, in the 1980s, neighboring countries Ghana and Nigeria expelled millions of each other's workers due to the growing unemployment affecting their own citizens.

Fortuitously, since the 1960s, the demand for labor was growing in the industrial counties as a result of economic expansion and declining population growth. Changes in U.S. immigration policies in 1965 and 1990 that favored those with skills and education and their immediate families made it possible for the first time for more people from Nigeria and other Anglophone African countries to immigrate, whereas past policies discriminated in favor of those of European national origin. The selectivity of U.S. immigration policy resulted in a typical African immigrant who was the "cream of the crop" of their country's citizens. In 1990, the average African immigrant had almost sixteen years of education, and more Africans (43 percent) than any other immigrant group had college degrees. Equally impressive, 30 percent of all foreign-born Africans were employed in the highest occupational category as professional, technical, and kindred workers (PTKs).

Then in 1995, the diversity immigration lottery was expanded, which proved to be highly advantageous for skilled, educated Africans. This policy made available 55,000 visas each year to nationalities that had been disadvantaged by previous immigration policies. To qualify, applicants had to, as a minimum, have completed secondary school or be able to show evidence of two years of work in a skilled occupation. In 1995 alone, 37 percent of the diversity visas went to Africans. This policy, along with immigration via traditional channels, led to an increase in the percentage of African immigrants from 3 percent to 5 percent of all immigrants to the United States. Even more impressive, the percent of Africans in the 1990s that were PTKs had risen to 44 percent.

Both Nigeria's internal problems and the changes in U.S. immigration policies led to a large increase in immigration to the United States. Initially, Nigerian immigration began to climb upward in 1971. Most of the immigrants were Igbo fleeing Nigeria at the end of the civil war. Most of them were highly educated and skilled. Another group, also mostly Igbo, were students already in the United States for higher education who decided not to return to Nigeria. Here on student visas, they applied for immigrant (i.e., permanent resident) status. The 1970s oil boom in Nigeria led to additional students coming to the United States on student or other temporary visas. However, when economic and political conditions soured in the late 1970s and 1980s, many changed their status to that of permanent residents in order to avoid returning to Nigeria. Many others began to leave Nigeria to escape conditions there. Between 1974 and 1995, Nigerians comprised the largest number and percentage of immigrants in the United States from Africa—close to 70,000 (17 percent of the total).

Nigerians have become a significant presence in many countries. Approximately 15 million Nigerians, out of a population of perhaps 120 million, live abroad. Many are in developed countries with immigration laws that favor the educated and skilled. This exodus has produced a dramatic brain drain from Nigeria. It is estimated that more skilled, professional Nigerians now live outside of Nigeria than inside. In the United States alone, 1990 census data showed Nigerians to be the most educated group in the country. About 64 percent of Nigerians had at least a four-year college degree, and 84 percent were in the labor force. In 1995, included in this talented group were 21,000 Nigerian medical doctors and researchers. Each year, approximately 12,500 Nigerian academics move to developed countries, and the number of Nigerian academics in the United States is said to be higher than the number in Nigeria.

One of these academics is writer Femi Ojo-Ade. Ojo-Ade discusses the desperation that has driven so many educated Nigerians to leave their homeland. "Nigeria is the only country," he observes, "where exile, even if it means enslavement, is now preferred to life at home" (2001, 37). Ojo-Ade notes that Great Britain used to be the favored destination because of Nigeria's colonial ties to that country, which gave them favored access as members of the Commonwealth. The United States is now would-be migrants' first choice. Ojo-Ade recalls a popular Lagos joke on the subject. The gist of it is as follows: a slave ship going to the United States would be so overfilled with willing candidates that it would sink before it even got under way. On a more serious note, Ojo-Ade laments that so many professionals are "desperate people hell-bent on running away to greener pastures." Yet he understands that they are escaping the "robbers and rapists" who are destroying Nigeria (ibid., 211).

Migration and Identities

Becoming a resident of a different country creates conditions that often lead to significant changes in identity. Some may become assimilated and greatly reduce their identification with their original ethnic or national identities. They intend to make the host country their permanent home. Others see their stay abroad as temporary and have little interest in taking on the identities of the local population. Their primary orientation is to people and places from home. They prefer to, or out of necessity, remain in ethnic enclaves with people from home, which contributes to the preservation of their ethnic identities and reduces assimilation.

Most Africans, including Nigerians, migrate with the intention of furthering their education or economic fortunes and then returning home, at least upon retirement. Their primary goal is to earn money for themselves and their families and provide a share of their resources to help family members and communities back home. However, many Nigerians' expectations have been compromised by the adverse economic and political conditions back home. That is, they have found that they can't go home in the foreseeable future. Under these circumstances, in the United States at least, considerable assimilation, and thus identity change, occurs. Highly educated and skilled PTKs, which most Nigerians are, tend to be the most rapidly assimilated of all immigrants because they often live apart from concentrated ethnic enclaves due to their jobs. Also due to the nature of their jobs, for example, as university professors, they have most of their daily interaction with people who are not of their ethnicity. In other words, work and friendship relationships outside of the migrant's ethnic community encourage the formation of new or modified identities and interests.

Identity changes are reflected in high rates of permanent residence status and citizenship the longer Nigerians remain in the country, but these changes are not taken lightly. For one, citizenship means embracing a national identity as an American, which requires, at least formally, a lesser identification with Nigerian national and ethnoregional loyalties. Similarly, the emphasis on national identity in the United States makes Nigerians more aware of their common identity with others from Nigeria, regardless of ethnoregional identification. One reason is that, in the United States, Nigerians will be identified by most people and will often come to label themselves as "African" or "Nigerian"; few people will know or care that they are Yoruba, Igbo, or Tiv.

Despite such identity issues, taking permanent residence and citizenship have distinct advantages to the long-term immigrant and their family back home. Citizenship gives greater access to employment and rights and services in the United States. It is also a requirement for bringing family members other than the immediate family into the country. Given the climate of insecurity that has prevailed in Nigeria, many Nigerian migrants have been eager to get their families out as quickly as possible.

This does not mean that Nigerians lose their ethnoregional identities, of course. For one, most African immigrants (93 percent of the ones in the United States) are clustered in large urban areas and a handful of states. This has encouraged the creation of a multitude of ethnic associations. For many immigrants, ethnic and subethnic identities are actually rediscovered or created in the context of life as an immigrant. The concentration of immigrants in large cities can also reinforce ethnic, as well as religious, ties. For one, Christian churches are tailored to serve the Nigerian immigrant community. They help immigrants to maintain their cultural identities while adjusting to new identities and demands of American life. In many cases, Nigerian Christians do not feel at home in American churches, or they prefer to worship in a place and style that reinforces their cultural identity. One example is St. Cecilia Catholic Church in Los Angeles, where about 100 Igbos come for Mass and singing in Igbo. African drums and music play, and women wear traditional dress. The church helps to bring the scattered Igbo community together, lessens their sense of isolation, and helps them cope with the pressures of life in the United States. The church also helps to reinforce the culture and identity of Igbo youth. The children sing songs in Igbo and have relationships with other Igbo in order to foster a sense of community. One mother mentioned that her nineteen-year-old daughter now has a sense of pride in her Igbo identity, whereas before she shunned her Igbo name; now she corrects her friends who try to address her by her American nickname.

Protestant churches serve a similar role. For instance, the Brotherhood of the Cross has branches in several cities where Nigerian communities are located. The Brotherhood has about 2 million members worldwide. The Cherubim and Seraphim Church has a large Nigerian following in and around Washington, D.C. Many of these churches are especially attractive to less financially well off immigrants who are finding the adjustment to their new life stressful and alienating. The Cherubim and Seraphim Church provides both material and emotional support for new immigrants, who are able to stay at the church for up to two months.

Seven African immigrants—five from Nigeria, and two from Ivory Coast—sit aboard an inflatable boat before being arrested by Spanish civil guards at sea near the Spanish port of Ceuta, early August 12, 1999. Many Africans attempt to cross the Mediterranean Sea in makeshift vessels to reach the Spanish coast in search of a better life in Europe. (Photo by Marcelo del Pozo, Reuters News Media/Corbis)

A recent study of Nigerian Pentecostal churches in Great Britain illustrates how the church helps immigrants to both adjust to their host culture and at the same time maintain their identities from home. The specific church studied was the Redeemed Christian Church of God (RCCG). The RCCG started in Nigeria and has experienced enormous growth since the 1980s when economic and political crises mounted. It currently has about 2,000 parishes in Nigeria and another 1,000 worldwide to serve Nigerian Christians abroad. In Great Britain, the RCCG has more than fifty parishes and 200,000 members; it is the largest Pentecostal church there. Its emphasis on purity and strict morals is a way for church members to create identities for themselves that allow them to distance themselves from what they see as the corrupting influences of British society and to distinguish themselves from the negative stereotypes Westerners have of Nigerians as corrupt and criminal. Church members also believe that their lifestyle of self-control will pay off in terms of achieving prosperity and being "the best you can be" in all areas of life. In essence, the church provides immigrants with an adaptive ideology and a supportive community of fellow Nigerians in order to reinforce identities and behavior conducive to achieving success in their new surroundings.

One of the most widespread views Nigerians have, which reinforces their home identities, is the "myth of return." Paradoxically, this can promote both ethnoregional and national identities. Sulayman Nyang wryly observes that "immigrants entertain the notion of coming here [to the United States], striking it rich and then returning home with the golden fleece" (1998, 5). Actual experience is often much different, however. Because most immigrants are young and unmarried, they often get married in their new country (and not necessarily to another Nigerian) and start a family. They also end up staying for many years rather than only a few. Often their children grow up with only tenuous ties to Nigeria or the hometowns that mean so much to their parents. The children don't know their parents' native language, and they have been socialized primarily into American culture, not the customs of their parents. These Americanized children feel that the United States is home, and most would be unwilling to go to Nigeria to live even if their parents were able to return.

This suggests that Nigerians born and raised in Nigeria retain much of their ethnoregional cultural identity, but that identity is weakened after years away from Nigeria, especially if they have children. The effect this has on altering Nigerian ethnic identities is poignantly expressed by Dympna Ugwu-Oju in an essay she wrote for *Newsweek* magazine. Dympna and her husband are both Igbo professionals living in California. Like many Nigerians, she came to the United States (in 1974) for higher education and has lived here ever since. Now she has an eighteen-year-old daughter, raised her entire life in the United States, who is going to Princeton for her university education. Dympna reveals how, at least in the area of gender, her own identity has been modified and how little of her Igbo identity was transferable to her daughter.

> I'm a member of the Ibo [Igbo] tribe of Nigeria, and although I've lived in the United States most of my adult life, my consciousness remains fixed on the time and place of my upbringing. On the surface, I'm as American as everyone else. My husband, who was also raised in Nigeria, and I are both professionals. In my private life, my Iboness, the customs that rigidly dictate how the men and women of my tribe live their lives, continues to influence the choices I make. I see these American and Ibo aspects of my life as distinct; I

separate them perfectly, and there are no blurrings. Except for maybe one: Delia.

When I left Nigeria at 18, I had no doubts about who and what I was. I was. I was a woman. I was *only* a woman.

All my life my mother told me that a woman takes as much in life as she's given; if she's educated, it's only so that she can better cater to her husband and children. When I was Delia's age, I knew with absolute certainty that I would marry the Ibo man my family approved for me and bear his children. I understood that receiving a good education and being comfortable in both the Western and the traditional worlds would raise the bride price my prospective husband would pay my family. My role was to be a great asset to my husband.

I've struggled daily with how best to raise my daughter. Every decision involving Delia is a tug of war between Ibo and American traditions. I've vacillated between trying to turn her into the kind of woman her grandmothers would be proud of and letting her be the modern, independent woman she wants to be. At 18, Delia knows very little about the rules that govern the lives of Ibo women.

I wonder about the implications for people like me, women from traditional cultures raising American-born daughters. Should we limit their opportunities to keep them loyal to our beliefs and our pasts, or should we encourage our daughters to avail themselves of all experiences, even at the risk of rejecting who and what we are?

Or perhaps I've always known that Delia is her own person with her own life to lead. (Ugwu-Oju 2000, 14)

For many Nigerians living abroad, similar compromises resulted from the years of adjustment to American life. Those who grew up in Nigeria continue to identify strongly with their homeland, but many also experience relief because they have escaped the problems back home. At the same time, there is a sense of responsibility to make things better there. A sense of loss is tinged with guilt and typically expressed in nationalistic terms. That is, most longtime immigrants see themselves as Nigerians and expect all Nigerians abroad to do the same. They disapprove of the minority of Nigerians living abroad who say they never want to go back to their homeland and, according to Ojo-Ade, such people are referred to as "the lost tribe."

Despite the large geographical distances that often separate Nigerian immigrants from their homeland, most maintain close contact with people back home. One of the most important connections is economic. Remittances sent back home by those abroad provide a major source of foreign exchange earnings for many financially struggling developing countries. It is estimated that between 1995 and 1998, Nigerians abroad sent home $1.3 billion per year. This was about 10 percent of the value of Nigeria's exports and was equal to the total foreign direct investment in the country. According to Ojo-Ade, families in Nigeria are so dependent on remittances that people back home often want them to stay abroad so they can send back money. And, if Nigerians in Chicago are typical, most immigrants regularly send money home. Osili's study of Nigerian immigrant households in Chicago in the late 1990s revealed that 93 percent of them had sent money home in the past year. The average amount was $6,000, quite a sizeable and welcome sum considering the low incomes of most Nigerians in their nation's troubled economy.

Virtual Nigeria

Maintaining ethnoregional and national identities can be complicated when migrants are far from home for many years and have only limited means to maintain contacts with people back home or with other Nigerians like themselves in their host country. Today, Nigerians abroad have been able to maintain contact with each other in ways that were impossible until recently. Dympna Ugwu-Oju, the Igbo woman living in California, describes what it was like to be far away from home in the 1970s:

> My home country, Nigeria, was for all intents and purposes as far away as Mars. Back then, it was virtually impossible to reach my family by phone; we could communicate only through snail mail and, in an emergency, via telegraph. It wasn't until six years later, after I had completed both my undergraduate and graduate degrees, that I went home for the first time. (ibid.)

Since Ugwu-Oju came to the United States, much has changed for immigrants like her. Even if they can't physically be with their families and friends, many Nigerians are "wired" to each other thanks to computers, e-mail, and the Internet. This has allowed them to create a "virtual Nigeria," which connects Nigerians abroad to each other and to their country and people back home. In the author's research for this chapter, she has communicated by e-mail with Nigerian colleagues all over the United States and with some outside the country. She has read many Nigerian newspapers and chat sites for exchanges of opinions on current issues inside and outside of Nigeria, learned about many Nigerian ethnic and professional associations and other civil society organizations in the United States and elsewhere, and been informed of important Nigerian gatherings in major U.S. cities, all on the Internet and often with pictures. All of this reflects an astonishing variety of information-sharing linkages among Nigerians abroad to each other and to their homeland. As mentioned above, these networks, paradoxically, allow Nigerians to maintain ethnoregional identities but often foster a Nigerian national identity as well.

One of the most important Internet sites for discussion of social and political issues among Nigerians is Naijanet (http://www.naijanet.com), which was started in the United States in the early 1990s. Naijanet provides a forum for Nigerians abroad to openly express their views on any issue within Nigeria or within the diaspora community. Participants generally see Naijanet as providing them with a virtual nationalist community of people who relate to each other as Nigerians, not primarily as members of ethnoregional communities. Naijanet helps ease the loneliness Nigerians often feel when living far from home. Most of Naijanet's users are male, affluent, and highly educated. Unfortunately, relatively few Nigerians in Nigeria are able to participate in the discussions that take place, due to the lack of access to computers and the Internet in many areas of the country.

Naijanet has produced several spinoff online networks. Among these are Igbonet, which is ethnically based. Others are multiethnic, for example, ANA-Net (the Association of Nigerians Abroad). The issue that led to the Igbo starting their own discussion group was a heated exchange among Igbo and non-Igbo on Naijanet over the Biafran civil war. Among the discussion participants were a group of former Biafran soldiers, who resented the suggestion that they should just "get over" the war and concentrate on Nigeria's current problems. In 1994, one of these former soldiers decided to set up Igbonet. Igbonet has attracted a growing number of active subscribers who exchange ideas on such issues as the civil war, the relatively small number of women on the Net and other gender issues, Nigerian politics, and various gatherings of Igbo immigrant associations around the United States and Great Britain. Below, readers will see that the Biafra issue continues to galvanize many diaspora Igbo. The issue links them with Igbo groups back home that continue to favor a Biafran state separate from Nigeria.

ANA-Net was established by the Association of Nigerians Abroad (ANA). It describes itself as a "body of talented and highly skilled Nigerians in diaspora, formed out of Naijanet to address the wishes of these patriotic Nigerians and friends of Nigeria toward achieving the economic, educational, technological and democratic goals of Nigeria." Although not a political group, the ANA does see itself as a medium for communicating the views of Nigerians abroad to the Nigerian government. ANA is a truly global organization for building community among Nigerians of all ethnic groups in every country where Nigerians reside. It has members and officers in such countries as the United States, Canada, Australia, Great Britain, Norway, Finland, New Zealand, Saudi Arabia, Denmark, South Africa, Hong Kong, and Russia. Among its activities, the ANA has been active in promoting community development and education back in Nigeria (for example, through scholarships). ANA also has been active in the prodemocracy and human rights movements in Nigeria. During the 1994 political crisis, for instance, ANA was among the groups calling for an end to military rule. It also took out ads in Nigerian periodicals supporting the oil workers' strike. The ANA was a leader in international protests against the execution of Ken Saro-Wiwa and other Ogoni activists in the Niger delta.

Naijawomannet gradually emerged in the 1990s from the discussion of gender issues on Naijanet. One of the most controversial issues was the practice of female circumcision (also known as female genital mutilation, or FGM). A female Naijanetter from the University of Pennsylvania started the offshoot women's net to give women a space to discuss issues of special interest to them, although most women participate in both networks and postings are often forwarded back and forth.

Naijanet and other similar networks are having an impact back home in Nigeria, even though a limited number of Nigerians have the Internet access to dialogue directly with members of virtual Nigeria. For example, during the Abacha regime, many Naijanetters were sending home their opinions on events in Nigeria that were published in local magazines and newspapers. Some of the individuals active on the Internet also became internationally active through their positions in academia or business. They spread information on Nigerian issues, arranged conferences, and promoted foreign investment in Nigeria.

Activism by Nigerians abroad is not limited to Naijanetters, of course. There are many formal and informal associations of Nigerians abroad that are in close touch with each other and with issues and groups back home. Many of these organizations are for members of specific ethnic groups in a state or local area, such as the Yorubas of Atlanta. Others are for ethnic group members countrywide, such as the Ibibio Community in the Americas. Some are for people from a particular hometown in Nigeria, such as the Obosi Development Association (Obosi is a town in Anambra State). Others are umbrella groups for all the ethnic associations in a country, such as the Alliance of Yoruba Organizations & Clubs, USA. Some are even international, such as the Urhobo National Association (United States and Canada). Typically these groups profess to be educational, social, cultural, and information sharing groups rather than overtly political. Similar to ethnic associations back home, these organizations reinforce identities and connections with home while helping members adjust to a new, multicultural environment.

Many of these groups are active on the Internet but manage to get beyond the limitations of virtual Nigeria by holding gatherings at which people can meet and establish connections face to face. Some of these groups are overtly political and designed to promote specific ethnic group interests back home. In Great Britain, for example, there is a branch of the Yoruba political party, the Alliance for Democracy (AD). The AD (UK) on the Afenifere website mentions a visit in 2002 by the governor and chairman of Oyo State, who commended the group for assisting the AD in their election campaign in 1998–1999. It was clear that AD (UK) members had hopes of gaining government positions back home and in other ways becoming more active in politics and economic development in Nigeria, for example, by promoting foreign investment and trade between Western countries and Nigeria. At the same time, a new pan-Yoruba group, Igbimo Agba Yoruba (Yoruba Council of Elders), is trying to reconcile feuding Yoruba political leaders from the AD, APP (All People's Party), and PDP (People's Democratic Party), all active in the 1998–1999 elections. The Council held a World Yoruba Congress in Ibadan in 2001, where the top agenda item was the reelection bid of President Obasanjo in 2003. Diaspora Yoruba have been involved with Yoruba in Nigeria in efforts to hold similar meetings to promote Yoruba economic development and other interests.

In Ghana, where millions of Nigerians are living, an explicitly political group has formed to influence politics back home. Called the Grand Alliance of Nigeria (GAONI), the purpose of the group is to promote the reelection of Obasanjo to the presidency. The group claims to represent the sentiments of at least 2 million of the Nigerians in Ghana (without any reference to ethnicity). Among their activities in the fall of 2002 were efforts to prevent some members of the National Assembly of Nigeria from impeaching Obasanjo.

As mentioned above, a significant number of diaspora Igbo in the United States continue to support the creation of an independent nation of Biafra, despite the devastating civil war over this issue from 1967 to 1970. In Washington, D.C., the Biafra Foundation tries to rally support from Igbo at home and abroad to facilitate achieving the goal of liberation for the "40 million Biafrans in bondage in Nigeria." The Biafra Foundation exhorts "Biafrans" in the United States to rescue the motherland by providing generous moral and financial support to the foundation. The Biafra Foundation has close ties to MASSOB in Nigeria. In Washington, D.C., the Foundation recently opened Biafra House to commemorate the civil war. Supporters of Biafra have created new identities to reflect their political agenda. Nigeria is called BiafraNigeria, and its citizens are BiafraNigerians, which implies that there exists in fact, if not in law, two nations in what is now Nigeria. There is also a website, BiafraNigeriaWorld (http://www.biafranigeria.com), that posts important news and discussions by individuals from all over the United States and internationally. In one message exchange, there were messages from many states in the United States and also from Denmark, Great Britain, and Germany. At the opening of Biafra House in 2002, General Odumegwu Ojukwu, the president of Biafra during the civil war, was in attendance. Ojukwu praised Biafra Foundation and MASSOB and encouraged Biafrans in diaspora to support them. Also in attendance were Chief Austin Egwuonwu, former chairman of the World Igbo Conference, and Ralph Uwazurike, head of MASSOB. Part of the agenda at the open house was to raise funds for MASSOB activities back in Nigeria.

It is unclear how many Igbo actually support this new secessionist movement, but it does seem to reflect deeply felt grievances held by many Igbo. These include feelings of discrimination against them since the civil war; concerns about the imposition of shari'a in the north, where many Igbo live; and violence against Igbo in northern cities. Many diaspora Igbo, through their national organization, Igbo USA, are involved with politics in Nigeria, especially with efforts to elect an Igbo to the presidency.

Although there are many ethnically based associations for Nigerians, many associations are designed to bring diaspora Nigerians together regardless of ethnicity. These organizations help to reinforce a focus on national identities and interests. There are local groups, such as the Nigerian Community of Charlotte in North Carolina, and the Nigerian Association of South Florida. Many of these groups bring Nigerians of different ethnicities together by appealing to their common interests as a minority, immigrant community. Many of these groups are also focused on national issues back home in Nigeria. For example, the National Democratic Forum wants to create an alliance between Nigerians abroad and at home "to work together to make Nigeria a better place." The objective is "to promote the interests of all Nigerians for the benefits of all Nigerians." Their first meeting was held in New Jersey in June 2001. Participants came from all over the United States, from Canada, and from Great Britain. Meetings in London, Lagos, Abuja, Port Harcourt, and South Africa also were scheduled. Revising Nigeria's constitution is one widely shared issue across many ethnoregional groups, which has inspired some diaspora groups to form and to hold meetings. In 1998, for instance, Nigerians in the United States gathered in Washington, D.C., to debate the 1995 Draft Constitution. At this meeting, Nigerians from all over the world participated via the Internet. Other meetings have been held to discuss reform of the 1999 military-imposed constitution.

Sometimes ethnic and transethnic associations have coordinated their efforts in order to influence controversial political issues back home. One of these issues, discussed earlier in this book, concerned the Nigerian government's invasion of Odi in Bayelsa State (in the Niger delta) in 1999. Along with debating the issue, members from such groups as the Council of Ijaw Associations Abroad and Niger Deltans in the United Kingdom put pressure on President Obasanjo and Prime Minister Tony Blair in order to achieve a change in Nigerian policies in the Niger delta. One interesting group, Zumunta Association, USA, is trying to bridge the ethnic and religious divide in northern Nigeria. Zumunta was formed in New York in 1991 as an organization of northern Nigerians in the United States. One of its main goals is to develop the north technologically, socially, and economically. It hopes to bring together all groups from the region, for example, Hausa, Fulani, Tiv, Igbira, and Kanuri as well as Muslims and Christians. Zumunta maintains that it is dedicated to the peaceful coexistence of all Nigerians and to a unified Nigeria in which the common people will no longer allow the elites to exploit them and misuse the country's resources.

Using the Internet is not a monopoly of Nigerian immigrants; Nigerians back home also use the Internet to tap into the diaspora community. For example, the Internet is being used by organizations in Nigeria to seek financial assistance from Nigerians abroad. One such organization is Fantsuam Foundation, which is also registered in the United Kingdom. Fantsuam is appealing to Nigerians abroad to consider an alternative to sending money home only to family members. It would like some of those remittances to go toward development efforts in rural villages. Fantsuam (http://www.fantsuam.com) "partners" are invited to contribute their skills as volunteers, to send money, or to adopt a project or a community. The foundation describes itself as a "service civic organization comprised of women's community-based organizations." Its officers are all women based in both Nigeria and the United Kingdom. To lessen concerns about possible corruption and mismanagement of funds, Fantsuam promises that contributors can be incorporated into monitoring and evaluating the projects they help to fund during visits home.

Now that democracy has been restored in Nigeria, the Obasanjo government is making concerted efforts to contact and involve the diaspora community in Nigerian affairs. The government hopes to tap into their skills, connections, and financial resources to help develop the country through more than the provision of remittances. After all, nearly one in ten Nigerians lives abroad, and an estimated $50 billion of Nigerian money is outside the country. Up to now, political instability, corruption, and lack of investment opportunities and incentives have kept many Nigerians wary of risking money in investments in their homeland. Obasanjo faces a big challenge in trying to convince Nigerians inside or outside of the country that their money can be invested safely and reliably back home. Understandably, many Nigerians continue to be wary; they are uneasy about ongoing corruption and the possibility that the military could stage another coup.

Since his election in 1999, Obasanjo and members of his government have been meeting with and courting Nigerians in many Western cities. In 1999, for instance, he hosted a reception for Nigerians at the New York Palace Hotel, and in 2000, the government organized the Atlanta Dialogue with Nigerians there. Even the first lady, Stella Obasanjo, has gotten into the act by visiting Nigerians in such cities as Cape Town, South Africa. The government and corporations such as Mobil Oil are backing a new organization of Nigerian professionals in North and South America called the Nigerians in Diaspora Organization (NIDO). A European NIDO group is also planned. NIDO's objective is to get Nigerian professionals to use their expertise and resources to promote economic development back home. In March 2001, the first NIDO convention was held in Washington, D.C. More than 500 Nigerian accountants, lawyers, doctors, engineers, and other professionals attended to help organize the new group and hold elections for board members. NIDO's "Projects Committee" will assist Nigerian professionals in implementing development projects in the public or private sectors.

Although eager to gain access to the money and expertise of diaspora Nigerians, the government appears less willing to have their political participation. According to the 1999 constitution, Nigerian citizens living abroad (that is, those who are not residents) cannot vote in elections. This restriction has been evaded by defining a resident as anyone who lives in, works in, or originates in a local government area or ward covered by the voter registration center. It is also fairly easy for a Nigerian to vote if they have been home in the past three or four years. Another obstacle to political participation is Electoral Law 2001, which bans those with dual citizenship from running for office. The legislation also prohibits Nigerians residing in the United States, Canada, and Europe from voting by absentee ballot, effectively disenfranchising those who can't get home during elections.

These actions have outraged many diaspora Nigerians who were planning to vote or run for office in 2003. Polly Ubah, chairperson of the New Jersey branch of Nigeria's People's Democratic Party (PDP), expresses her resentment: "How do you ask Nigerian professionals to return home to help in reconstruction, while at the same time downgrading them to the position of second-class citizens?" (Eze 2002). Some Nigerians argue that unless these policies change, many Nigerians abroad will wash their hands of further involvement with the country. Several Nigerians abroad are running for state governorships on PDP or AD tickets. The Washington, D.C.–based Nigerian Democratic Movement and the New York–based United Committee to Save Nigeria were reported to be planning a court challenge to the 2001 law.

Can One Go Home Again?

The big question for many Nigerians abroad is, can they go home now that despotic military rule has ended? "The myth of return" is based on the hope that going home would someday be possible. This view is so deeply held that it has become normative; that is, Nigerians who admit they don't want to go home or who embrace the national identity of their host country are often castigated by their peers. Most Nigerians have been like Femi Ojo-Ade, who writes, "We envy those at home. We wish to join them, sit with them, and map out strategy for a struggle that would use all of our capacities for the good of the community, including ourselves" (2001, 224). Ojo-Ade adds, "If we Nigerians want to influence the future, we must go back home" and "put your money where your heart is" (ibid., 224).

Obasanjo hopes to capitalize on such sentiments by getting Nigerians to invest their money back home, but he hasn't stopped there. He is also trying to get Nigeria's most able citizens to come back home to live. As Stella Obasanjo said in Cape Town, "I am inviting you to please come home and rebuild our nation" (Singer 2001, 7). Government officials are conveying this message in their meetings abroad with Nigerians and also through personal phone calls asking them to at least consider a period of national service. And, as an article by journalist Rena Singer reports, some Nigerians are responding positively to these appeals, but there are many misgivings as well. Omorede Osifo, a Chicago resident with a college degree and four years of banking experience, is one of those who is planning to move back to Nigeria. Her goal is to start a real estate or home mortgage business. Other Nigerians are also willing to start businesses, but most are not prepared to move to Nigeria.

One reason many Nigerians are unwilling to go home is the fear of violence. The governor of Lagos State, where a great deal of crime and religious and ethnic violence has flared up recently, acknowledges that Nigerians abroad will not return unless they feel their lives and property will be secure. He also mentions that, since Obasanjo became president, many Nigerians who have returned have been killed by armed robbers. This is hardly encouraging news to possible returnees! Omorede Osifo admits that her Nigerian friends and family in the United States are skeptical of her decision to go back to Nigeria. They worry that democracy won't last and that a civil war, coup, or fall in oil prices could plunge the country back into turmoil.

As Singer's article concludes, given all of the uncertainties, diaspora Nigerians seem to be taking a cautious approach to going home again to live. They want to see that democracy will be lasting and that they can have a decent existence in Nigeria before they uproot themselves. Basheer Abdullahi, a surgeon living in Dublin, Ireland, represents what many Nigerians abroad are thinking: "Right now, I'm just waiting and seeing. I have the belief that I can help my state and if given the opportunity, also my country. But the way things are going now, it is still difficult to tell if this will work out" (ibid.).

Conclusion

Nigerians abroad are not the only Nigerians worrying about whether or not things will work out in their homeland. Nigerians at home are also concerned. Millions of those who could do so have left Nigeria for greener pastures elsewhere. Many more at home would like to join them. Because many of those who left are Nigeria's "best and brightest," critics have lamented that Nigeria has experienced a debilitating brain drain to industrialized countries. Nigeria and its economic, political, and educational institutions have been left weaker and less able to develop the country as a result of this mass exodus. Some argue, by contrast, that many of those who went abroad were underutilized in Nigeria's relatively underdeveloped economy. By going abroad to work, diaspora Nigerians lessen employment pressures at home and contribute valuable foreign currency to the home economy through their remittances and investments back home. The immigrants' experience, knowledge, and networks acquired abroad can also contribute to national development. In this way, the brain drain becomes a brain gain.

Perhaps a less tangible gain of the Nigerian diaspora is the expansion and re-creation of identities that occur when people leave home. Many Nigerians abroad are exposed to new people and more cosmopolitan values and ways of life that expand their horizons beyond the confines of region, ethnicity, and religion back home. It is not that these identities are no longer important. They are, and most Nigerians in diaspora strive to maintain cherished identities and ties to hometowns, regions, and ethnically related people. At the same time, those identities become modified as Nigerians find themselves living abroad for many years. Partly, this comes from more inclusive national identities and labels attached to them by others, which then influence self-concepts. In this author's research on virtual Nigeria, as discussed above, she discovered that many websites and associations are for "Nigerians," not for any specific ethnic group. Moreover, Nigerians from a variety of ethnic groups participate in open discussions about the issues affecting them and their country. They have become accustomed to an open, democratic society in which people of diverse ethnic and religious backgrounds can freely debate their differences, yet strive to live and work together in peace and tolerance. They have experienced achieving success and working in a system in which personal advancement is not dependent on government or corrupted by the ethnoregional politics of home.

In an interesting essay by a member of the Nigerian Democracy and Justice Project in Washington, D.C., the government's NIDO (Nigerians in Diaspora Organization) initiative is criticized for being under too much control by the Nigerian government. The writer's remarks show clearly that many Nigerians abroad are a transformed people. He notes that, in the United States and Europe, there is a large number of well-run, grassroots, nongovernmental organizations, including Oduduwa, Igbo, Zumunta, Ijaw, and Edo ethnic associations, as well as professional, cultural, and social organizations. They do not need the Nigerian government running things as the government often does in Nigeria. He adds that Nigerians abroad are already a potent force for change in Nigeria through the kinds of programs they have undertaken while abroad, including medical relief efforts in Nigeria and donations of books and equipment. In the United States, Nigerians have learned what they can do for themselves. He comments, "Listen Nigerian government officials! This is America and not Nigeria where your hand is in everything and nothing is happening or being achieved." (Harris 2003)" Nigerians abroad want to bring their knowledge and experience to bear on solving the problems in Nigeria by leading the way or, at least, in an equal partnership with the state. It will be important for the future of Nigeria whether or not Nigerians abroad return home so that the new values, knowledge, skills, and identities they have developed can become a model for their countrymen and women.

So far, it remains uncertain how many will return and what the future holds for Nigeria. This book's final chapter will examine some of the major issues, especially ethnoregional and religious divisions, which will determine

Nigeria's future. Elections in 2003 and the aftermath, for one, will be an indication of how much influence parochial identities continue to have on the government and on party behavior and issues. Chapter 11 will also discuss whether or not the much-resented power of the northern ethnomilitary oligarchy is being reduced by the formal return to democratic institutions and civilian control of the government. As part of this discussion, the upcoming chapter will explore what Nigerians think about the major issues that will determine whether or not Nigeria will be able to overcome its ethnoregional and religious differences and become a livable home for Nigerians abroad as well as for those who have remained behind.

Timeline

1965, 1990	U.S. immigration laws make Nigerian immigration easier
1970s	The first period of immigration of Nigerians to the United States begins
1980s–Present	Migration of Nigerians to the United States and Europe grows; European immigration policies become more restrictive
1990s	Naijanet and other Internet sites for Nigerians are established
1995	The United States expands the diversity immigration lottery, benefiting Africans

Significant People, Places, and Events

COMMONWEALTH The British Commonwealth is made up of fifty-four nations that were former British colonies. Among other privileges of commonwealth membership are liberal rights to immigrate to Great Britain.

EGWUONWU, CHIEF AUSTIN Egwuonwu was a former president of the African Students' Association at Rutgers University in the early 1970s. He is the founder of a number of regional Igbo ethnic associations in the United States, and he cofounded the national group Igbo USA. This led to the formation of the World Igbo Congress, whose chair he became in 1997.

FEMALE GENITAL MUTILATION (FGM) FGM is also known as female circumcision. It involves excision of some or almost all of the external genitalia. This controversial practice occurs in many countries of Africa, and an estimated 80 to 100 million females have undergone some form of the procedure.

OBASANJO, STELLA The Nigerian First Lady is from Anambra State and is a Christian. She has accompanied her husband on many overseas trips, including one on October 27, 1999, to visit with President Bill Clinton. She has been instrumental in aiding her husband in his efforts to improve his relationship with the eastern states in Nigeria.

OJUKWU, ODUMEGWU The former head of state of Biafra, Ojukwu was a candidate for the presidency in Nigeria in the 2003 elections. His political ambitions may explain why he now disavows any sympathy for an independent Biafran state.

PERMANENT RESIDENT Acquiring permanent resident status in the United States is often the first step toward naturalization (citizenship). Temporary residents include students or those with work permits, who are allowed to stay for a limited period of time.

REMITTANCES By some estimates, Nigerian immigrants in the United States send home about $1.3 billion per year. Worldwide, remittances from immigrants are worth an estimated $100 billion to their home countries.

UWAZURIKE, RALPH The leader of MASSOB, Uwazurike is an advocate of Biafran independence. He has described Biafra as the "fourth kingdom of God on Earth." Nigeria's main pan-Igbo association, Ohanaeze Ndigbo, has rejected calls for secession.

Bibliography

Bastian, Misty. 1999. "Nationalism in a Virtual Space: Immigrant Nigerians on the Internet." *West Africa Review.* http://www.westafricareview.com (accessed July 17, 2002).

Eze, Chukwu. 2002. "A Coup against Nigerians Abroad." http://www.indypressny.org (accessed July 19, 2002).

Gordon, April. 1997. "A Demographic Portrait of Africans in the United States." Presented at the November 1997 meeting of the African Studies Association, Columbus, OH.

Harris, Ugo. 2003. "Nigerians in Diaspora Organization (NIDO)—Agents of Body and Mind Control." http://www.nigerdeltacongress.com (accessed February 8, 2003).

Hunt, Stephen. 2000. "The 'New' Pentecostal Churches in Britain." Presented at the Fourteenth International Conference of the Center for Studies on New Religions, Riga, Latvia.

Jumare, Ibrahim M. 1997. "The Displacement of the Nigerian Academic Community." *Journal of Asian and African Studies* 32 (June): 110–119.

Nyang, Sulayman S. 1998. "The African Immigrant Family in the United States of America: Challenges and Opportunities." Presented at the May 1998 meeting of the Center for African Peace and Conflict Resolution, Sacramento, CA.

Ojo-Ade, Femi. 2001. *Death of a Myth: Critical Essays on Nigeria.* Trenton, NJ: Africa World Press.

Osili, Una Okonkwo. 2001. "Immigrants and Home Country Ties: What Does It Mean for Chicago?" http://www.globalchicago.org (accessed July 29, 2002).

Singer, Rena. 2001. "Nigeria Calls Expatriate Sons and Daughters Home." *Christian Science Monitor* (February 26): 7.

Ugwu-Oju, Dympna. 2000. "Should My Tribal Past Shape Delia's Future?" *Newsweek* (December 4): 14.

Wipsa, Leslie. 1998. "At L.A. Mass Ibos Re-Create Home Villages." *National Catholic Reporter* (March 27): 3.

CHAPTER ELEVEN

The Future of Nigeria

"THE DISINTEGRATION OF NIGERIA MEANS THE END OF AFRICA. Nigeria is Africa. It is Africa's beacon of hope." The fate of West Africa is "tied to the destiny of Nigeria." These words were part of an impassioned commentary from the president of Gambia, Yahaya Jammeh, made in December 2002 (World Peace Foundation 2003). Although perhaps overstating Nigeria's importance to the growth and progress of sub-Saharan Africa, what happens to Nigeria is understandably of great concern to its African neighbors. Given Nigeria's size, wealth, and power, if it were to break down economically or politically, the disastrous consequences would be widely felt. Nigeria's fate is also of critical importance to the United States. Nigeria is the fifth largest supplier of oil to the United States and a key player in its efforts to promote political stability and democracy in the West African region. With so much at stake, Nigeria-watchers have been anxiously monitoring the progress of the latest return to civilian, democratic governance in the country.

The return to democracy and the inauguration of the Fourth Republic, beginning in 1999, was initially viewed as a new day for Nigeria after years of autocracy under the military. There were high hopes that the lessons of past mistakes had been learned and that democracy and development would bear such fruit as a decline in the forces of narrow communalism and sectarian violence. President Obasanjo was hailed as an embodiment of the new dispensation. It is also important to note that Obasanjo's victory at the polls showed the extent to which Nigerian politics had moved beyond the politics of narrow, parochial loyalties and appeals. The 1993 national elections had already shown the electorate's willingness to vote outside of ethnoregional and religious lines. A Yoruba Muslim, Moshood Abiola, had gained broad support throughout Nigeria, including among Christian and non-Yoruba northerners. In the 1999 election, Obasanjo, a Yoruba Christian, received more support in the Muslim north than he did among his fellow Yoruba in the south.

Audu Ogbeh (left), chairman of Nigeria's ruling People's Democratic Party (PDP), listens as President Obasanjo addresses party supporters March 6, 2003, at a presidential campaign rally in Kano for his reelection. President Obasanjo reaffirmed his commitment to deal decisively with culprits involved in political thuggery and assassinations following the March 5 murder of Harry Marshall, a stalwart of the opposing All Nigeria People's Party (ANPP). (AFP PHOTO/PIUS UTOMI EKPEI)

Obasanjo promised that he would serve the nation and be his own man. He would not be beholden to any ethnic or religious community or to the ethnomilitary elite who helped to put him in power. To his credit, he initiated some significant reforms. The media, civil society organizations, and political activists found their freedom restored. The government passed a tough new anticorruption law, and some of the billions stolen by former dictator Sani Abacha and his family were returned. Human rights violations and corruption by previous governments have been investigated. Antipoverty and educational programs have been introduced in an effort to improve the lives of ordinary people. The president has used his international popularity to travel to several Western countries to encourage foreign investment in Nigeria and to court the many Nigerians living abroad.

Despite these positive steps, Obasanjo has faced enormous, deeply entrenched problems that may be too great for any leader to handle, at least in the short term. This last chapter will focus on what progress has been made since 1999 in lessening the ethnoregional and religious divisions that threaten Nigeria's stability and future. The discussion will look first at the continuing political dominance of the northern ethnomilitary elite, ethnoregionalism and corruption in politics, and communal violence. This will be followed by a discussion of the outcome of the 2003 elections and then with conclusions about what changes Nigerians feel must be made for Nigeria to survive as a unified nation.

The Ethnomilitary Elite

Nigeria's military has been a northern-dominated institution since the 1960s; both military and civilian rulers have governed with the military's consent and have been removed when their military support was lost. Although popularly elected in 1999, Obasanjo would not have become the president of Nigeria without the political and financial support of such powerful northern generals as Ibrahim Babangida. The military remains the single most powerful group in Nigeria, with power to unseat any president who might threaten to go too far in the direction of reforms that could threaten their interests. Many critics conclude that Obasanjo has not pushed the investigation of the human rights abuses and financial misdeeds of living ex-presidents because this would be going "too far." For the same reason, Obasanjo has not been in favor of overhauling the federal system or of lessening federal control over the oil revenues that allow the ethnomilitary elite to line their pockets and maintain their patronage networks.

Realizing the potential of the military to be his undoing, in 1999 Obasanjo began to purge many northern military officers from the armed forces. All officers who had political posts during the last three military regimes were retired, as were about fifty members of the former provisional ruling council during the Abacha regime. This was viewed as necessary to ensure the survival of democracy, to subordinate the military to civilian rule, and to help rein in corruption. In April 2002, all three chiefs of the armed forces (army, navy, and air force) were replaced. In all of these moves, Obasanjo was trying to consolidate his position and undermine Hausa-Fulani dominance of the military. Obasanjo's concerns about the military are real, because as of 1985, 70 percent of the senior officers were from the north or the Middle Belt. It is not surprising that most of the officers retired by Obasanjo are northern Hausa-Fulani Muslims. Two-thirds of the replacements are southerners, with another third being from the Middle Belt. As could be expected, Obasanjo has alienated many of his powerful northern military backers, including Ibrahim Babangida. Some of the generals are also angry because they view the Oputa panel investigations and the efforts to prosecute Muhammed Abacha, Sani Abacha's son, for murder and embezzlement as part of a vendetta against northern leaders.

Although northern dominance of the military is less than before, there are still many powerful active and retired northern officers, and they wanted to see Obasanjo replaced in the presidency in the 2003 elections. Several of them, including former presidents Babangida, Buhari, and Abubakar, considered running against him in the April 19, 2003, elections. Buhari was the first of the generals to declare his candidacy, but he was joined by former general and senator Ike Nwachukwu and former leader of Biafra General Odumegwu Ojukwu. Babangida and Abubakar decided not to enter the fray. It is too early to tell whether this trend of ex-generals running for the presidency is propelling Nigerian presidential politics into a system in which coalitions of generals and their backers, rather than civilian politicians, run against each other. Nigerian journalist Bolaji Aluko has aptly named the general-politicians the "militicians." If the generals are unable to oust Obasanjo through elections, there is still a possibility for the military to stage another coup should they decide that Obasanjo must go. Although newly appointed southern military officers are likely to be loyal to Obasanjo, Nigeria's 80,000-man armed forces still have a preponderance of northern common soldiers whose support for the Obasanjo government could be questionable if they came to view it as biased against the north. Although a coup remains unlikely at the present time, if a return to military rule were to occur, it would almost certainly tear the country apart in civil strife.

Ethnoregionalism and Corruption in Politics

Opposition to Obasanjo has mounted since his election in 1999, which is reflected in intraparty feuds and a proliferation of new political parties. Much of the opposition is associated with current ethnoregional and religious divisions. Although most parties have mixed membership and had to appeal to voters from across the country to win in the recent national elections, to a large extent the political parties and politicians selected and rejected candidates, jockeyed for position, jumped from one party to another, created new parties, or forged intraparty alliances largely on the basis of ethnoregional interests. For example, some members of Obasanjo's own party, the PDP, actively worked to replace him as the party's candidate for president. Some were northerners who felt that Obasanjo has implemented antinorth policies and betrayed them. Along with his purge of northern military officers, the northerners believe that Obasanjo has been antagonistic toward shari'a and has favored southern Christians in political appointments and business contracts.

Some northern and Igbo members of the party also wanted to dump the president because his run for a second term undermined an alleged agreement made with the party (and the northern generals) that he would run for only one term as part of a rotational "power shift." One version of the power shift arrangement is that the presidency was to rotate from the south back to the north in 2003. The version espoused by some prominent Igbo members of the PDP, such as Chuba Okadigbo, is that there was to be a rotation, or "power shift," from the north to the southwest in 1999 and then to the southeast in 2003. This would facilitate the long-standing Igbo goal of having one of their own in the presidency for the first time. At first, Okadigbo planned to contest the PDP nomination for the presidency, but he decided instead to defect to the All Nigeria People's Party (ANPP). The ANPP—which is being financially backed by Babangida, who is now an anti-Obasanjo defector from the PDP—selected northerner Buhari as its presidential candidate and Okadigbo as his running mate. Another Igbo leader, Alex Ekwueme, decided to challenge Obasanjo's candidacy within the PDP. Ekwueme was reportedly backed by some of the country's generals and some governors from the north and the oil-producing south. In the end, Ekwueme lost, and Obasanjo was renominated early in January 2003.

One of the most troubling trends in Nigerian party politics is the continuation of past "win at any cost" practices that undermined democracy in the past. One manifestation of this was the December 2001 murder of justice minister Bola Ige, a key Obasanjo supporter among the Yoruba. It was mentioned in a previous chapter how state governors, such as the governor of Anambra State, have employed ethnic militias to kill and terrorize their political opponents. The nearer the country got to the April 2003 elections, the more violence there was. In March 2003, Harry Marshall, a close aide to Buhari, was gunned down in his home. Dozens of other Nigerians were killed in political clashes around the country. From local elections on up to the national level, the competition for office was intense and many worried that elections were unlikely to be conducted in a fair or impartial way. The term *second term syndrome* could be applied to the phenomenon, in which incumbents and parties from the 1999 elections were resorting to bombings and assassinations in a desperate effort to keep their advantages and positions. Politicians continued to use appeals to parochial interests to gain support, so it was not surprising that both ethnoregional and religious tensions were increasing before the April 2003 elections. Critics contend that issues-based platforms still did not matter much compared to ethnic or religious identity and getting one's own candidate into office in order to gain access to the rewards of power.

This brings up the issue of corruption among officeholders. Despite Obasanjo's early efforts to punish corruption by government officials, little seems to have changed for the better. Nigeria remains at or near the top of corruption watchdog Transparency International's dubious honor roll of the most corrupt countries in the world. It does not bode well that Nigeria's national legislative officials secretly awarded themselves extravagant pay increases and allowances. At a time when a large majority of Nigerians are living on less than $1 per day, top lawmakers in 2000 awarded themselves a salary of more than $9,000 per month. Both national and state legislators remain among the most corrupt of Nigeria's government officials, and several were removed from office, including two presidents of the national senate. Such greed by officeholders has a corrosive effect on society and undermines respect for and faith in the government. Corruption not only perpetuates economic inequality and poverty, it also undermines the climate for investment necessary for economic growth. All of these negative results reinforce ethnic, regional, and religious tensions. Although northerners dominate the federal government and are, therefore, disproportionately responsible for corruption at that level, malfeasance in office appears to be an equal opportunity Nigerian vice.

Ethnoregional and Religious Conflict

Since Obasanjo took office, ethnoregional and religious violence has gotten worse, not better. Between 1999 and 2003, more than 10,000 people died in communal strife. Both ethnicity and religion have been involved in outbreaks of violence that continue to erode what trust and tolerance exists among the involved ethnic groups and between Christians and Muslims. One recent episode involved the Miss World pageant held in Kaduna in November 2002. Instead of showcasing Nigeria's cosmopolitanism to the world, the ugly and embarrassing face of ethnic and religious insensitivity and intolerance was shown instead. What sparked the violence was a journalist's comment in a local newspaper that the prophet Muhammed (founder of the Islamic religion) would have approved of the pageant and maybe even married one of the contestants. Muslims were outraged at the blasphemy and disrespect this comment represented to them. The controversy led to four days of riots and violence involving Muslims and Christians. When the violence ended, 200 people were dead, 1,000 were injured, and more than 30,000 were displaced from their homes. The Zamfara State government authorities issued a fatwa (religious edict) for Muslims to kill the reporter who made the offending remarks. To its credit, the National Supreme Council for Islamic Affairs overruled the politicians and accepted the apology of the newspaper for the incident.

Additional sectarian violence struck the mostly peaceful city of Jos as well as Kaduna. In 2002 in Jos, politicians allegedly goaded their respective Christian and Muslim followers to attack each other. At least 500 people were killed, and homes, churches, mosques, and stores were destroyed. Reports from dismayed local residents indicate that Christians and Muslims used to live in peace with each other, but each group now sees the other as the source of recent conflicts. As one Christian remarked, "The Muslim northerners started getting jealous that the president is a Christian. They claimed he was ignoring them and they started attacking us. Now we are divided." A Muslim neighbor saw things differently. He claimed, "The problem is with the Christian politicians. They are inciting the youngsters for selfish reasons. They are trying to tell us we do not deserve as much as them because we are Muslims" (Harman 2002, 6). Similarly, in Kaduna in 2003, Christians and Muslims who had lived and worked together for years are now moving into segregated enclaves to escape sectarian violence. In most cases, religion is not the cause of the violence; it is sparked by such issues as who gets jobs, political offices, and police protection.

Along with religious violence, ethnic clashes have also increased in many parts of the country, as was discussed in previous chapters. For instance, in February 2003, fighting occurred between rival Urhobo and Itsekiri gangs in Warri, the headquarters for oil companies in the Niger delta. The conflict was related to competition over the delineation of electoral wards in advance of the April elections. As many as twelve people were killed and several homes were set on fire before police and soldiers moved in to stop the violence. In March 2003, Ijaw and Itsekiri youths were involved in attacks on each other. Itsekiri villages were burned down, and oil company activities were disrupted by attacks on workers. The conflict was linked to the February dispute between the Itsekiri and Urhobo over political representation. The Ijaw, siding with the Urhobo, believe they are politically marginalized and want local electoral boundaries redrawn. By the time of the elections in mid-April, an uneasy calm had been restored to the area.

Some observers attribute the increase in violence since 1999 in part to the return to democracy and greater freedom since Obasanjo came to power. Under military rule, conflict and violence were more readily and ruthlessly repressed. People are now more able to express views and advocate policies, such as the implementation of shari'a, that may provoke ethnoregional and religious antagonisms. Communal groups also feel freer to question territorial and power arrangements and to challenge institutions imposed by previous regimes, such as calling for secession or a "power shift." Whatever the causes and flash points for violence, how to stop ethnic or religious violence and protect lives and property poses a major dilemma for the government. Under military rule, the government could act as it chose, more or less with impunity. Now the government is more likely to be held accountable for its actions. Moreover, when there is violence, each side tends to accuse the government of complicity or favoritism toward its rival, of not acting quickly or forcefully enough, or of acting too forcefully and with disregard for human rights.

The charge of human rights violations has recently been leveled at Obasanjo and suggests a worrisome tendency on the part of the government to overreact in the use of force in dealing with ethnic and religious conflict. Human Rights Watch, an international human rights monitoring group, reports that Obasanjo's human rights record so far is mixed. The Oputa panel and its investigation of human rights abuses is praised, but the government is sharply criticized for excessive violence against civilians, such as the 1999 massacre of hundreds of civilians in the town of Odi in Bayelsa State. Soldiers are alleged to have killed the villagers in retaliation for the murder of several police officers by some militant youths. Soldiers are reported to have gathered the villagers together at a meeting; then they shot them down in cold blood. Soldiers also killed at least 200 Tiv civilians in several villages in another revenge case in which armed militants had murdered a number of soldiers. In both cases, government forces were initially called in to stop ethnic conflicts.

One effort to stop ethnic and religious violence has been to clamp down on militant ethnic organizations, such as the Oodua People's Congress (OPC) and the Movement for the Actualization of the Sovereign State of Biafra (MASSOB). For instance, MASSOB offices have been broken into, their meetings disrupted, and their leaders arrested. In the Niger delta, the center of Nigeria's oil industry, reports of violence and brutality by the police and soldiers against protesters and ethnic group associations have been a black eye for Obasanjo and have undermined his credibility as a champion of democracy and human rights. Such heavy-handedness is also counterproductive, as it does little to defuse or lessen ethnic or religious strife.

The issue of shari'a in northern states is perhaps the single most explosive issue dividing the country. To many Muslims, support for shari'a is a means to combat rampant crime, moral breakdown, and political corruption in the north after secular institutions have failed. Their beliefs are analogous to those of conservative Christians in the United States who feel that only by restoring God's law and following the Bible can the country be a moral and upright nation. Clearly, such ideas are divisive when not everyone shares the same moral and religious beliefs. For this reason, in Nigeria, a commitment to a secular state has been regarded as being essential to political stability and democracy. Because Christians are a minority in the country and in the north, they understandably feel threatened by the imposition of shari'a in twelve of the northern states and by other signs of Islamization of the country. Northern Muslims resent Obasanjo's statements that he would intervene in the northern states to prevent the imposition of harsh punishments for crime under shari'a. They believe they have a right to choose their legal system. So far, no one has been able to resolve this divisive issue, which interpenetrates and worsens ethnic, regional, and religious antagonisms over resource and opportunity issues that are not religious in nature.

The 2003 Elections

The conduct and results of the 2003 elections are considered to be a major test of Nigeria's democratic transformation. For one, since independence, Nigeria has never succeeded in having two consecutive elected governments in power uninterrupted by a coup. Also, there have been doubts whether or not Nigeria could conduct genuinely free and fair elections, especially in light of the violence and contentious politicking before the elections. It appeared to many observers that the politicians and parties were repeating the discredited practices of the past and that the outcome at election time would be widespread fraud and rigging of the votes.

Although domestic and international election monitors were in place around the country to observe the elections, many of the monitors admitted that their standards for validating that the elections were free and fair were set low. To declare Nigeria's struggling civilian government illegitimate was considered too destabilizing to Nigeria and to the West African region after years of autocratic military rule. Most monitors acknowledged that the election process was likely to be imperfect and that some cheating would take place, but that that would not be enough to declare the election results invalid.

Indeed, these low expectations were fulfilled. In elections held on April 12 and 19, Obasanjo and his People's Democratic Party (PDP) won a landslide victory. The PDP won control of twenty-one of the thirty-six state legislatures and twenty-eight of thirty-six governorships, as well as a majority of seats in both houses of the national legislature. The All Nigeria People's Party (ANPP), headed by Buhari, was a distant second place, winning mainly in some states in the Muslim north. Obasanjo defeated Buhari for the presidency by a nearly two to one margin. Even before all of the election results were in, Buhari and the opposition parties were crying foul and calling for a cancellation and rerunning of the elections in most of the states. Otherwise, Buhari threatened there could be a massive and violent reaction against the newly "elected" government and even the possibility of a breakup of the country. In other statements, Buhari vowed that there would be no government on May 30, with May 29 being the date Obasanjo was to be sworn in as president.

Election monitors agreed that there were serious irregularities in the conduct of the elections, including ballot box stuffing and falsification of results. In some places, such as Enugu State, voters were disenfranchised because polling stations never opened. Abuses were worst in the oil-rich states of the southeast. In Rivers State, Delta State, and Bayelsa State, for instance, there were widespread implausibly high voter turnouts of 90 percent or more reported. Apparently, all parties were guilty of dubious practices, not just the victorious PDP. Despite these and other problems, most monitoring groups felt that the abuses were insufficiently bad to discredit the election outcomes in most cases, especially in the reelection of Obasanjo.

On a positive note, the threatened mass action and other dire consequences against the government did not take place. Challenges to the electoral results thus far have been largely peaceful and lawful. A coalition of seventeen opposition parties joined Buhari and the ANPP in demanding the formation of an interim government until new elections could be held. This effort failed, however, and Obasanjo was sworn in on May 29 as president for a second term. The only hint of major violence was a disclosure by the police that they had uncovered a plot by "some groups" to use explosives to stop Obasanjo's inauguration. To date, there remains considerable bitterness over the elections, as indicated by the following opinion piece in a Lagos newspaper by Gani Fawehinmi, a presidential contender and one of Nigeria's foremost human rights activists.

> I woke up this morning at 65 deeply saddened by the events in my country concerning the 2003 General Elections. Undoubtedly, our brand of democ-

racy defies plain logic. It does not accommodate honesty and integrity. Everything about the 2003 elections is unnatural. If the results of the elections are a reflection of the votes of the electorate then they (the electorate) voted or were induced to vote for continuation of poverty, hunger, starvation, depressed economy, looting, corruption, low quality of life, weak currency, mass unemployment, insecurity of life and property, lack of water, epileptic electricity supply, and bad roads. THAT TREND IS ABNORMAL. If the results do not reflect the votes cast, then the elections were massively rigged and grossly manipulated. Either way, the fate of this country is doomed. And I pity the people, particularly the masses. Nevertheless, my heart bleeds that my country continues to be governed directly or remotely by unrepentant Lucifers and obdurate satans revelling in political and money debauchery and belching out falsehood, lies, and all forms of distortions to hoodwink the people into believing that what is abnormal is normal, and what is unreal is real. May God Almighty deliver us from this rot in which money manipulations and Mafioso reign supreme and honesty and integrity are jettisoned. However, I made bold to say that the future of this country is bleak, dark, and disturbing. (Fawehinmi 2003)

Despite the shortcomings of the elections, there are some noteworthy ethnoregional and religious aspects of the elections. For one, Obasanjo's victory signals that power sharing between the north and the south, if not a power shift, is occurring. Obasanjo has managed to dilute the power of the north in both the military and the federal government. Second, as mentioned previously, major political parties are becoming more ethnoregionally and religiously inclusive, which is reducing bloc voting along such lines. Moreover, politicians and parties that are associated with narrow ethnoregional and religious interests and groups are not finding as much success as in the past. For instance, one reason Buhari lost the presidency is that he was reported to be exhorting Muslims to vote only for Muslim political candidates. He also charged that PDP candidates and Obasanjo were nonbelievers who didn't deserve the vote of good Muslims. Not only did this alienate many southerners, it also failed to win him or the ANPP some of the northern states. Indeed, many Muslim northerners are PDP members. Consequently, the Muslim northern vote was split. The effects of this were shown in a recent meeting of the Arewa Consultative Forum, the northern umbrella political association designed to promote northern Muslim solidarity. In discussions over whether Arewa should join the chorus of demands for new elections, the group was unable to arrive at a consensus because Arewa itself was divided between ANPP and PDP members.

The drubbing the Yoruba AD (Alliance for Democracy) party took at the polls (losing every governorship except in Lagos State in the southwest) reveals the split among Yoruba voters and also that an avowedly ethnoregional party can have limited appeal even in its home region. Obasanjo's victory in the southwestern states attests to his success in mending fences with his fellow Yoruba, most of whom voted against him in 1999.

The Igbo too face divisions in the ranks. Obasanjo and the PDP put in a very strong showing in Igboland, despite the fact that civil war leader Ojukwu was running for president on the All Progressive Grand Alliance (APGA) ticket. Although Ojukwu believes the southeastern Igbo states were stolen from him, the Royal Fathers of Igboland, a group of traditional leaders, paid a solidarity visit to Obasanjo after his reelection, despite the dispute over electoral fraud.

Although legal appeals of the election results are ongoing, it is likely that the victors in most cases will retain their offices. The main question now is how the politicians will govern and if they can improve on the less-than-impressive record of those who gained office in 1999.

The Future of Ethnoregionalism and Religious Divisions

Despite setbacks and disappointments, most Nigerians continue to have faith that Nigeria can manage, if not solve overnight, its ethnoregional and religious problems. Among the optimists is Dr. Chukwuemeka Ezeife, a special advisor on political matters to Obasanjo during his first term. In one of Nigeria's leading newspapers, the *Guardian,* Ezeife gives an impassioned plea for national unity and urges the winning and losing parties to unite for the sake of the country. Among his remarks are the following:

> Nigeria can be made good. I can see Nigeria, re-organised after a national dialogue, and things begin to work. A re-organised One Nigeria will be in the long-term best interest of every Nigerian. Any intelligent Nigerian who can think in terms of the costs and benefits to him, of his continued membership of such One Nigeria, should see that his costs are smaller than his benefits. This is true for a Hausa/Fulani, Tiv, Junkun, Zuru, Member, Kanuri, for an Igbo, Ijaw, Itshekiri, Eggba, Effik, Ibibio, etc. It is even true of the Niger Delta peoples, as a group. It is true for every deep-thinking Nigerian, whether he is a Christian, a Moslem, a traditional religionist, whether he is from the North or South or in between North and South; whether he is from the Western or Eastern part of Nigeria. One Nigeria, re-organised so that things begin to

work, is in the best interest of every Nigerian. Only negative emotions and shallow, short-range thinking can lead to a different judgement. The British were merely in the hands of God when they brought together elements of the country we call Nigeria. God, not the British, created One Nigeria. And God does not make a mistake! (Onwubiko 2003)

Although there is no consensus on what changes to the current system are needed, many believe that a helpful beginning would be to reorganize the framework of government inherited at independence to allow more autonomy for the various states and local governments. The push for restructuring the relationship between federal, state, and local governments is in large part motivated by the belief that the current system is unfair and gives more of the nation's resources to some groups than others. This belief sustains the pervasive fear that ethnic and religious groups have of being dominated by other groups. This fear fuels a hypersensitivity to perceived slights or discrimination. Insecure and distrustful of each other, ethnic groups and even subethnic groups seek more autonomy and control over resources to ensure that they are getting their share.

Southerners are most likely to favor restructuring to create "true federalism," that is, a more decentralized political system that gives more autonomy to the states. Although Nigeria is formally a federal system, currently with thirty-six states, reform advocates contend that Nigeria has never had a true federal system. Instead, the elite compact made by British colonial authorities and Nigerian leaders when the country was formed gave too much power to the north and to the federal government at the expense of the southern states. The centralization of power at the national level increased over time under successive military regimes. One of the most contentious problems of the current system is that the federal government controls most of the nation's oil revenues and then distributes them to the states based on a revenue allocation formula. Unable to raise their own revenues through taxation, the states are dependent on the federal government for their operating budgets. Southerners, especially those in the oil-producing Niger delta states, want the allocation formula changed so that they get a larger share of oil revenues. Another decentralization issue is the demand by the states for their own police forces and the abolition of the federal police system.

During his first term, Obasanjo opposed demands for decentralization. He argued that a radical change in the revenue sharing and resource ownership systems would result in a worsening of regional inequality and even more bickering over resources among Nigeria's ethnoregional groups. Indeed, "true federalism," which would enable the oil-rich states to control more of their resources, is especially unpopular in the nineteen northern states, which are heavily dependent economically on their current share of oil revenues. This is a major reason the north has been so determined to maintain its control of power at the national level.

Restructuring of the government has so far been limited to the creation of new states and local area governments without changing the fundamental dominant position of the national government. Instead of promoting regional autonomy, however, the proliferation of states has weakened rather than strengthened the position of the states in relation to the federal government. It also has exacerbated patronage politics and government inefficiency. The use of "federal character" in determining rights and resources within states favors indigenes while making second-class citizens of outsiders. This worsens ethnic relations, intensifies the importance of ethnic identification, and lessens a sense of national identity. Furthermore, some observers argue that the desire for more local autonomy and independence is now so great that the federal system is vulnerable to breaking apart.

Already there are overt calls for secession, including among some elements of the Igbo. Others call for a "sovereign national conference," which would include representatives from all of Nigeria's ethnic groups. At this conference, Nigerians would discuss whether they wish to stay together as one nation and, if so, how they want to govern themselves. The idea of a national conference is, like true federalism, largely supported by southerners. In the north, both ideas are seen as a plot by the south to shift power away from them. The north is also hostile to the idea of a breakup of the country, as northern states would lose access to the resource revenue produced mostly by the south.

Akin to the demand for a sovereign national conference, but less controversial, is the popular call to revise the 1999 military-imposed constitution. Obasanjo has supported this idea and has already created a Presidential Constitutional Review Committee. The committee has begun the review process and is expected to solicit popular input from across the country. Revising the constitution is widely seen as a means of creating new governance arrangements that could result in greater legitimacy for how the country is run.

Although Nigerians of all ethnicities and religions have many obstacles to overcome, most Nigerians want their country to remain unified, democratic, and equitable for all. And, there are many Nigerians within and outside the country willing to work for democracy and national unity. Unfortunately, though, after years of economic and political crisis and ethnoregional and religious strife, there are growing numbers who see little future in maintaining what they consider to be a fiction of nationhood. Nigeria, these pessimists argue, has never been a nation and never should have been created as such by its colonial masters. They believe that there are too many fundamental and irreconcilable differences between the Muslim north and the mostly Christian south, and that each should go its separate way. As Ojo-Ade worries, how can reconciliation take place when there are such "diametrically opposed cultures, principles, and peoples?" (Ojo-Ade 2001, 71).

What does seem certain is that if Nigeria is to hold together and make real progress in healing its wounds, fundamental changes will have to be made. It will be necessary for Nigerians to come together and frankly discuss their differences and then be willing to compromise in order to create a country in which they can live together. Below are some general proposals that concerned Nigerians themselves have suggested in a variety of writings and public forums:

- There is a need for more political and financial autonomy for the states and local governments.
- There should be a change in the revenue allocation formula to make more resources available to states and local governments.
- Governance issues must be addressed, for example, corruption, professionalism, fairness, and the delivery of public services.
- Improving the accountability and transparency of government is essential.
- Government needs to be more decentralized and participatory.
- Human rights, freedom, and equality of all citizens in all parts of the country need to be safeguarded.
- Citizens' peace and security must be protected (for example, from crime and from official abuse) in order to promote national unity.
- Citizenship should be defined on the basis of residence rather than ethnic, religious, regional, or gender identities.
- The military must be made subordinate to civilian control.
- The oil-producing states should have more control over oil revenues produced in their territory.
- Nigeria's character as a secular state and protection for freedom of religion must be upheld.
- Nigeria must diversify and grow its economy by encouraging entrepreneurship in the nonoil sectors of the economy. This is necessary to alleviate poverty, improve living standards, encourage the retention of Nigeria's trained and educated citizens, and give ordinary citizens a meaningful stake in peaceful coexistence with others in a unified state.

To define and achieve these goals, Nigeria will need strong, effective, and honest leadership from both government and civil society. So far, many

Nigerians feel that the government under Obasanjo has failed to deliver. Although he promises to do more in a second term, many believe that Obasanjo has lost the goodwill he had at the beginning of his first term and that it could be even harder for him to undertake the necessary reforms in a second term. Unfortunately, none of the other parties, especially those that backed discredited ex-generals as their presidential candidates, seems to be taking seriously Nigeria's need for untarnished and effective leaders. Perhaps this is why most Nigerians voted for Obasanjo despite the problems of his first term.

Some Nigerians and commentators despair that Nigeria will be able to overcome its problems. They believe that Nigeria could eventually disintegrate into civil war and become another one of Africa's "failed states." They fear that ethnoregional and religious conflicts have become too great for reconciliation to be possible. Although the difficulties are admittedly formidable, this writer rejects this conclusion. She hopes that this book's study of Nigeria's history and peoples has shown that Nigerians are not inherently "tribalists" with primordial and unchanging identities and loyalties that are inimical to national cohesion. Identities in Nigeria have not been fixed and unchanging; they have developed and changed over time in response to changing conditions. Today's ethnoregional and religious identities and conflicts are rooted primarily in recent historical, economic, and political circumstances. Constructed in response to these forces, identities can be modified if circumstances and interests change. Creating the conditions for identities compatible with national unity is the challenge that must be met if a democratic Nigeria is to survive. As Nigerian civil society activist Oronto Douglas states, "We don't have a choice but to hold onto our democracy. What is the alternative? The old brutal military dictatorship?" Such an outcome is clearly unacceptable to Douglas. Speaking for many of his countrymen and women, he adds, "Someone will rise who cares about national equalities and is able to stabilize this vast country. And we will vote for that person" (Harman 2002).

Timeline

1999	Obasanjo is elected president, and the Fourth Republic begins
1999	Obasanjo purges the military
1999	The massacre in Odi, Bayelsa State, takes place
2002	The chiefs of the armed forces are replaced
November 2002	Riots in Kaduna over the Miss World pageant occur

2002 and 2003   Sectarian violence strikes Jos and Kaduna
April 19, 2003   National elections take place

Significant People, Places, and Events

ABACHA, MUHAMMED Muhammed is Sani Abacha's oldest son. He was charged with, but not convicted of, the murder of Moshood Abiola's wife after Moshood's election to the presidency was annulled. Muhammed has also been charged with embezzling millions of dollars during his father's rule.

BABANGIDA, IBRAHIM Babangida and Buhari became enemies in 1985 when Babangida led the coup that overthrew Buhari and when Babangida imprisoned him for twenty months. They have now reconciled, and Babangida backed Buhari's presidential bid to defeat Obasanjo in the 2003 presidential elections.

FAILED STATES In some countries, including some African countries, the breakdown in the ability of the government to control its territory becomes so complete that there is effectively no functioning government. These failed states are usually the result of war or civil war.

OIL To lessen its dependence on mideast oil, the United States is turning to Africa, especially Nigeria, to increase its oil output. Production is projected to double from the current 2.2 to almost 4.4 million barrels per day by 2020.

OKADIGBO, CHUBA Okadigbo was the former president of the senate. He was the vice-presidential candidate on the ANPP (All Nigeria People's Party) ticket in the 2003 elections. He still faces charges of embezzlement and corruption.

REVENUE ALLOCATION FORMULA In the current system, the federal government collects the oil revenues and disperses them to the thirty-six states and 774 local governments. The share each government unit receives is based on a formula that includes population size, interunit, equality, and land mass.

TRANSPARENCY INTERNATIONAL Transparency International is an international organization, in which Obasanjo was a founding member, that monitors perceptions of corruption in countries around the world. Nigeria regularly rates as the most corrupt among the most corrupt countries in the world. It is currently number two (behind Bangladesh) on the list.

Bibliography

Ajaero, Chris. "Second Term Syndrome." http://www.newswatchngr.com (accessed January 13, 2003).

Aluko, Bolaji. 2003. "The 2003 Presidential Elections—The Militicians vs. the Civilians." http://www.dawodu.com (accessed January 28, 2003).

Falola, Toyin. 1998. *Violence in Nigeria: The Crisis of Religious Politics and Secular Ideologies.* Rochester, NY: University of Rochester Press.

Fawehinmi, Gani. 2003. "My Sadness." *The News* (Lagos). http://allafrica.com/stories/200305050322.html (accessed May 5, 2003).

Harman, Danna. 2002. "Nigerian Leader Faces Test of Unity." *Christian Science Monitor* (June 25): 6.

HRW (Human Rights Watch). "Nigeria: Government Must Disband Vigilante Groups." http://www.hrw.org (accessed May 20, 2002).

Ojo-Ade, Femi. 2001. *Death of a Myth: Critical Essays on Nigeria.* Trenton, NJ: Africa World Press.

Onwubiko, Emmanuel. 2003. "Ezeife Urges Unity, National Conference." http://www.guardiannewsngr.com (accessed April 22, 2003).

Stratfor.com. 2001. "What's Behind Nigeria's Military Shake-Up?" http://www.globalpolicy.org/security/natres/oil/2001/0502nige.htm (accessed May 2, 2001).

World Peace Foundation (WPF). 2003 (January 6). "Nigeria on the Brink of Failure?" *Policy Brief #2.* Cambridge, MA: Harvard University John F. Kennedy School of Government and WPF.

Index

Patron-client system *(continued)*
  defined, xxii
  ethnoregional abuse of, xxii–xxiii,
    116–118, 155–156
  of Hausa-Fulani, 35–36
  as national unity threat, 120
PDP. *See* People's Democratic Party
Pentecostal Fellowship of Nigeria, 216
Pentecostalism, 115
People's Democratic Party (PDP), 245
  election abuses by, 174–175
  in 1999 elections, 173–174
  "power shift" arrangement of, 172, 259
  in 2003 elections, 264, 265, 266
People's Redemption Party (PRP), 162, 163
Pepple, William (king of Bonny), 63
Pidgin English, 228, 231
Political parties
  Abacha's control of, 171–172
  in census controversy, 127–128
  corrupt election practices of, 157–158,
    164–165, 174–176, 264
  economic issues of, 163, 165
  ethnic unions' ties to, 207–208
  ethnoregional affiliations of, 127, 152,
    153–154, 258–259, 265
  with minority interests, 154
  in 1978 elections, 161–162
  1978 reforms of, 160–161
  in 1998–1999 elections, 172–174
  patron-client abuses by, xxii–xxiii,
    117–118, 155–156
  two-party system of, 167–169, 180, 189
Port Harcourt, 87, 137
Portugal, 46–47, 54, 58, 69, 140
Pottery artifacts, 5–6
Praise singers, defined, 41
Presbyterian missionaries, 61
Presidential system
  Babangida's reform of, 167
  election problems in, 161, 162–163
  military dependency of, 196–197, 257
  transition to, in 1978, 160

Prodemocracy groups, 223–224
PRP. *See* People's Redemption Party
PTKs (professional, technical, and kindred
  workers), 235, 237

Qadiriyya Islam, 84, 99–100, 220
Quakers, 55
Quinine, 58

Racism
  of British colonialism, 82, 89
  of Christian missionaries, 62
  tribalism notions of, xvi–xvii
Ranger, Terence, 38
Ransome-Kuti, Beko, 224, 231
Rational-legal, defined, 122
Redeemed Christian Church of God
  (RCCG, Great Britain), 239–240
Regionalism
  as civil war factor, 145
  of colonial policy, 82–83, 93, 102–103,
    127, 152–153
  conflict management of, 266–267
  defined, 122
  economic/cultural factors of, 86
  of First Republic government, 106–107
  Gowon's restructuring of, 132–133,
    137–138, 184
  Ironsi's response to, 131–132
  migrants' weakened ties of, 228–229,
    233, 250–251
  as national unity threat, 94–96, 104–105,
    108–109
  in 1993 election, 169–170
  in 1999 election, 173–174
  political patronage of, xxii–xxiii,
    116–118, 155–156
  population disparities of, 96–97, 127–128
  post–civil war reforms of, 159–161
Religion
  conflict management of, 221–222, 223,
    266–267
  indigenous forms of, 22

About the Author

April A. Gordon is a professor of sociology at Winthrop University in South Carolina and the coordinator for the women's studies program. She has written numerous publications on African issues, including *Understanding Contemporary Africa* (3d ed., 2001) and *Transforming Capitalism and Patriarchy: Gender and Development in Africa* (1996).